AMERICAN SOCIETY

Note on Authors

Joseph Bensman is Distinguished Professor of Sociology at the City College and the Graduate Faculty of the City University of New York. Born in Two Rivers, Wisconsin, he studied at the University of Wisconsin and at Columbia University. Mr. Bensman's writings have ranged widely, beyond sociology, to include psychology, anthropology, philosophy, politics, and literature. His first book with Arthur J. Vidich, *Small Town in Mass Society,* is considered a classic in its field. He has also written *Mass, Class, and Bureaucracy* (with Bernard Rosenberg); *Reflections on Community Studies* (with Arthur J. Vidich and Maurice Stein; *Dollars and Sense*; and (with Robert Lilienfeld) *Craft and Consciousness*; and *Between Public and Private; Lost Boundaries of the Self.*

Arthur J. Vidich is Professor of Sociology and Anthropology in the Graduate Faculty of the New School for Social Research in New York. He grew up in Milwaukee, studied at the University of Wisconsin, the University of Michigan, and Harvard University, and was a Fulbright Scholar at the University of London. In addition to his book *Small Town in Mass Society* with Joseph Bensman, Mr. Vidich is the author of many sociological essays, editor of *Sociology on Trial* (with Maurice Stein); *The Political Impact of Colonial Administration; American Sociology;* and *Worldly Rejections of Religion and their Directions* (with Standford Lyman). He edits the journal *State, Culture and Society.*

AMERICAN SOCIETY

The Welfare State & Beyond, Revised

Joseph Bensman
&
Arthur J. Vidich

BERGIN & GARVEY PUBLISHERS, INC.
MASSACHUSETTS

First published in 1987 by
Bergin & Garvey Publishers, Inc.
670 Amherst Road
South Hadley, Massachusetts 01075

789 987654321

Printed in the United States of America

Library of Congress Cataloging-in-Publication Data

Bensman, Joseph.
American society.

Previous ed. published as: The new American society. 1971.
Bibliography: p. 337
Includes index.
1. Social classes—United States. 2. Middle classes—United States. I. Vidich, Arthur J. II. Bensman, Joseph. New American society. III. Title.
HN90.S6B448 1987 305.5′0973 86-17458
ISBN 0-89789-108-2
ISBN 0-89789-109-0 (pbk.)

Contents

Preface

In the original version of *American Society* we attempted to define and describe the emergence of a new America, an America dominated by a new middle class and its lifestyles.* This new middle class was in large part a product of the bureaucratic social service state, a corporate managerial economy, and the sustained economic prosperity of the post World War II period. Its lifestyles were more sophisticated and more liberal than those of the traditional older Protestant middle classes. By 1964, with the election of President Lyndon Johnson, it seemed that the new middle classes were dominant and that the older American conservatism had been defeated. Yet we then recognized that the only way the victory of these classes could be reversed was by excesses committed by its representatives and by a reaction, i.e., a backlash of the "rednecks" and older conservatives.** This, in fact, did happen in the latter's response to protests against the war in Southeast Asia, the excesses of the civil rights and black nationalist movements and the youth re-

*The first edition of this work was titled *The New American Society.*

**See Chapter 15, pp. 270–72 of this volume. For a similar observation see *Small Town in Mass Society: Class, Power and Religion in a Rural Community,* Chapter 12, "A Theory of the Contemporary American Community", p. 347, (second revised edition), Princeton University Press, 1968.

bellion in the universities. The effect of the reaction was an emphasis on law and order and on what we have called budgetary racism, i.e., the attempt of the older middle class to withdraw budgetary support for liberal economic and social policies in aid to students, minorities, and less favored social and ethnic groups. Since its beginnings in 1968, the reaction has become deeper even though no one, not even President Reagan, cares to reject explicitly the New Deal and the Welfare State. Instead, its specific policies are continuously being whittled away by changes in legislation, taxation and budgetary policies, and the deregulation of industry or the nonenforcement of existing regulations. The term "safety net" was President Reagan's concession to an attenuated Welfare State.

At the same time that the political liberalism of the fifties and sixties was being reversed by Presidents Nixon, Ford, Carter, and Reagan, the cultural radicalism of the sixties was being institutionalized; thus pornography, obscenity, sexual freedom, new family forms and lifestyles, homosexuality, nudity, have been largely legitimated at the level of public tolerance and recognition. Drugs have become a major problem at both high, middle, and low levels of society, partly because they are chic and not because of the pain of poverty as in older peasant and ghetto societies. The cultural revolution of the sixties also was reflected in new styles of dress, personal appearance, and self-presentation. In sum, the revolution of the sixties had its greatest effect on the personal bearing and lifestyles of the new middle classes and relatively little long-term effect on American politics and social organization. The cultural revolution of the sixties permeated the lifestyle of all social classes even as the original bearers of those lifestyles became politically more conservative along with the rest of the nation.

The American affluence of the late forties, fifties, and early sixties was based on a political agreement in which all parties—labor, farmers, the middle class, business—restrained their demands on the system in exchange for moderate increases in profits, wages, prices, and tax and fiscal benefits. This moderation of claims on the system has been called the Keynesian political bargain, which meant that all demands upon the system were moderated by a beneficent federal government and thus subject to management and control. This

Keynesian bargain, which we describe in Chapter 16 of this volume, was largely abrogated by American business after the inauguration of President Nixon in 1968, when American corporations increased prices to previously unheard-of levels. Previous administrations had restricted price and wage demands within the terms of the Keynesian bargain. At the same time, the central control over prices, credit, and the movement of capital was lost, partly because of President Nixon's insistence on an international economic policy based on a fixed relationship between the dollar and the other major currencies of the world, and partly because the rise in oil prices after 1973 gave the oil-producing states vast reserves of dollars that they could move about at their own discretion. At the international political and monetary level, the United States discovered after the fact that the Western world had the equivalent of an international Keynesian political bargain, with it being the central bank. But by the mid-sixties the United States had lost much of its political and financial leadership as well as control of the flow of its own currency. At almost the same time the Keynesian "political bargain" began to disappear at both the domestic and international levels.

In the late sixties and early seventies, Keynesian theory seemed to be appropriate to the study of some aspects of American society and international relations. By the eighties it became apparent that an economic and political Keynesian solution would have to be made at the international level in order to restore stability at the domestic level.

Our original analysis of these changes failed to give sufficient recognition to the inability of American business and industry to compete with the new and foreign industrial powers, Germany and Japan, and to a lesser extent, with the host of other nations that modernized segments of their industry. American industry, while investing in both advanced and underdeveloped nations in order to acquire lower cost components and imports—and in some cases becoming importers of manufactured goods, primarily consumer durables, rather than their producers—failed sufficiently to recapitalize its own plant. By the seventies the tenfold increase in the cost of oil appeared to have reached a plateau, threatening permanent stagnation in the American economy, a virtual freezing of unemployment, then at a 9–10 percent level, now stabilized at 7 percent, underemployment of even greater levels and a poverty rate of over 15 percent. During most of the period from 1965 to the present, inflation has been a constant factor reaching a maximum of 20 percent during the last years of the Carter administration, but falling to 5 percent in 1982 by means of induced unemployment and reduction of the utilization of industrial capacity to 67 percent. The 1983 recovery, while modest, seemed to be the product of an unintended Keynesianism: a budgetary deficit of nearly $200 billion caused primarily by defense spending and high interest payments, occurring at the same time as cuts in social service payments, induced unemployment in the civilian economy. Consumer spending was further stimulated among the affluent by tax cuts of over 25 percent. In one sense the only solution we have had to the depression of the thirties is a Keynesian defense-oriented deficit whose beneficiaries have been the upper and upper-middle and yuppie classes.

Some of the negative changes mentioned above were anticipated and described in our essay entitled "The Crisis of Contemporary Capitalism and the Failure of Nerve" originally published in *Sociological Inquiry** and appearing here as a concluding chapter. This essay, published in 1976, still understates the extent of the changes that occurred since that time.

A significant aspect of *American Society* is the joint domination of the United States and the Soviet Union over the international political order. After World War II the United States assumed the obligation to sustain the "free world," its economies and politics, and expected free-world nations to accept American leadership and policies. It particularly expected these nations to follow the United States's lead in dealing with Russia and Communist China in a cold war. This policy, lasting for about 20 years, was defined by Henry Luce as the American Century. Its articulation and problems are elaborated in Chapter 14. We develop the interplay between domestic and foreign policy and the effects the oil embargo and OPEC would have on American domestic economy or on the economies of other nations. The Middle Eastern assumption of control over oil prices weakened

*Vol. 46 (3–4), 1976, pp. 207–17.

America's control over the world economy and subjected it to unpredictable and, from this point of view, irrational influences. We noted some of the implications of these developments in our chapter, "The Crisis of Capitalism and the Failure of Nerve." In addition, the rise of a new international division, that between the North and the South, especially when combined with OPEC, Arab nationalism, and Moslem religious fanaticism fostered a climate of international anti-American opinion which, however, was not consistently pro-Soviet. The United Nations had, in part, become dominated by a third-world bloc. However, this bloc has its own internal tensions and contradictions which are repressed when it finds itself in opposition to American policies and, less so, to those of the Soviet Union and its satellites. All of these conflicts are complicated and exacerbated by the ominous threat of a nuclear war, one that might be generated not only by American, Soviet, or Chinese initiatives, but also by less responsible or more desperate leaders of third-world nations.

The net effect of all these changes suggests that American society is in permanent conflict with itself. We in the United States are entrapped in self-images based on a glorious past and on illusions of an unlimited future of affluence and power. At the same time we are increasingly being forced to recognize our own incapacity to police ourselves and the world and our inability to maintain economic and political leadership over our ascendant allies, especially Japan. We remain the single most important economy and polity in the world, especially as the world's largest single market for international trade, and one to which the free world looks for leadership. But the brand of leadership that we have to offer is quite often rejected. President Reagan symbolizes and expresses these contradictions. His conservative nationalism, patriotism, single-minded unilateral rhetoric, and international and domestic actions seem to affirm not only the ideology but also the policies of the cold war. Yet, as President and Commander-in-Chief of the Armed Services, President Reagan is forced to recognize the limits of American power and resources in dealing with the Soviet Union, the third world, and America's allies. From time to time he has appeared to recognize some of the dangers of an unqualified cold-war policy and the needs and desires of a substantial segment of the American population for nuclear disarmament and the avoidance of another Vietnam and global war.

None of these problems has been resolved. Our society, with all its problems and contradictions, seems to be in a permanent state of transition. It appears to be doubtful that we can ever achieve that state of inner confidence that characterized much of American society in the fifties and sixties. President Reagan attempts to provide us with that inner assurance by acting friendly, self-confident, engaging, and good-humored, and for a majority of Americans he appears to be successful. The social policies that would transcend the difficulties that emerged in the late sixties and seventies have not been defined in the eighties. Such a definition would, we believe, have to take into account the issues and problems presented and analyzed in the chapters that follow.

J. B.
A. J. V.
New York City

AMERICAN SOCIETY

I.

Origins of the new society

1. The new society

Since the beginning of World War II, American society has been changing continuously. This change has been in direction as well as in rate. The total amount of change has been so vast and radical that it can only be recognized as a social and cultural revolution. This revolution is so deep and pervasive that all traditional analyses of American society no longer hold.

Four major causes have brought about the New Society:

1. There has been a tremendous increase in productivity due to automation, the continuous growth of industrialization, and the greater productivity of capital.
2. This increase in productivity has been achieved through the use of large-scale, bureaucratically organized corporate giants. Paralleling the bureaucratization of business has been a bureaucratization of the organizational apparatus of almost all other institutions. Bureaucratic styles, language, culture, and personality have become the dominant matrix for life within the New Society.
3. A new middle class has emerged. In large part this new middle class is college educated. It is a class of white-collar employees, managers, professionals, junior executives, and service workers

in the higher-status services such as education, recreation, leisure, social work, psychiatry, and the other service occupations.

4. The Keynesian solution of sustaining full production and employment in the American economy has laid the basis for large-scale expenditures by the federal and state governments which stimulate and sustain the total economy. Expenditures are in the hundreds of billions of dollars each year. They not only sustain the total economy but are a major source of income for individual firms. The attempt to control and direct the flow of these funds to more or less favored contractors is an independent political consequence that goes far beyond the purely economic aspects of Keynesianism.

In combination these factors point to a new direction in the evolution of American society. At the simplest level, Keynesianism distinguishes between the individual firm and the total flow and size of national income. National income is subject to different dynamics than is an individual firm or a business. With repeated deficits an individual firm would go bankrupt, but when one looks at the role of government and the federal budget, one finds that this is not the case. The economy may prosper precisely because it has repeated deficits. Even though a firm may have unused productive capacity, it ordinarily does not increase its output beyond the limits of the market demand. For the firm, total demand is accepted as a given. The federal government can, however, affect, create, or diminish the demand itself. By increasing the amount of credit or of money in circulation, it can increase national income or investment and thereby increase effective market demand for the individual firm. With an increase in effective demand the Gross National Product (the total value of all goods and services produced) can be increased by employing unused capacity up to a point at which full employment is reached. The federal government, by the use of repeated deficits, by tax cuts, or by lowering the interest rate, can therefore increase the GNP or, by reversing these policies, can limit effective demand. In the Keynesian perspective, federal spending and taxation policy are evaluated by their effects on GNP and not by regarding the government as just another business firm. This change in perspective has added considerable flexibility to the national economy.

But there is an even greater justification for such policies: the "multiplier effect" of federal fiscal policies. Either by spending or by tax cuts the government can increase the GNP far beyond the amount of funds released. The multiplier effect is based on the fact that one man's income is another man's expenditure. Therefore the initial injection of additional money into the system is multiplied by the fact that it is spent and respent by successive purchasers and spenders of the same dollars.

Thus, for example, a government expenditure of a million dollars represents not only a million dollars of income to the prime contractors; it also represents incomes of up to a million dollars to subcontractors and employees of the prime contractors, the secondary beneficiaries of the expenditures. When these secondary beneficiaries spend their portion of the million dollars, that portion becomes the income of a tertiary group. The process continues infinitely. Theoretically, the infusion of a million dollars into the income stream by government expenditures (or by tax reductions) results in an infinite increase in income. In fact, the income-producing effects of a government expenditure are limited by two processes.

First, the primary (secondary, tertiary, and so on) beneficiary does not spend all of the income received. The leakage decreases the number of dollars involved in each subsequent series of spending.

Second, the time lag between the initial government expenditure and each subsequent spending diminishes the income-creating function of the original expenditure. The greater the time interval between spendings, the less effect the initial expenditure has. If the time interval is very long, the result is the same as if the money had been hoarded. In that case, the expenditure of a million dollars by the government would produce only a million dollars of income. If there were absolutely no time interval between spendings (a condition that empirically could not exist), the income generated would be infinite.

The effect of governmental expenditures on the total economy varies with both the level of utilization of labor and capital in the economy at the time of the expenditure, and the segment of the economy which receives the expenditure. If the economy as a whole or the segment of the economy which is the focus of the expenditure is operating at capacity or close to capacity, then the expenditure's major effects will tend to be inflationary, and will not generate much employment of capital and labor. If the economy or sector is operating at much less than full employment, the expenditure will produce a genuine (non-inflationary) rise in the GNP.

A true measure of the effect of governmental increase in the amount of money made available, then, is not the simple dollar value of the initial injection but the cumulative effect of this injection through spending and respending. In the optimum case the initial expansion of income flow could be great enough to produce tax revenues in excess of the original "deficit spending" or the "tax cut," so that deficits are not only smaller than the increased GNP but are recouped. In Keynesian economics the fundamental point of government policy clearly is not budget-balancing but spending in the event of unused productive capacity and unemployment. Spending increases productivity. This productivity resulting from federal spending has overwhelmed the older economic myths of the balanced budget where government is conceived of as just another business firm.*

In allowing for tax write-offs and high depreciation allowances, American tax policy has operated to subsidize capital investment and economic growth at low cost to business. The cost to government is an initial loss of potential tax revenues, recouped in the long run by economic growth. Such policies are effective as long as there is less than full employment of capital. In periods of full employment, the same policies have brought about inflation accompanied by unemployment in some sectors of the economy. The redistributive effects of these tax-exemption policies necessarily favor those groups who own or control investments. The gains to these groups tend to be hidden because the benefits are indirect.

Despite the fact that this analysis has been fully understood since the late thirties by all but a few intractable classical economists, the explicit application of Keynesian economics has been resisted by all but liberal economists. This is because the social and political implications of Keynesian economics have not been understood by laymen, politicians, businessmen, and Presidents until the administration of John F. Kennedy. With the onset of the Kennedy administration, and under the influence of Walter Heller, his economic adviser, a historical

* The economic basis of the New Society and the role of federal fiscal policy in controlling aggregate demand are analyzed in detail by John Kenneth Galbraith in *The New Industrial State* (Boston, 1967).

watershed in economic understanding was reached. The new generation of political leadership felt free to abandon the older myths of classical economic thinking.

So long as federal spending stimulates the growth of GNP (without inflation), the administration has freedom to use its spending and taxing powers to influence social policy. In this framework fiscal policy can be used to restructure the very basis of society so long as such policy does not produce an undesired decline in the GNP. Thus Keynesian economics allows political-fiscal intervention to be productive in quantitative economic terms while it produces qualitative changes in the structure of society. Understanding this insight makes it possible to control the previously segmented and unplanned process of expanding the public sector of the economy. Keynesian economics has thus provided a theory of political economy for the United States.

President Kennedy understood this and acted accordingly, within the limits imposed by a very narrow electoral margin; but it was Lyndon B. Johnson who, until the Vietnam War began to dominate his domestic policy, applied the formula fully.* Keynesian economics was highly compatible with Johnson's political impulse to give something to everyone who enters the political arena. Under his administration, federal tax and spending powers were used to fashion a new approach to politics, the budget, taxes, and to society. While President Nixon has indicated a preference for relying on interest and discount rate manipulation and tax incentives and deterrents as a means of controlling and directing the economy, he has been forced to maintain levels of spending in part consistent with the pressures and responsibilities that past spending policies have imposed on him (as with any President). Where he has had the option he has altered patterns of taxation or expendi-

* The limits of this formula are, of course, full employment. Beyond this point, inflation becomes a serious threat. For various reasons this point is difficult to determine, but it was reflected in the fear of a falling growth rate and economic crisis in the fall of 1966 and in the uncertainty of President Johnson and his advisers as to what precisely should have been done with regard to tax cuts and increases. Another limitation in the system is foreign expenditure, in terms of balance-of-payments consequences. Thus President Johnson's uncertainties over imposing tax increases and cutting government expenditures were resolved by the balance-of-payments problem resulting largely from the Vietnam War and the fiscal uncertainty it has introduced in the Western monetary system. President Nixon is subject to the same pressures and problems. In his case the pressures are increased because of promises to cut expenditures and taxes.

tures which favor established interest groups, particularly the banks, and which disfavor a broad spectrum of already disadvantaged groups. Yet Nixon has been unable to limit expenditures, despite inflation, because of the Vietnam War and domestic political commitments. To the extent that political commitments are a primary consideration, American economic policy has remained more traditional in nature.

CONTEMPORARY CAPITALISM AND THE NEW MIDDLE CLASS

The relationship between automation, mechanization, the greater efficiency of capital, and the rise of the new middle class is vital to our analysis. Some observers who have studied the middle-class revolution have noted that this new middle class produces services more than products. Even where they are employed within the industrial structure, the new managerial and professional classes are primarily engaged in the planning, facilitating, and administering of production —not in production itself.

The percentage of the population engaged in primary production—that is, in the movement of objects and in the growing, the extraction, the gathering, and the transformation of the fruits of nature—has declined with the advance of the industrial revolution, and continues to decline even more precipitously with each new advance in automation or capital intensification. Thus the new middle classes produce other kinds of economic functions—administrative, professional, and personal services—which were previously performed as part of the voluntary leisure activity of those whose paid work was primary production. For example, education has left the home and has become professionalized. But this is not a singular case. Leisure, too, has become increasingly professionalized, and in recent years we have seen many more social services become professionalized as the family becomes regarded as less and less a source of social and psychiatric strength. Professional workers have increasingly assumed professional responsibility for what were previously family functions. These developments are all the more interesting because they defy much of our traditional social and economic theory.

According to Marxian analysis, every increase in labor productivity resulting from capital intensification should result in an increase in the proportion of income and wealth going to the capitalists and a decrease in both the relative and absolute amount of income and wealth going to the primary producers, the workers. Thus the development under capitalism of capital intensity would result in a shrinking of markets for those goods and services which the increased efficiency of capital would produce, because the workers as consumers would be less able to buy them. This was defined by Marx as the dilemma of capitalism —a dilemma that would result in the increasing impoverishment of the poor and a crisis that would lead to capitalism's collapse. It is obvious that this has not happened.

Later Marxists—especially Rosa Luxemburg in her book *The Accumulation of Capital,* and Lenin in his book *Imperialism*—in attempting to save Marxian theory from its failure to predict social and economic reality developed the idea that imperialism was capitalism's solution to its internal dilemmas. According to this concept, international competition for markets, international war, and the competitive struggle of the capitalist nations to industrialize the underdeveloped world and to export their social system would result in the export of both capital and consumer goods. In short, imperialism provided the needed markets for the increasingly efficient exploitation of nature and of men under advanced capitalism. Thus under the theory of imperialism the dilemma of capitalism and the crisis of capitalism would be postponed. But though capitalism would not be defeated directly by these internal contradictions per se, imperialism would still fail to provide an adequate solution to the dilemma of capitalism. Capitalism would be destroyed by the international wars caused by the various capitalist nations as they attempted to control the underdeveloped nations in a race to preserve their own capitalist system against its own contradictions. And yet, despite international and world wars and despite world competition for markets, this prediction has not come true.

Nevertheless there are those who still argue that foreign aid, the Cold War, and other wars like the one in Vietnam are the means by which capitalism preserves itself in the face of its internal contradictions. For these observers, history has not yet made its judgment. But this Marxist argument founders on the fact that the standard of living of all classes, including the industrial proletariat, has increased in all of the advanced capitalist nations of the world to levels which were not imaginable by even the most roseate defenders of capitalism in the nineteenth century. Capitalism has not failed in its ability to produce internal markets, even though all classes have not shared equally in the new affluence. Internal markets have developed, and the dilemma of capitalism as posited by Marx has not become reality.

Instead, due in part to trade unionism, to the development of social legislation, to minimum-wage laws, to increases in social services, and to political programs like the New Deal and the Fair Deal, internal demand has created internal markets that absorb a substantial part of capitalism's increasing productivity. This solution, through the creation of internal markets sufficiently large to take production off the market, is a twofold one:

1. It is relatively easy to point out the enormous market provided by a federal budget of over $200 billion and state and local government budgets that in total are even larger. These budgets sustain military industry, science industry, social welfare industry, educational industry, and the civil service. These sectors are supported not only directly in their pattern of expenditure, but indirectly through the multiplier effect: secondary, tertiary, and even more indirect expenditures help to sustain demand in the nongovernmental aspects of the economy. Thus government expenditures supported by taxation, borrowing, and monetary policy produce the markets and income that, according to Marx, would have disappeared due to the dilemma of capitalism.
2. In a second sense, capitalistic enterprises—in a form which would not be recognized by Marx—have produced their own nongovernmental counterpart to the Keynesian solution. As the productivity of industry owing to the application of science, technology, automation, and capital intensity has increased, the structure of industry itself has changed so that the number and kinds of jobs—the occupational structure—has been altered by new forms of industry.

The rise in social service and bureaucratic occupations within each firm creates a kind of labor force whose function is not only to increase the efficiency of industry in its internal operations but also to provide markets for the increased productivity of capital throughout industry.

If we were to project the labor force composition of 1900 into the industrial structure of 1971, the work done by that labor would result in much higher rates of unemployment than we now have; this is because the technology of 1971 is capable of producing much more with a much smaller labor force than was employed in 1900. Unemployment has not increased in phase with increase in productivity. The expected oversupply of labor has not developed because the development of secondary, tertiary, and other indirect forms of labor and services has absorbed the decline in primary labor. To be sure, certain types of unemployment have increased from time to time. Most frequent has been the unemployment of semi- and unskilled marginal workers whose economic vulnerability has placed them in marginal industries. Secondly, unemployment has occurred due to changes in the structure of federal spending, especially spending for defense. This form of unemployment is located in skilled blue-collar, higher white-collar, engineering, and middle managerial positions. A third form of unemployment occurs among those whose occupations are located in the higher consumption industries—stock salesmen, brokers, furriers, jewelers, art dealers, and others whose services cater to the affluent. Yet, in spite of these forms of unemployment, the growth of secondary and tertiary and more removed occupations has increased the amount of employment, thereby increasing the demand resulting from the growth of these new occupations upon the total productive enterprise.

One may ask legitimately whether these new jobs are necessary to the productive enterprise—necessary apart from their function in the production of demand.

1. The very large expansion in the leisure industry is not necessary from the standpoint of production, but appears to be quite necessary from the standpoint of demand.
2. Much of the same can be argued in relation to the economic functions of education. The kinds of technological education that colleges produce can be produced equally well, if not better, by apprenticeship, in-shop, or on-the-job training. But the colleges and advanced technical schools operate to take youth off the labor market at precisely the time when science, automation, technology, and capital intensity decrease the demand for workers in

primary industrial production. The extension of education and the increase in its complexity and ritual absorb much potential labor which would otherwise be unemployed.

3. Old-age insurance and early-retirement plans take older employees off the labor market at precisely the time when the demand for primary labor decreases.

Thus the consumption functions of all these groups are retained while their production functions are curtailed. In exactly the reverse sense, early capitalism employed children, women, older workers, and entire families, and imported masses of immigrants when there was a need to expand the size of the labor force. With the growth in the degree of capital intensity, more segments of the population have either been barred by law or encouraged by financial alternatives to abstain from the labor market. As a net result, capitalism decreases the percentage of individuals engaged in primary production and increases the percentage of people whose primary economic function is to be that of consumer. As a further result, the consumption aspect of the society is stimulated while the production function continues to expand as a result of the autonomous growth of science and the increased capitalization of the economy.

Many of the occupations of those in industry and government are totally unnecessary for any economic function other than that of providing consumption. Much of the development of the higher occupations represents only the growing application of Parkinson's Law, whereby the expansion of higher-level, abstract, administrative services requires further growth in order to cope with the unnecessary work the higher occupations produce. Humorous as this may seem, it should not be scorned, for Parkinson is wrong if he would say that these jobs are not functional. The function of these new nonproductive classes is to provide the demand that the expansion of productive industry requires. Thus the private segments of the economy, just as the public ones, continuously operate as a gigantic WPA for the middle, the professional, and the administrative classes.

Modern industry increasingly takes a more familistic attitude toward its upper-level employees and enlarges the size of the population that it defines as being covered and protected by Parkinson's Law. The evidence for fairly heavy upper-white-collar featherbedding is seen in any period of retrenchment where corporate industry, under pressure of external events, discovers that it can reduce the size of its labor force without affecting production. By dropping secondary and tertiary employees, by cutting frills, administrative work, and paper work, costs can be reduced while production is maintained. It is quite clear that the number of employees and the number of fringe services sustained by industry are far greater than are necessary. As a result, industry, by these internal operations that provide for higher levels of wages and employment, develops within its own structure sources for demand which collectively help to produce the markets for its output. In part, the liberal corporate tax laws as well as the growth of managerial prerogatives promote these forms of managerial dole and benefice. Under present tax rates, federal and state governments absorb a major part of the costs of keeping unnecessary managerial and white-collar officials employed, because their salaries are computed as costs before taxes.

The result of all these Keynesian solutions, whether intended or not, in addition to producing an expanding economy and the ability of capitalism to generate the markets that absorb its own productivity, is the creation of a new middle class. Its major functions—even if the middle class is primarily located in industry—include that of consumption. The rise of the new middle class, then, is not independent of technology, capital intensity, and Keynesian budgetary policy, but rather is a product of these factors. Together with the planned and unplanned Keynesian solutions to the dilemmas of capitalism, the new middle class reflects the economic dimension of the new social system. This new economic system is a phenomenon that we in the United States, according to traditional Western social and economic theory, were not prepared to receive. None of the economic or social theories or ideologies of the past could anticipate the phenomenon that we have discovered after the fact.

The fundamental aspect of the New Society is an ever-increasing flood of new productivity which, when distributed, has raised the standard of living not only of the upper classes, as it has done in the past, but also of wider and wider segments of the middle classes, which have increased in numbers sufficiently to become the numerically dominant class. Simultaneously the working classes have been provided with growing income levels which, compared with their past expectations, are almost inconceivable. The only groups who have not profited materially from this new economic system are the "poor," the aged, the ill, the totally unskilled, and a large proportion of the blacks, American Indians, Latin Americans, and Appalachians wherever they are located—groups that have not, for complex reasons, been able to accommodate themselves to capital intensity and the Keynesian economy. The exclusion of the blacks has in large part provided the basis for the "black revolution." Meanwhile, the growth of the new middle class has been the most dramatic feature of the American economy in the past two decades. We have been and still are unprepared to imagine the full consequences of the growth of both productivity and the middle class in the New Society.

POLITICAL DIMENSIONS OF THE NEW SOCIETY

The political effects of the new economy are different for different groups. In the past decade, business, the upper class, and the middle class have been satisfied by tax relief and by a swelling of the income stream: the upper and middle classes have received disproportionate shares of the wealth. Negroes and the poor have been offered civil rights and poverty programs, but at a level of expenditure that is proportionately much less than that granted to the middle classes in the form of tax relief and increased income opportunities. Organized labor has been promised (but not accorded) a revision of the Taft-Hartley Act and continuous—but modest—wage increases on the condition that they refrain from striking. Business has tended to accept these concessions to organized labor because it has received tax benefits and a right to pass on increased labor costs to the consumer in the form of moderately but continuously rising prices. Business and organized labor each has shown a remarkable willingness to accept peacefully the concessions offered, though business sometimes passes on proportionately higher price increases than would be "suggested" either by wage increases or by its agreements with government economic advisers.

These violations of a tacit deal between business, organized labor, and government cause labor to feel that it has been betrayed both by recent Democratic administrations and by business. Democratic administrations, meanwhile, could feel that they had been betrayed by business. The Nixon administration, pursuing a laissez-faire policy, has permitted business to state its own terms, though the administration has had to apologize for the consequences of those terms. Businessmen, in overstepping the traditional price boundaries imposed by their agreements with government and organized labor, or when being given freedom to state their own boundaries, challenge labor and Washington to upset American prosperity by making reprisals. When labor, especially labor in the public and service sectors, where it is difficult to pass on wage increases, has struck, it has had to bear the onus for upsetting the ongoing equilibrium and for having inconvenienced the middle classes. Unorganized labor, still a substantial percentage of the labor force, is in the least advantageous position. Because it is unorganized, it lacks the force to apply pressure on either the government or business and so receives a disproportionately small share of benefits. Its wages fail to keep pace with either the wage increases of organized labor or with the rising cost of living. Unorganized labor thus helps to pay a disproportionately high share of the costs of the New Society.

American farmers, who were penalized during the twenties, have been heavily subsidized since the thirties both by direct grants and by the right under price controls to tax the consumer. In addition, subsidy programs favoring large producers have encouraged farmers to leave the land. At present only slightly more than 5 per cent of the labor force, as compared with 12 per cent in 1950 and 35 per cent in 1900, is engaged in agriculture. The result is that more and more farm subsidies go to fewer and fewer farmers. Those farmers who survive the liquidation process—that is, the least marginal and most prosperous farmers—join the mainstream of the preferred subsidized groups in America. Small businessmen, despite fair-trade laws designed to limit competition among retailers, and despite the Commerce Department's Small Business Administration, have also received a lesser share of federal largess. Lastly, Southern urban and rural white Protestant "redneck" groups have partly lost their privileged position with respect to the federal government and its budget, both in terms of civil rights legislation and contingency clauses in subsidy or grant programs to the states. Although redneck Southern Protestantism retains some privileges at the local level, these are declining too. Their last-ditch defenses have resulted in a reassertion of their "traditional" values. New political movements have emerged which have given them national recognition. As a result they can influence the policies of national parties to recognize their demands and compete in complying with them.

The universities and a favored segment of intellectuals and academicians, on the other hand, have been subsidized by grants that would have been unimaginable even during the WPA days. The defense, space, and electronics industries have subsidized a corps of engineers, professionals, and technicians while in turn being subsidized by the federal budget. The college-bred and educated, who are middle class or, in the case of state universities and city colleges, lower middle class in their origins, have increasingly joined the ranks of the subsidized. They receive benefits far in excess of the tuitions they pay. The same is true of secondary school teachers in both secular and parochial schools, for whom there are now innumerable specialized programs geared to their needs, interests, and aspirations. The middle class has been the beneficiary of a vast educational subsidy.

All of these subsidies are based on the recognition that spending cannot hurt so long as the income thus created expands or at least does not diminish the gross national product. The unorganized consumer, if he is not at the same time a subsidized producer, bears the cost of subsidy through higher prices and higher taxes, while organized groups claim the right to raise prices and pass on the increased costs to the consumer.

The Keynesian budget philosophy, besides placing direct costs on specific groups, can also be seen in terms of relative income benefits. Insofar as the Keynesian perspective emphasizes effective demand and consumption by making the GNP its central criterion, the government's ability to affect the income flow becomes a key element in society. Production gains in American society, however, are not simply the result of monetary policy. Productivity has continued to increase in recent years because of technological improvements, increased capital investments, and population growth; but participation in the gains of this productivity is not equal or proportionate to previous income shares. Because total income has been growing for twenty-five years, almost all groups have had at least minimal increases in income, but some groups have had greater increases than others. Which groups have gained and the relative amount they have gained have been in large measure a function of their relation to the federal budget and federal legislation. It appears that all organized groups have made greater gains than unorganized groups, which suggests that *political pressure* is a greater economic factor than is *economic function* by itself. Analysts have noted that political pressure is a factor in determining who gets what in local politics, but they have not focused on national politics with respect to this issue.

Labor peace has given industry a sustained period of "production rationality." Industry has also gained by successive modifications of the tax laws which allow it to retain greater percentages of the profits, and by changes in tax regulations which allow it to conceal profits. Through such legal devices as the carry-over of losses, tax write-offs, depreciation allowances, complicated changes in accounting procedures, and cost-plus agreements on federal contracts, big business has been able to maintain and increase its profits. For a small sector of big business consisting mainly of the giants, there has also been, until recent restrictive legislation, the mechanism of mergers of profitable and unprofitable companies, wherein the losses of the merged company become an asset that can be used as tax credits against the profits of the prosperous firm. In all such mergers the federal government assumes the burden of the cost of business expansion and "integration" in the form of a loss of tax revenue.

The economic gains that have accrued to big business and corporations have benefited the upper and upper middle classes in the form of salaries, dividends, or capital gains. Organized workers have benefited from wage increases that have been granted in order not to interfere with the production and high profits that business has enjoyed. Next to unorganized workers, organized labor has gained greatly. As unorganized or poorly organized groups, Negroes and the poor have gained through poverty programs, but their gains have been much less than the tax relief provided to the upper middle and upper-income classes. Moreover, much of the gains made by the Negroes and the poor as a result of the poverty programs has been canceled out by the amount of collective income wiped out by unemployment and price increases. Even these pittances are the result of unorganized pressures caused by riots, the fear of riots, and the increased discontent of black masses and their leaders, caused by the failure of legal gains to produce economic benefits. The blacks' loss of confidence in the urban Democratic parties has encouraged the national administrations to use poverty programs in the same way that food baskets were used to gain the votes of immigrants at the turn of the century. The poverty programs have most benefited black professionals, black and white social workers, administrators, social scientists, and black college graduates. These groups, which live off poverty and which started from relatively low levels five or six years ago, have experienced the greatest relative gains.

The relative distribution of gains and losses produced by automation and mechanization and by federal "management" of the flow of income to and away from various groups seems to have a definite contour.

1. The organized elites in all sectors of the society appear to have gained the most from the structure of income distribution under the Keynesian system.
2. The disorganized, the poorly organized, and the underorganized have gained least or suffered most. A lack of organized power to apply pressure for legislation affecting income redistribution favorable to their cause seems to be the crucial factor determining their economic fate.

That freedom of income management which is not part of the federal power thus ultimately rests upon political pressure. Those groups that are best organized and possess power and resources are most successful in gaining favorable income opportunities—and vice versa.

Under this system a new consensus, a new pluralism in American society has been a consensus among organized *elite groups*. These groups represent interests as widely divergent as those between big management and big labor. Or they represent such structurally differentiated groups as big universities and agencies of the government like the Pentagon, the Central Intelligence Agency (CIA), or the National Institutes of Health. At another level, local and state governments find themselves in alliances with large industrial and commercial enterprises.

In other words, instead of there being a conflict between vested interests, the new consensus has produced cooperation between them, because all have a stake in sustaining the consensus from which they benefit. This, of course, does not necessarily deny competition between cooperating and organized vested interests, but such competition as occurs is designed to achieve a more favorable position within the new consensus and stops far short of anything resembling an open confrontation between competing groups.

THE BUREAUCRATIC ETHOS

One important aspect of the New Society is the ever-increasing growth of the administrative structure of bureaucracy and of the scale of large organizations. Government, industry, education, trade unions, and churches carry out the internal and external operations of the society by use of the bureaucratic mechanism. It is critical to note that the exact counterpart of the growth of the middle class is the growth of the administrative structure of bureaucracy which administers this enormous productive and service-oriented society.

In describing the characteristics of bureaucracies and especially European political bureaucracies, Max Weber provided the foundations for the technical description of large-scale business organization. The key theme in Weber's description of bureaucracy is the separation of the administrator from the means of administration, just as the soldier in an earlier epoch had been separated from the ownership of his weapons, and the worker from the means of production. Bureaucracies are characterized by relatively fixed hierarchies and spheres of competence (jurisdictions), and they depend on files and legalistic regulations for specifying their operations. The entire bureaucracy depends on technical experts who are engaged in a lifelong career and who are dependent on their jobs as their major means of support. Thus discipline, obedience, loyalty, and impersonal respect for authority tend to become psychological characteristics of the bureaucrat.

Even more important, however, is the bureaucrat's habit of making standardized categorical decisions which are rationally calculated—in form if not in content—to administer thousands of cases which become relevant because they fall into a category predescribed by administrative regulation and procedure. Weber describes bureaucracy as a giant machine in which all individuals, both administrators and subjects, are cogs. This Weberian nightmare is so awesome and horrifying in its portrayal of the dehumanization of men and the disenchantment of society that it has been hard to swallow in all its implications. It is only Weber's academic style that has prevented him from being treated as another George Orwell.

For Weber, bureaucracy did not arise out of a devilish plot. Rather it was a dominant institution emerging from the administrative efficiency that results from size, scope, and categorical application of cases. Bureaucracy is adaptive to large-scale enterprises in all areas of society, as governmental and private activities expand in response to the growth of societies from localistic (feudal) and small units to giant large-scale enterprises that are national and international in scope. In many respects, Weber saw bureaucracy as almost self-generating, with one important qualification: the desire of leaders of large-scale enterprises to extend their own freedom, autonomy, and opportunity for rational decision-making by limiting the assertiveness, the interference, the power, and the irrationality of others within their sphere of administration. Thus those who control large-scale institutions limit the freedom of others in order to maximize their own freedom. Seen from the point of view of leadership, bureaucracy must always be something more than a technical system of administration. It is also a system for the organization and distribution of power and the formulation of policy within institutions, between institutions, and within societies. From this perspective, bureaucracy, in its full form, is diametrically opposed to the Jeffersonian and Jacksonian image of a viable democracy.

American social and political scientists did not find it easy to accept Weber's discussion of bureaucracy. For the most part they reacted against the image of the officious, legalistic bureaucrat and criticized Weber for universalizing the image of the uniform-happy, tyrannical German bureaucrat, later overdrawn in the image of the Prussian Junker or the Nazi official. Americans contrasted the German stereotype to the oft-perceived style of the American official, who appeared to be easygoing, equalitarian, breezy, friendly, personal, and nonofficious, even though a bureaucratic official. What they failed to realize was that the American tradition, stemming as it does from the Jeffersonian and Jacksonian frontier style, causes the power holder to conceal his power in proportion to its growth. The Weberian bureaucrat does not look like the American manager because the *cultural* style surrounding bureaucracy is different in America. As a result of this mask, the subordinate in any organization has at subliminal levels the ability to make precise estimates of the actual power positions of each officeholder in the organization. With this as his framework, the formal, equalitarian, personal, and friendly responses of co-workers are based on these estimates. In the American system the official knows how to be informal and friendly without ever intruding into the office of the superior, and the superior knows how to be equalitarian without ever losing his authority. Thus bureaucracy functions in the classical Weberian way while retaining an air of American friendliness and informality.

This special bureaucratic by-product of Jeffersonian and Jacksonian democracy creates a bureaucratic style in which it becomes a major requirement to mask authority relations. As a result, very substantial changes have taken place in the ideology of the social worker, the human relations specialist, the psychological counselor, the personnel officer, and in interpersonal relations in almost all bureaucratic job situations. In the United States a whole range of bureaucratic subspecialties have been created in welfare, government, and business bureaucracies for the express purpose of concealing bureaucratic authority. In American bureaucracy it is possible to sustain a rhetoric of agreement, respect for the individual personality, and rewards for technical ability as the critical factors governing the relationship between boss and subordinate.

In actual bureaucratic practice the subordinate is expected to agree voluntarily with his superior and to suggest the conditions for his subordination without ever openly acknowledging the fact of his subordination. The rhetoric of democracy has become the *sine qua non* of bureaucratic authoritarianism.

So complex is this masking process that in a literal sense a linguistic revolution has taken place that allows us to conceal from ourselves the inequalitarianism of bureaucratic social relations. Bureaucracy, like any dominant institution, has developed a structure of linguistic euphemisms which allow the retention of an equalitarian, friendly, personal ideology while concealing the authoritarianism and at times the harshness of bureaucracy. The following expressions, placed opposite their euphemisms, are intended only to suggest some of the possibilities.

EUPHEMISM	REAL MEANING
Obedience:	
We expect your cooperation.	Obey.
I'd like to have consensus on this issue.	I expect you to repress all differences.
Obligation and duty require this.	My job and responsibilities require your obedience.
Being reminded of one's place:	
It's a wonderful idea, but at the present we don't have the time to give your idea the attention and consideration it needs.	Drop it.
You're kidding, aren't you.	You're out of line.
That's an interesting idea that needs further developing.	Let's not discuss it now.
We must respect the autonomy and individual rights of others.	You're overstepping your authority.
You can do that if you want to, but I'll take no responsibility for it if it gets out of hand.	You do it at your own risk, but I'll take the credit for it if it's successful.
With some development and elaboration, the germ of your idea could be useful.	I'm stealing your idea; forget it, the idea is no longer yours.
That was a good idea you had at our meeting yesterday.	I'm giving it back to you.
Ways to get fired:	
You've been late three times in the past month.	Warning of forthcoming dismissal.
Your work is not up to your usual standards.	Warning of forthcoming dismissal.
You haven't reached your full potential in this job.	You're not fired, but don't expect a raise or promotion.
We feel that this organization can do no more to further your career.	You're fired.

EUPHEMISM	REAL MEANING
We can't stand in the way of your growth.	You're fired.
You're too well trained for this job.	You're fired.
We'll give you excellent references.	Please leave without making a scene.
We'll give you an extra month's severance pay.	Please leave and forget you ever worked here.
At other levels:	
Free lunch.	A small, somewhat ambiguous bribe setting the stage for bigger bribery.
Fringe benefits.	Fairly serious bribery.
Hanky-panky.	Serious bribery.
A preliminary meeting.	Setting out to rig a forthcoming meeting.
A well-organized meeting.	A rigged meeting.
An informal coffee meeting.	An incipient plot.
A private meeting.	A plot.

Although this whole area of linguistic usage is central to the functioning of society, few writers apart from George Orwell, Hannah Arendt, and Shepherd Mead have emphasized it. The bureaucratic aspects of the New Society could well be studied through the revolution in linguistics of which we have suggested only a few examples.

THE INDIVIDUAL IN THE NEW SOCIETY

The development of centralized bureaucracy has meant that each individual, at least in his work, must submit to the objective and impersonal requirements which are necessary to maintain the system as administered by its managers. Bureaucracy implies—at least at the level of work—a series of external, objective, legalistic constraints which make each individual surrender—for the sake of the organization and his personal success within it—his own autonomy, his own rhythm of work, and his own ability and desire to define goals for himself and to execute them on an individual basis.

In the 1930's the ideological enemies of society were either from the extreme right—National Socialism and fascism—or from the extreme left—communism, totalitarianism, Stalinism. In that period, intellectuals who were not themselves committed to extreme solutions saw the danger to society coming either from the outside or from extremist groups within it. Forms of freedom were denied by external enemies who were repressive, irrational, and totalitarian. Now the "rational" bureaucratic organization of society and the Keynesian solution to internal problems combine to produce entirely new forms of constraint upon the individual. In contrast to the denial of freedom by external enemies, we began to discover by the late 1940's and 1950's new but gentler, more hidden forms of constraint, new sources of conformity, and the drying up of old forms of freedom, liberty, and individualism. These losses occurred not because of irrational forces but because of forces within the framework of a bureaucratic, middle-class, service-oriented, Keynesian society.

Paralleling the bureaucratization of the occupational world was the discovery that the new industries of mass recreation, mass leisure, and the mass media prescribe predigested ways of thinking and behaving, of relating to others when not at work. The providing of standardized solutions to individual problems, and standardized styles of thought and action, has made it more comfortable for the individual to be a passive receptacle for the standardized product of the mass leisure and communication bureaucracies in which so many of the new middle class are employed. As a result, a new form of personal constraint lies in the ease with which one can surrender his desire to define his own form of thought, his own form of leisure, and his own work. The invitation to succumb to premanufactured patterns, including those of dreaming, is easily accepted. Thus the new forms of leisure, recreation, and mass communications increasingly describe standardized ways by which one experiences one's private life.

The discovery of these processes by intellectuals and students has caused them to rebel against these easily acceptable constraints and comfortable forms of conformity. Both these groups have tried to uphold the ideal of authentic individualism by glorifying nonconformity, individual freedom, and spontaneous but often unfocused romantic and revolutionary action. But for different reasons they have had difficulty in finding ways of doing so.

1. Most simply, resistance has been difficult because acceptance of the constraints, at least in terms of work patterns, has been relatively easy. The poets, writers, and artists who work in the mass media are well paid. The intellectuals, scholars, academicians, and scientists who are employed in large-scale industry, government, and foundations discover that the opportunities and rewards are so great for those who would submit to the external demands of these bureaucracies that the cost of maintaining genuine autonomy is too great. Apart from being easier, it is also more pleasurable to accept the economic rewards of premanufactured surrender.

2. In the past the autonomy of the intellectual was imposed upon him because the society had no means to absorb even the small number of intellectuals produced by the impractical universities. Until recently, with the exponential growth in the demand for "scientists" in the great bureaucracies, the universities were not able to meet the production demands for technicians, administrators, intellectuals, writers, and artists whose work is necessary primarily in terms of Parkinson's Laws as they apply to industry. But now, because one has the *choice* between being autonomous or not, it is easier to surrender than in the past when autonomy was forced upon the intellectual by the lack of economic opportunity and appreciation.

As a result of these almost unlimited opportunities to enjoy a pleasant, materially satisfying, consumption-oriented life based on work which is intellectually meaningless, there is a significant malaise among the intellectuals. On the one hand, the comfort, the ease, the security, and the standard of living are all pleasant and acceptable. Yet, on the other hand, there is continuous doubt arising from a self-conscious self-examination. The questions that force themselves on one's consciousness are: Are all these pleasant, tepid things worth it? Isn't there more to life than consuming—something that has meaning independent from and above it? Isn't consuming senseless without a dedication to causes that are meaningful in their own terms? It appears that the answers to these questions are not self-evident.

Intellectuals, scientists, and educated administrators, comprising a significant part of new middle classes, have attempted to resolve these same problems in the following ways:

1. Some try to enjoy a prestigious cultural life. Culture may include support of the symphony or beyond—rock music, the ballet or the pornographic dance, Shakespeare, *Hair* and *Oh! Calcutta.* In film it ranges from the new pornography to the old camp. Novels whose real-life characteristic is proven by the calculated illiteracy of their authors can be read in conjunction with novels whose vocabulary and complexity of style make them unintelligible to highly literate audiences.
2. Others play at small-scale "PTA and local improvement" politics, which have as their major quality a capacity for giving expression to kinds of idealism not permitted on the job and which do not rock the boat on serious political waters. This kind of activity has become a major form of politics throughout the country, especially in those places where the new middle classes are a sizable segment of the community.
3. Others become members of the "radical" upper-class white Bohemia who, at the political level, support groups like the Black Panthers by sponsoring and attending fund-raising parties. Playing at revolution for them is a chic social requirement.
4. Others pursue images of the life styles of older upper classes, which they do at precisely the time when the older upper classes have lost their political and economic functions.
5. Others participate in civil rights movements, in SANE, in anti-war and anti-nuclear-testing protests, in World Federalist and U.N. support organizations. In such activities some middle-class suburbanites (especially housewives) attempt to address themselves to the large issues of our times.
6. Others express anti-establishment sentiments by engaging in "far-out" modes of self-expression. These include new forms of dress and sexual styles, attachment to op, pop, and folk art, avant-garde theater and literature—or in general by becoming "swingers." Drugs are frequently served as alternatives to cocktails or cigarettes. Swingers who exhibit one or more of the new forms of mod culture are often able to do so without jeopardizing high-paying positions in the business and professional worlds.

This attempt of segments of the new middle class to find for itself meaningful activities and meaningful forms of consumption and recreation constitute a major force in the shaping of a new culture. That culture is based on a continuous effort to democratize the forms, images, and stereotypes of what was previously an upper-class life style. If this process continues at its present pace, or if it should intensify, it will result in the total transformation of American social and cultural life. It will erase and destroy the character type of the hard-working, materialistic, democratic, equalitarian, Boobus Americanus who has been the epigone in American life. In short, the penetration of new forms of middle-class values—a consequence of a dissatisfaction with bureaucratization—is a major revolutionizing influence in American life.

Certainly the quality of class values alters the tone of the society, but the Keynesian solution in its explicit governmental terms goes far beyond these cultural and consumption forms in revolutionizing the structure of American society. The Keynesian revolution's astronomical governmental expenditures have several consequences:

1. The amount spent—almost regardless of what it is spent upon—serves as a stimulant to the economy. In a much more limited sense, this was once known as pump-priming.
2. At another level, the direction of expenditures—the specific activities upon which money is spent—can result in the modification and remodification of society. At this level, the social policies behind the expenditures represent an opportunity for the "society" to remake and recast itself along lines which in turn determine subsequent expenditures.
3. In fact, however, the pattern of resentments and jealousies over what constitutes a fair share of societal rewards becomes polarized. These conflicts affect the production of governmental expenditures (and taxation). And, of course, they also alter and quite frequently determine the pattern of governmental expenditures and taxation.

As a result of these consequences we now have what some observers call a "contract state," in which a large number of giant institutions depend on the government as the major source of their income. The fate of these institutions is determined by both the level of government expenditures and by their ability to influence government decisions that will make them prime contractors. So critical has the function of "influence" become that the lobbyist who was once despised has become a respected professional in his own right.

The amount of money involved in government expenditures is so large and so highly profitable for its recipients that the attempts to control and direct the flow of funds constitute an unforeseen political effect of Keynesian economics that goes beyond all past political tradition.* In our society it represents a genuine revolution, for in the past the competition for the scarce fruits of government operation was so great that the entire class structure of society represented a war of "class" against "class" to determine who would be the major beneficiaries of government policy despite the scarcity. With the new volume of production and expenditures, the problem is no longer one of scarcity but rather of the *relative* distribution or allocation of the rewards within a wide framework. While the distribution is not considered equitable (the rewards still being thought of in terms of the differential advantage that each is eager to get), the totality of production is a solution to the problem of scarcity. The political economy thus begins to operate under new budgetary principles.

Under these principles there are three criteria for the efficacy of the federal budget:

1. The effect of the total volume of expenditures on the society.
2. The technical efficiency of the expenditures within the framework of the total volume.
3. The political consequences of a given level and direction of expenditure.

The way in which decisions are made under these criteria serves to define the foundations for the New Society.

In its political dimension, the managers of this New Society are forced to allocate expenditures to different segments, groups, classes, interests, firms, and so on, so as to avoid what previously might have been a struggle of each class against the others and against the regime itself. Thus, by the system of allocations, extreme conflicts between

* Except, perhaps, in the late Roman empire when both monopolies in tax farming and construction *and* concessions in the use of conquered land determined the leadership and policy of the empire.

competing interests and groups can be stimulated or avoided; this is the politically determined redistribution of economic rewards. In short, it is possible for an administration to prevent or exacerbate forms of group conflict by making or not making concessions to the various claimants. If one wishes to use a vulgar term, this is a policy of massive and calculated bribery and punishment. Under this politics, funds can be diverted, allocated, reallocated, shifted, or increased so that any dissatisfied group, depending on how much noise it makes, its numbers, and the effectiveness of its organization, can find a reward for its activities in the federal budget. If one wishes, one can call this the politics of consensus. Up to now, at least, the demanding and threatening groups, with the exception of youth and the Negroes, have been bought off with concessions in approximately those proportions necessary to make the purchase. In a real sense this achieves a kind of social equilibrium that replaces any self-regulating, automatic process which society naturally achieves under liberal free-market conditions.

The profile of American society suggested by the foregoing sketch defines the emerging society. Now we will develop and elaborate the outlines of its profile. A large part of our discussion will be concerned with describing the processes by which the New Society works. Finally, we will analyze the effects of shattered dreams and new "realities" on the lives of the members of this society.

2. *Historical background to the new society*

THE CIVIL WAR AND ECONOMIC GROWTH

The Revolutionary War did not alter the class and social structure of America beyond achieving independence from colonial overlords; but the Civil War represented the triumph of industry and the free farmer over slave labor and the plantation system. An entire class was destroyed, the "free" Negro was created, and the regional distribution of power was drastically altered. Unresolved aftereffects from this second revolution have added new dimensions of complexity to American society.

The revolutionary effects of the Civil War in favor of Northern business, industry, and farming laid the groundwork for extensive changes in American society; but what was known as business and industry in the post–Civil War period bears almost no resemblance to what we now know as business and industry. Nor does our present large-scale agribusiness bear any resemblance to earlier notions of the free farmer. In fact, the triumph of business and the defeat of the plantation system did no more than set the stage for the corporate explosion and for agricultural industrialization, both of which occurred with state and national aid from governments subservient to business and industry. The Civil War enabled America to emerge as it now appears, but it did not shape the result.

In the first half of the nineteenth century, industry consisted mainly of small, local operations. The entrepreneur or manufacturer used machine labor, but based his operations in a single industrial plant. The factory formed the basis for all of the manufacturer's business operations. Business, so to speak, was only an aspect of manufacturing, and manufacturing itself was still based on the relatively autonomous plant. All of this changed drastically during and especially after the Civil War. The demand created by the war stimulated manufacturing, and the new postwar political climate of Northern victory created the conditions for the rapid growth of business.

After the Civil War both the financial and natural resources of the country were placed in the hands of business entrepreneurs. Through the political support and sympathy of the federal government, these entrepreneurs were given sway to develop railways, exploit forests, open the plains, develop the mines, and so on. Public lands and resources were given away, and vast subsidies were provided primarily for railroads: all this for the purpose of advancing the practice of business and its laissez-faire ideology. The Supreme Court neutralized the restrictive efforts of labor and of the government itself whenever the latter was inclined to restrict business. As at other times, only more so in this epoch, political support came from entrepreneurial quarters through the massive bribery of state and national legislators and through direct control of the Republican party by business interests.

Structural changes in American business organization included the following:

1. During and immediately after the Civil War the size of industrial and business units increased, but there was as yet no change in the organizational structure of business itself. Not until the beginnings of the merger movements in the 1870's did business organization begin to take on the new forms of corporate collectivism.
2. Mergers, combined with powerful fiscal intervention into industry by Eastern banking (Boston and New York), resulted in the first major steps toward horizontal and vertical organization of firms. The structural pattern for the vertical and horizontal control of industrial "sectors" of the economy was established at this

time and formed the basis for the increasing size of industrial enterprise.

3. This process of almost total horizontal and vertical absorption has continued to the present time and has resulted in the giant enterprises we now know. In recent times even the concepts of horizontal and vertical integration have changed so that they need not include firms and industries from a single sector of the economy. The diversification of business seems to be restricted only by opportunity and the businessman's imagination.

In the second half of the twentieth century the form of industrial organization is best described as a giant state within the state. Enterprises like Ford, du Pont, and General Motors, to mention only a few, are complexes which spread over the globe and seek to absorb other firms wherever on earth they may be.

General Motors' gross receipts of $24.3 billion in 1969 exceeds the national budget of all countries in the world except the United States, Russia, England, Japan, and France.* Standard Oil (N.J.) and Ford Motor Company, with sales of over $14 billion, lag only slightly behind. A number of corporations in the United States have gross annual sales which exceed the gross income of New York State, and hundreds of corporations have gross incomes which exceed those of the smaller American states. According to Gabriel Kolko, "In 1955 the 200 top non-financial companies—most of which dominated their respective industries as price and policy leaders—directly owned 43.0 percent of the total assets of 435,000 non-financial corporations." According to *Fortune* magazine (July 1965), the five hundred largest industrial corporations in the United States employ nearly three-fifths of all people working in United States manufacturing and mining companies. The assets of these same companies were valued in 1965 at $224.6 billion. The extent of capital concentration and pyramidization in industry and banking has gone far beyond the imagination of even the New Deal's Temporary National Economic Committee reports on industrial concentration in the thirties. And still the trend toward concentration, rationalization, and technological penetration continues, especially in areas affected by new technol-

* As reported in *Fortune,* May 1970, p. 182.

ogies and in areas previously neglected by efforts at concentration.

Given the economic trends toward immensity now prevailing in our society, one has a curiously mixed image of American business and its impact on society. Since the 1950's blue-collar workers, the raw materials on which industrial bureaucracy works, have ceased to occupy a majority position in the composition of the labor force. White-collar and managerial classes have in numbers become the dominant class in our society. The American farmer is becoming an insignificant part of the labor force numerically; small business appears to hold its own, though our definitions of smallness in business tend to become larger, so that many small business enterprises are in fact organizationally complicated. This is particularly true of the small manufacturing plant which supplies a specific part or unit to a giant corporation. Other small enterprises which still function at the fringes of the economy do so because the unit cost of absorbing them would be too great for the fixed and administrative costs of big business. This accounts for a fairly large number of small firms with one, two, or three hundred employees, which, however, are small only in comparison to the giants.

Economic concentration and growth in size of firms are directly related to the organizational requirements of business. The greater a firm's markets, the greater its organizational requirements and the more complex its organizational structure. The tendency since the Civil War has been for a continuous growth in size, irrespective of legislative efforts to the contrary. With corporate giantism, the possibilities for the survival of small firms is greatly reduced, and when they do survive, their existence depends on a specific constellation of circumstances.

When a large corporation enters a new area of production or distribution, its overhead costs, particularly in the form of salaries to middle and top management, are so great that it must anticipate a mass market to achieve profitability: the product or service must be sold on a mass basis in order to absorb established overhead costs. In any area of production or distribution where a high level of craftsmanship of product or service is a condition of production, the market for the item may be so small that these overhead costs prevent the large corporation from competing with smaller firms not burdened with heavy administrative, organizational, and other fixed costs.

For example, a giant corporation such as General Electric or the Radio Corporation of America can profitably mass-produce low-cost stereo or television sets. But these superefficient giants have found it difficult to enter the market for expensive, handcrafted stereo, hi-fi, and, until recently, color television sets. Given technological breakthroughs, a handcrafted product may submit to mass production and thus result in the elimination of small producers: this is the history of the automobile industry. So long as technological know-how and workmanship rather than capital are basic in an industry, relatively small firms may still exist in large numbers and perhaps even dominate a given market area.

In agriculture it appeared for a long time that dairying could not be reduced to mass production. The limit on the size of a milking herd seemed to be related to the size of the farm, feed, labor, bovine habits, and markets. It now appears, in Iowa, at least, that milk production too can be industrialized on a mass basis. Centralized feeding, transport of food to the cow, and continuous milking make this possible. Increase in the size of the herd makes it possible to run milking machines and milkers on eight-hour shifts in a manner exactly equivalent to the automobile assembly line. The farmer-herdsman who knew the name of each cow is eliminated and is replaced by a technician-milker who for eight hours a day stands in the milking pit processing an endless stream of cows. Under this method, productivity is so extremely efficient that Midwestern markets cannot absorb it all. This has prompted researchers in Iowa universities to devise a method for freezing a milk concentrate, which when unfrozen and diluted will retain the original milk flavor. When this is perfected, Iowa milk will be sold in New York, like frozen orange juice, and the smaller Eastern milk producers will lose their competitive advantage now based on their nearness to the fluid milk markets. These trends will lead to the elimination of smaller producers and an increase in the size of remaining producers.

The dairy industry is only one example. Lettuce, nut, grape, asparagus, carrot, apple, citrus fruit, and other kinds of agricultural production and distribution have submitted to automatized industrial procedures. Agriculture in California and Florida has been a leader in this process. In the case of cotton, as noted by Lauchlin Currie, mechanization has reduced the man-hours necessary for its production from 160 about twenty-five years ago to ten to twelve now. Production units of between 5,000 and 10,000 acres are quite common in Texas and California, and one farm consists of 86,000 acres. The large-scale corporate farm has replaced, or will in short course replace, the small agricultural business.

Elimination of small firms by the use of technological efficiency and capital intensification is only one method. There is also the method when, in the process of competition, a small firm becomes large enough to develop a wide marketing base through quality and reputation, and becomes ripe for acquisition by larger firms. In business circles this is known as a corporate acquisition, a process which since 1945 has been carried out on an unprecedented scale. The tendencies for horizontal, vertical, and diversified growth in the modern corporation make the small firm a choice object.

Finally, even where handcrafted technology cannot be industrialized for technological reasons, its marketing may be taken over by a retailing giant. Thus the rationalization of retailing becomes the marketing vehicle for the "handicraft" technology of small scientific and quality products.

The results of this revolution in business size and organization are not only economic in effect but have consequences for the occupational, social, and personal lives of those who fall within the revolution's area of impact. The large-scale organization has developed means of administration which structure both the character of relations between people and the relationships between business and other institutions in American society.

Since World War II the giant U.S. corporation has flexed its muscles on the international scene as well, especially in petroleum, minerals, and manufactures. Corporations in these areas now operate on a worldwide market far more than most governments of the world. They thus conduct international relations, make diplomatic and economic development policy, and perform higher-level public relations in their dealings with foreign governments. For the most part a representative of a major firm will deal directly with heads of state as if such relations existed on a state-to-state basis. In the case of large firms, their policies can result in the economic development or nondevelopment of a country, as is true, for example, of Venezuelan and Middle Eastern oil interests. In some cases such political and economic activities can make and remake governments and stimulate revolutions. Through economic investments in local politics, large American corporations can build constituencies and affect the social structure of "host" countries. It would be naive not to acknowledge these structural changes in the position of corporate institutions in the United States.

IDEOLOGICAL RESISTANCE TO BUSINESS DOMINATION

The enormous growth in the size and scope of business units since the Civil War crosses the ideological grain of the American population, especially its liberal segment. A substantial part of American ideological ethics was founded on Jeffersonian and Jacksonian democracy, whose cultural "hero" was the strong, independent, free-speaking farmer. This is the image of the sturdy, proud yeoman beholden to no one, yet fundamentally decent.* The values of this heritage are equalitarianism, self-respect, and those democratic virtues that stem from belief in individual responsibility, economic independence, and a self-assertive manliness based on taking pride in one's accomplishments and creativity. This earlier heritage of rugged American individualism has always come in conflict with organized "bigness."

American populism was built on the foundations of Jacksonian democracy. After the Civil War this populism supplied the farmers with a rhetoric and ideology that allowed them to reject in part their alliance with business when they saw that government policy in this area constituted an attack on the small independent farmer. Post–Civil War monetary, tariff, and pricing policies all disadvantaged the farmer. The growth of industry and business organizations left the farmer vulnerable even in those instances when he formed his own organizations to protect himself. The conflict of the farmers with "Eastern" money has continued until today to be part of the farmer's rhetoric in areas where there are still small farmers. But in the long run the small farmer has been defeated not by business directly but by the industrialization of

* America historically has not had a peasant class, though in colonial society bondmen were a large part of the population. The nearest thing to a peasant class were imported black slaves who were brought to America because the indigenous Indian population did not easily lend itself to bondage and the sedentary habits of farming.

farming itself and by federal agricultural policies.* Even in defeat, however, farmers, more tenaciously than any other group, have held to nineteenth-century populist ideologies and rhetoric.

Other groups in post–Civil War America have reacted to corporate giantism in different ways. The ideology of small businessmen has always been shaped partly by their illusion that they too could become big businessmen. This particular illusion has been part of the basis of strength of the Republican party, even when the party has weakened small business through its national policies. Because its hope has been to become *big* business, small business has vacillated between opposition and advocacy of restraints on competition which would protect it from the onslaughts of organized bigness. Small business has been ambivalent and for the most part politically emasculated in the face of corporate dominance.

Labor, mainly immigrant in origin, experienced most directly the financial and physical exploitation of the new industrial giants. In the latter part of the nineteenth century, and in this century up to the 1930's, labor had at times been driven to desperation and to sporadic rebellion against big business. Because of its immigrant character (multiplicity of origins and languages), however, labor has been difficult to organize. The growth of business was therefore never seriously threatened by labor organizations. Labor remained pliable and weak in spite of the heroism of some of its early leaders, while the continuous influx of new immigrants up to 1924 provided industry with a continuously expanding and almost always disorganized labor force. Not until the thirties did this situation change, but by that time labor had acquired the habit of distrusting big business.

American intellectuals have generally resented business, a resentment which has several sources. One source is the "worship" of an American "aristocratic" past. For the North, Henry Adams in his *Education of Henry Adams* conveys his distaste for the whole tone of

* American agricultural expansiveness was subsidized by the land-grant system of agricultural and mechanical colleges in all parts of the country. While the original intention of this system was to stimulate agriculture, in fact the land-grant colleges focused on technology and the rationalization of production processes. The development and production of agricultural machinery stimulated and shaped the growth of American manufacturing as much as it accounted for increases in agricultural productivity.

American business life in the postbellum period. The defeated Southern aristocracy saw the *nouveau riche* businessmen of the North as alien to the gentility they had known. This was also true of the "aristocracy" of Virginia. In fact, a major aspect of the American literary tradition, as seen in such writers as Herman Melville, Mark Twain, Edward Bellamy, Henry George, Sinclair Lewis, and H. L. Mencken, can only be understood as a reaction against the vulgarity, immorality, tastelessness, and greed of big business. The other source of intellectual disgust with American business was expressed by the muckrakers—Lincoln Steffens, Gustavus Myers, Ida Tarbel, Jacob Riis, and Upton Sinclair, among others. Their disgust was with the brutal qualities of business, especially as it related to politics and economic exploitation. American intellectuals, in their self-appointed superiority, have lived off their excoriation of business.

But almost all major groups from the 1880's to the recent past have been hostile to large-scale business enterprise. Ironically, even though big business became the dominant institution in American society, the dominant ideology of America was based on attacking its dominant institution. In its legal forms, the curse of bigness was defined by Louis Brandeis, and this ideological theme remained extremely potent in American life until the late 1930's.

Throughout the period beginning in the late nineteenth century and to the present, "populist," labor, intellectual, "aristocratic" opposition to big business resulted in a succession of reforms. Every major business scandal, corrupt practice, and unethical excess gave anti-business groups grounds for regulatory legislation. These reforms nevertheless had a piecemeal quality, as indicated by the Sherman and Clayton anti-trust laws, the federal Food Laws, the Interstate Commerce Act, the Norris-LaGuardia Anti-Injunction Act, the Federal Reserve Act, the Securities Exchange Act, and so on. In spite of continuous efforts of reformers and their success in achieving reform and amelioration, the final product *in toto* has been curious and unanticipated.

Even though business resisted every reform and regulation that would limit its economic power, it never succeeded in wholly defeating the reform and control legislation. In a curious way, however, the attacks on the curse of big business were translated into a legitimation of it. The long-term effect of all such legislation was to assure increasing segments of the American population that business was being controlled and that its corrupt practices were being eliminated, or at least that they were improved because of the safeguards being provided by a benevolent and watchful government. The popular psychology has been so haunted by the issues raised by populism that it has concentrated all of its hostility on the ethical practices and external relations of big business. As a result the public has been blind to the enormous growth in size and power of the American corporation as well as to its internal structure. With every attack on big business, followed by regulatory legislation and federal control commissions, the size of the corporate giants has increased and their number decreased. In the end, the federal bureaucracy which was designed partly to control business simply coexisted with it. The history of the New Deal and the Fair Deal are excellent illustrations of this growth and the blindness.

FDR AND THE RESCUE OF BIG BUSINESS BY THE NEW DEAL

The indisputable place of big business in American society at the present time contrasts with its position in the 1930's. At that time the New Deal was caught between a philosophy of anti-big-business legislation best symbolized by the Banking Act and the Federal Power Act, which prevented holding companies from operating at more than three tiers, and the National Industrial Recovery Act, which invited big business to set up councils within the framework of government to regulate and civilize competition among, primarily, the industrial giants. Though Franklin D. Roosevelt's rhetoric was always anti–big business ("the economic royalists"), his politics vacillated between an attack on business and a defense of it. Though business rejected Roosevelt with hatred, it was Roosevelt who rescued business from its own greed and incompetence and, at times, even furthered the role of business in national policy-making. It is hard to say now what the success of Roosevelt's domestic policies would have been if World War II had not intervened. In any event, the international crisis and World War II resulted in the incorporation of big business into the highest councils of government.

Those were the heady days of dollar-a-year men in government serving the purpose of gearing war production needs to requirements of business organization. It was during this stage just before and during

World War II that federal funds began to be made available to business in previously unimagined doses. These funds assured business of stable production schedules and "cost-plus" contracts on a scale incomparable with all previous experience. Business was able to achieve in a few years a stage of scale in organization which might otherwise have taken decades to accomplish if the development had depended on intrinsic growth. Ironically, this growth occurred despite the reluctance of business to suspend domestic production in favor of war production. At the time business apparently feared an overdependence on government orders and excessive government controls, and was uncertain about the liberality of government contracts. But the government controls that were ultimately established were those of big business over itself. This was a specific role of the dollar-a-year man: a businessman in government who acted for business. In fact, these controls resulted in the largest growth of business. With time, business has learned the advantages of the government contract and federal regulation of competition. C. Wright Mills was correct in stating that American business is led by mediocrities: they were so completely lacking in imagination that they fought against almost every policy and law that ultimately brought them expanded profits and economic opportunities.* The businessman's conservative mentality has frequently been his greatest enemy; Roosevelt persisted in the late thirties, and by the end of World War II business had recovered completely from its defensive position of the 1930's.

After World War II President Truman, more the populist than Roosevelt, attacked big business in terms that were even more opprobrious than any used by FDR. Yet during the Korean War, Truman, under the National Production Authority, allowed big business to dominate pricing, production, and the spending policies of the federal government. It appears that it was during the Truman years, a relatively

* Most of the technological innovation and increasing efficiency of American business has not been the product of the "captain of industry." By and large such leaders were financial manipulators. At lower levels were craftsmen (such as Edison) with the "American genius for improvisation." The genius of American business was its knowledge of when to exploit and restrain these technological virtuosos.

In the modern era, the stimulation of innovation and capital replacement has been achieved by depreciation allowances, by protective capital reserves, and by federally subsidized research and development programs.

neglected area of study, that American society came closest to being a corporate economic state. Truman, more disliked by business than other recent Presidents, had the least power when it came to controlling business. Yet it was under the Truman administration that American big business, perhaps for the first time, fully realized that its interests were coincident with those of big government.

The long-term trend in the growth of size of corporate units has been noted by a number of contemporary social scientists. Thorstein Veblen, Adolf Berle and Gardiner Means, James Burnham, Peter Drucker, and Robert Brady, to mention a few, were able to convince some segments of the public through their writings that the giant corporation had become a dominant institution in American society. Collectively, such writers described the revolutionary impact of corporate penetration into all aspects of American life to the point where the trend was irreversible.

We are now at the point, whether we like it or not, where we live in a society where big business is a dominant institution. Our knowledge of this situation has come relatively late and is repressed because it disturbs the comfort and prosperity of a middle-class America that is primarily employed by big business.

3. *Business, bureaucracy, and personality*

BUREAUCRACY AND THE CONFORMING PERSONALITY

In his now classic work, *Capitalism, Socialism and Democracy,* Joseph Schumpeter first reopened the question of bureaucracy and modern business enterprise. In that book Schumpeter attacked the problem posed by Marx in his theory of the inevitability of crises in capitalism due to its internal contradictions. Schumpeter refuted this central idea of Marx on both economic and sociological grounds. As an economist he argued that capitalism continually renews itself through the process of "creative destruction." This means that the processes of continuous innovation, invention, and new technologies under the impetus of competition result in constant obsolescence, all of which creates demands for new investment and capital. The continuous production of new automobile models and the growth of the range of household electrical appliances are two simple illustrations. At a more fundamental level, a change in the process of steel production by the use of taconite or forced oxygen methods makes the existing plant obsolete. Finally, military hardware, especially airplanes and rockets, may be made obsolete by new designs even before it is used, or if used may be destroyed the first time it is used. Innovation, invention, and obsolescence provide the basis for renewed expansion and counter the tendency for the contraction in capitalism which, according to Marx, occurs whenever a given form of capital reaches a high degree of development. Thus the tendency for capital investment to fall off with the consequence of unemployment and underutilization of capital, as described by Marx, does not become a reality because under such competitive conditions each tendency in this direction is accompanied by new forms of technology and capital. The net result is a further expansion which counteracts the effect of the "inherent dilemma of capitalism."

Schumpeter places great stress on the entrepreneur's role of creative destruction in the competitive industrial structure. For him the entrepreneur has a restless, dynamic, and destructive temperament which acts against the stabilizing and contracting tendencies of the capitalistic system. In utilizing this idea, Schumpeter paralleled Weber's earlier work, *The Protestant Ethic and the Spirit of Capitalism,* which emphasizes the role of the freewheeling, unbureaucratized entrepreneur in providing creativity, imagination, and an irreverence for all established forms in the pursuit of his conquest and domination of the world. But Schumpeter, being a pessimist, foresaw more than any other commentator of his day the tendency for business to become monopolistic and bureaucratic, and as a result to produce a new social type—the business bureaucrat whose chief characteristic is a desire to keep things moving routinely, on an even keel. This business bureaucrat would hope to avoid disrupting existing procedures and would thus routinize capitalism, a tendency which if it became dominant would suppress the innovation that was the salvation of capitalism. The business bureaucrat would thus be the major enemy of the system of capitalism which he espouses ideologically.

Moreover, Schumpeter said, the development of capitalism would result in the destruction of older feudal, military, and landowning classes whose function in the past was to provide a protective governmental or ideological framework for the economy. Since businessmen were incapable of exercising these functions, the destruction of these classes would leave capitalism naked and governed by incompetents. Schumpeter's pessimism may have been warranted when he wrote in the depths of the depression, but he failed to see that government itself could provide the necessary impetus for innovation. It is in this sense that government spending, that is, Keynesian economics, has assumed a crucial role in maintaining a "capitalist" system.* In addition, as we shall see later, American business has produced a third generation of political and ideological leaders—men such as John D. Rockefeller, Laurence Rockefeller, August Hecksher, Averell Harriman, Robert F. Kennedy, and William Scranton—who have begun to demonstrate competence in those functions which Schumpeter argues they were incapable of exercising.

Since 1936, and especially during and after World War II, world capitalism has been supported by a whole range of new forms of technology and capital in chemistry, petroleum, steel, aluminum, transport, electronics, pharmaceuticals, atomic energy, and space and military hardware. Moreover, these new forms have been supported by government expenditures, particularly in military investments and technological innovations. The billions of dollars of support of research and development by government and "private" industry has not only provided a new motive for innovation but has rationalized it and made it a stable industrial institution. At the level of private business, research and development is supported by tax exemptions insofar as it is regarded as a current cost or business expense. In this way it becomes a form of capital accumulation subsidized by taxes. Thus the economy has continued to expand to levels which would have been unimaginable even to Henry Wallace in 1948 when he called for 60 million jobs. The discussions and arguments about mature capitalism heard in the thirties have been wholly forgotten in the light of subsequent events.

Yet a significant aspect of Schumpeter's work was to call attention to the existence of the business bureaucrat and to point out some of the implications of his psychology for the large-scale business organization. This "organization man" did not possess the restless, creative,

* Schumpeter's argument runs as follows: The firm in a competitive industry (i.e., an industry in which no single firm is large enough to influence price of inputs or outputs) makes no profits. The entrepreneur seeking profits wishes to create at least a temporary monopoly. He does so by innovation (of any kind) which he can introduce to give him a cost advantage or new market, etc., to gain temporary monopoly and thus profit. The other firms, however, do the same thing, and industry tends to return to competitive conditions. Thus a process is created which produces a steady stream of innovations as sources of investment and capital formation. Schumpeter also saw that tendency toward bureaucracy and centralization would destroy the conditions of innovation; but he did not see government taking the place of competition.

destructive energy of the entrepreneur, but, rather, was interested in conducting business as usual, getting along, and being mainly concerned with his career within the framework of a stabilized, established business. In thus applying Weber's formulation of the government bureaucrat to the business world, Schumpeter opened up a whole new dimension to the discussion of modern business.

Schumpeter's idea became popular and reached the general public through William H. Whyte in his book *The Organization Man,* which describes the development of the new social ethic of the man who works in a large business organization. This ethic consists of getting along, cooperating, limiting one's mobility aspirations, not being offensive, and adhering to an ideology of democratic decision-making in business. This business bureaucrat willingly accepts his place *within* the organization. Whyte also described the ideologies of schools of business administration and management which train and support the type. In the emphasis which these schools place on human relations, cooperation, and democratic ethics in business, would-be aspirants to the business world are taught to be more accepting of moderate goals at respectable levels. Thus Whyte, like Schumpeter, saw a fairly deep erosion of the older competitive and buccaneering spirit of the business entrepreneur. Instead, the new bureaucratic capitalism and its supporting agencies such as the business schools and management training programs reject ruthless competition and intensive mobility in favor of a more placid and comfortable world. In their totality these tendencies point in the direction of a stabilized managerial class and a class system in which each group accepts its status at given achieved levels.

David Riesman contributed to this image of a society composed of pleasant mediocrities whom he called "other-directed" men in his book *The Lonely Crowd.* But Riesman did not base his description or his argument on developments within industry. Rather, he saw population density, the mass media, and the unavailability of the father as a strong point of authoritative identification as root causes for producing an individual who is mainly concerned with pleasing others because he lacks standards of his own. With his other-directed, spineless men, Riesman produced a powerful image of the fifties. The influence of McCarthyism may have reinforced this image for Americans who worried about the lack of courage and strength in their political leaders, and for academic intellectuals who somewhat spinelessly submitted to the errant gall of McCarthy, Cohn, and Shine. The serious weakness of Riesman's work is that he was not able to demonstrate the specific institutional dynamics which produced his other-directed man.* Nor did he see him as a product of institutional changes in American life.

The link between the other-directed man of the fifties and the American past is provided in Weber's essay on the "Protestant Sects in America," in which Weber showed that the businessman of nineteenth-century America slavishly conformed to the manners and morals of his religious sect and of service groups like the Rotary Club, emulating others in order to prove among other things that he was morally worthy of credit in narrowly financial terms. The other-directed type has been well known on the Main Streets of America and is not unfamiliar to the readers of de Tocqueville and Sinclair Lewis, each of whom examined the type in detail without using Riesman's term. Nevertheless, Riesman reopened the issue and emphasized the society-wide extent of the other-directed conformist.

Seen in the context of Weber's essay, Riesman's other-directed man is linked to the tradition of the Protestant sects (small businessmen and independent farmers), whereas Whyte's organization man, paralleling Schumpeter, is linked to large-scale bureaucratic enterprise.

Undoubtedly, large-scale business is much more "sociable" in its form than small business or farming, in which the product rather than the personality of the businessman tends to be the measure of personal value. In either case, however, to understand the sources of other-directedness one would have to understand the social institutions that reward or penalize sociability as a positive or negative virtue. Since Riesman does not do this, he describes a relevant and observable social type without explaining its basis.

CONFORMITY AS A MASK FOR THE MANIPULATION OF BUREAUCRACY

The connection between Schumpeter, Weber, Riesman, and Whyte, and the work of C. Wright Mills is at face value not clear. Mills's image of the bureaucratic personality, especially as portrayed in *White Collar*

* Riesman accepted this criticism in later editions of his book.

and *The Sociological Imagination,* is substantially different from the other-directed and organization men. For him the bureaucratic world is a jungle in which struggles for power, back-stabbing with a smile, cliques, cabals, and Machiavellianism are everyday norms. Bureaucracy generates a whole range of types which include inside-dopesters, five-percenters, Bobby Bakers, con artists, Billie Sol Esteses, influence peddlers, sycophants, hatchet men, and organizational pirates and ahabs. But Mills agrees with Whyte, Riesman, and Schumpeter that the personality type of the bureaucrat is on the exterior smooth, sociable, agreeable, cooperative, bland, unaggressive, friendly, and rotarian, while, however, seeing that these traits are necessary for survival in the bureaucratic jungle.

In Mills's perspective, the other-oriented organization style becomes the character mask of the bureaucratic entrepreneur which enables him to conceal the special styles of competition, throat-cutting, and warfare characteristic of bureaucratic settings. Mills's imagery comes closer to describing a courtlike setting where the participants in the action are smiling, self-seeking, calculating, opportunistic Machiavellians.*

* In fact, it would seem that descriptions of what actually takes place within the managerial ranks (when not glossed by official ideology) corresponds to Mills's and not to Whyte's or Riesman's imagery. Melville Dalton's book *Men Who Manage* suggests a managerial world of cliques, competitive cooperation, use and abuse of the privileges of rank, capacity to make the ruthless decision when a sale, a contract, or a job is at stake, and so on. Any novel of the business world portrays exactly the same picture. Books like Hawley's *Executive Suite,* Robin Moore's *Pitchman,* Burnett's *The Brain Pickers,* and Laine's *The S Man,* except for their humor, make jungle warfare look relatively tame. To take almost at random a passage from *The S Man:*

> The success is a master of duplicity, yes; but one pole of his character is appalling honesty. There is nothing so completely disarming as complete honesty about oneself, whether it be true or false. We have shown that you can secure the allegiance of a man by encouraging him to "give himself away" to you; there is also the reverse: a kind of tolerant affection and confidence in you can be secured from others by letting slip for a moment the mask of charm and insouciance which is so much a feature of your character, and revealing the sure countenance of ambition which is on duty beneath it. This device of unexpected frankness is invaluable in cases where the man to whom you are speaking has already shown that he already suspects what you now frankly confess (New York, 1962, p. 149).

In business the degrees and levels of consciousness are fabulously intricate and complex; presumably it requires the literate insider to provide sensitive portrayals. Compared with novelistic reports, even Dale Carnegie seems pale. In

This conflict in images of the business bureaucrat in the managerial society is best resolved by Karl Mannheim, whose work on this particular point precedes that of Whyte, Riesman, and Mills. In *Man and Society in an Age of Reconstruction,* Mannheim describes a process which he calls self-rationalization. In this process the aspiring, would-be bureaucrat takes inventory of his personal characteristics, his skills, his assets, and his liabilities. Insofar as possible he treats himself as an object. He then analyzes the needs of the market to which he intends to address himself, and undertakes a systematic effort to make himself over into the smooth, agreeable, bland, tailored, other-directed official that will enable him to succeed. In this respect the self-rationalized man resembles Benjamin Franklin, who, in his effort to improve himself, made himself over into the embodiment of the classic Protestant virtues which he described in his autobiography. But Franklin transformed himself not only to become economically successful but to improve himself morally, ethically, intellectually, and personally. The self-rationalized man, in contrast, performs this act primarily as a means of getting ahead in business or politics. He adopts a character mask designed to conceal his intention.

Thus the other-directed man has, in fact, all the features described by Whyte and Riesman, but the act of acquiring and of acting out these external character forms implies a self-consciousness and intention that are not revealed by the forms themselves. To accept the concepts of the other-directed or the organization man on their face value is to miss the major point. Working in the tradition of G. H. Mead, Erving Goffman, in his book *The Presentation of Self in Everyday Life,* and especially in his later essay "The Moral Career of the Mental Patient," in his *Asylums,* describes the process of masked performances, which is entirely applicable to the organizational personality. Though Goffman's later work was done in the mental institution and would appear for this reason to be a special case, it is really the generic case of bureaucratic life, for the mental patient is located in a segregated, totally bureaucratic institution. As Goffman describes it, the art of survival and success in the total institution requires an ability to develop the

---

any case, we would argue that these reports are much more accurate than those based on academic interviews with businessmen who on such public occasions tend to respond in terms of ideology rather than of the reality of business.

arts of dissimulation in their highest degree. The mental patient is cured when he has perfected the art of impression management, and it is precisely at that point that he is permitted to enter the outside world, where adjustment and success demand the possession of this skill. In this sense, Goffman's work is a curious transvaluation of the social psychology of Mead, who postulated the growth of a generalized other (conscience) out of relationships with specific others. It would appear that survival in bureaucracy depends upon suspending conventional moral codes and developing a multiplicity of moralities, each specific to specific significant others. Bureaucracy destroys all older forms of conscience.

While the aforementioned authors have seen important aspects of the consequences of bureaucracy for personality, C. Wright Mills explored these trends more directly and comprehensively. His work is especially important in focusing upon at least two different aspects of bureaucratic giantism. In *The Power Elite* Mills points to the same processes of bureaucratic centralization in politics as have occurred in business, a problem we shall deal with in Chapters 5 and 6. Actually, Mills's discussion of political bureaucracy goes back directly to Weber's examination of the entire issue of bureaucracy in modern society. In *White Collar* Mills deals more directly with our present problem of personality and bureaucracy. Given the changes which we have noted in the American business and occupational structure, he saw that the central personality type of American society has become the white-collar managerial worker.

Modern bureaucracies, both in business and government, are for Mills competitive jungles in which the form of social competition is the denial of that competition. The bureaucrat is expected to be warm, friendly, sociable, congenial, and apparently bland, unless one casts himself in the role of a "genius" or a technically creative artist, or unless one does not aspire. The major personal virtue, apart from possession of the technical skills necessary to a job, is a self-control which does not allow the raw personality to be perceived and which conceals anger, spontaneity, and warmth, except when such qualities can help to attain specific objectives. At the same time, success in such competition requires that one be aware of all the technical, political, social, and psychological undercurrents without ever revealing one's awareness. Social and psychological sensitivity is maximized, even though the naive observer may find little visible evidence of it. In the back corners and interstices of the organization there are informal agreements, plots, cabals, and so on, in which, depending on the relationships between the parties, only the manifest content of the intention is revealed even within these groups themselves. Only occasionally, in drinking bouts and in office parties, and sometimes in satire and humor, are the undercurrents revealed.* Insofar as the bureaucratic *form* has come to permeate all areas of modern life, it can be expected that its accompanying psychological *consequences* will be expressed in all areas. Thus in its psychological overtones, life in business bureaucracies is not much different from life in political, educational, or religious bureaucracies.

EDUCATIONAL TRAINING FOR PARTICIPATION IN BUREAUCRACY

The creation and function of the "bureaucratic personality," with all its characteristics of dissimulation through image-making and maintaining a personable façade, takes place long before the individual's first encounter with the occupational world. It is the widespread requirement of a college degree that traditionally has provided the anticipatory socialization for life in the outside bureaucratic world. Four years of work at acquiring the diploma provides training and skills in academic infighting and provides the individual with acceptable rhetorics and sophisticated sociability. In the typical classroom the aspiring collegian competes with his peers at all levels of the collegiate experience. He knows that ideologies of honesty, integrity, and "doing one's own thing" are frequently strained to the breaking point because a competitive advantage accrues to those who use "unconventional" methods to attract attention and define themselves as leaders. Collegians often demonstrate a high degree of combative cooperation to nullify what have been traditionally regarded as objective measures of performance. Thus the "pass grade" increasingly replaces more specific letter grades, forcing employers and graduate schools to rely either

* Fictional writing by former bureaucrats frequently reveals much more of the working of the organization than of the public atmosphere, as is illustrated, for example, by the work of Shepherd Mead in his book *How to Succeed in Business Without Really Trying*.

on subjective criteria or on ever more complicated rating and recommendation procedures. As administration and the bureaucratic ethos more deeply pervade the entire structure of the modern university, a major unanticipated function of the college experience has become one of training in the arts of public and organizational combat and confrontation.

The neophyte's recognition of this preparation for bureaucratic warfare, and the knowledge that he is about to enter the castrating bureaucratic machine has been a major stimulus to the emergence of the New Left. The major tenets of its ideology include hostility to all forms of bureaucracy and an affirmation, however impractical, of a wide range of spontaneous, activist, and democratic methods of participation. In short, the new college radical responds to images of bureaucratic society by rebelling against the form of bureaucratic organization that is nearest to him, that is, the university. This is true despite the fact that compared with business or government organizations, the university is not especially bureaucratic. The student is responding more to his image of his future outside the university, than to the university: his response is one of anticipatory frustration. In part, this may be caused by the appearance of bureaucratic administrations in universities, and, ironically, it may also be a by-product of his image of contemporary society as received from liberal or "left" professors.

Even the child in nursery school or in the primary grades learns to compete with his colleagues for the attention, affection, and recognition of his teachers. Insofar as schools are organized by administrative rules, even under a regime of "creativity" ideology which attempts to organize the process of instilling individuality, the innocent child learns the rules of the system. Thus, for example, in the Montessori system, regardless of his own goals, he learns to act out simulated spontaneity, to be his true self while being watched, judged, and evaluated by teachers who reward the performers according to their (adult) standards of juvenile individuality. All administratively imposed standards of creative performance destroy the possibilities of spontaneity. In the nursery school in the modern system of education, the child begins to learn the limits and boundaries of permitted expression if he wishes to survive successfully. Instead of learning spontaneity, which by definition cannot be learned, he learns to act out those predefined gestures of spontaneous creativity that earn him the immediate rewards of recognition and success in the group. In these terms the nursery school for the middle class becomes the primary training ground for participation in the world of occupational bureaucracy.

In the educational system from nursery school to college a genteel atmosphere has traditionally pervaded. The expression of competition is suppressed while competitiveness nevertheless remains the basis of the system, no matter how much it is submerged in forms of gentility. This educational system, which in reality is preparation for the occupational and commercial world, has until the recent past appeared to be wholly removed from mundane considerations. Rarely in the educational system are money-making, promotions, production, and competition overtly stressed. The college campus permits the neophyte competitor to think that he can act strategically as a gentleman while making his success in the world. Thus college trains for competition without fully revealing the seriousness of success or failure. The college graduate is prepared for the competition, but is left with the impression that he is engaged in a game.

Before his first postgraduate job, the collegian prepares for the adult world by simulating both the gentility and competitiveness of bureaucratic competition in a game. In this sense college, secondary, and elementary schools are war games for adult life. But because they are games, they can be played tongue-in-cheek, with humor, satire, and burlesque. The player may recognize that a single or even a series of defeats are instructional, so long as he is not forced to drop out of the game.

When he graduates, the collegian enters the lower ranks of the bureaucracy. In his first job he begins to see the world in a different light than he did while he was in college. The world is now bigger. It no longer has the protective shield of the nonserious collegiate atmosphere. Rank, income, and status differentials become more meaningful than before. The consequences of defeat are more serious. In recognition of that seriousness, the forms of warfare, while masked, are often more destructive. Thus college students can riot and burn down buildings with a sense of joy, levity, and euphoria, and bureaucrats can destroy each other while pretending to be friendly, cooperative, and comradely.

His first job in a bureaucracy has a radical effect on the world view of the collegian. First of all, rank in the bureaucracy becomes patently visible to him for the first time. Upon reflection, if he is sensitive, he may even see in a wholly new light the politics of bureaucracy in the collegiate department which he once felt was protected from such base considerations. The initiate to the "real" world of bureaucracy looks upward and sees a vast hierarchy which, if he is to be successful, he must climb. Except for the unresurrected collegiate rebels, who become aware of and reject the differences between reality and appearances, the average American middle-class youth still accepts the challenge of success, though at times he uses the techniques of moral blackmail, existential honesty, and democratic equalitarianism to gain success in a hypocritical authoritarian bureaucracy.

THE BUREAUCRATIC MILIEU

Once in the bureaucracy, youth tends to participate in its culture no matter how narrow or sectarian it may be. If one becomes involved, he becomes committed in his area of specialization. And in every area there is a bureaucratic culture of house organs, publications, rewards, personnel management, linguistic style—all of which set the norms for success. The initiate learns which steps he must climb in order to "make it" in the field. He becomes involved with the culture of his field, which means that he accepts as his guidelines the income and occupational norms appropriate to the ladder he must climb in order to "reach the top." In the immediate postcollege period almost all individuals still entertain the idea of success.

The workaday world not only has a sobering influence, however, but takes its toll. Each aspirant begins to see that there are many income stages and alternative promotional possibilities. It does not take long, in spite of secrecy about salary and privilege, for the individual to acquire a fairly good notion of where he stands, not only in the firm but in the industry as a whole and in the ranks of his technical or professional specialization.

Nor does it take him long to learn that not all his chosen competitors advance at equal rates. Types and rates of success within the firm or the profession provide the basis for forming friendship groups and cliques among those whose general level of success or failure is roughly similar. Each of these groups within the bureaucracy begins to develop a subculture of its own, so that it is possible for a myriad of subcultures to exist within the formal apparatus of the organization. For present purposes we wish only to describe two polar types of mentality that are characteristic of bureaucracies.

Those individuals who feel they are advancing at rates equal to or above the rates imputed to their age and occupation tend to develop an optimistic, aggressive, and positive firm-oriented or industry-oriented approach and personality. They identify with the firm, live for the profession, and find their ego supported by official recognition and success, defined in company terms. Their own judgments and aspirations become inseparable from those of the organization. They become spokesmen for the aspirations of the company, occupation, or profession, and, in this sense, they are the embodiment of the institution. One might say that they become walking institutions. In so doing, they exhibit a public personality that is official and impersonal, and they socialize primarily with others who are in a position similar to theirs or, hopefully, with their superiors. If they are both successful and culturally advanced, they will behave like swingers. They will pretend to be above organizational goals, importing new mod styles of speech and dress into the organization and using their leisure to become full-fledged swingers. Even in the midst of the greatest anxieties about their success, they appear to be totally other-directed. The concept of the self-rationalized personality applies especially to this type of official.

At the other extreme are those individuals who, because of technical, personal, or psychological inabilities, find they cannot compete successfully in terms of the standards of the bureaucracy they are in. Because they do not expect success, they are much less likely to identify with the public norms. But in order to survive occupationally, a minimal compliance with the norms is necessary simply to hold the positions they have achieved, which frequently involve at least moderate status, salary, and privilege. The critical factor in the orientation of this type of individual is his estimate of his chance for advancement to higher positions. If he feels there is still some chance of success (which to some extent is correlated with age, the young entertaining more hope than their elders), he may look for a better job with greater opportunities elsewhere. The high rate of job-changing among the young in the great business bureaucracies is related to this factor. He may get his "break" in another organization, but this avenue can also close after five or six job changes. It is clear simply from the limited number of top positions available that most individuals are destined to hold moderate positions at moderate income levels. When the individual begins to realize that his chances are limited, and accepts this fact, he is quite likely to develop other approaches.

First, he is likely to be more prone to express openly his dissatisfaction with his job, his employer, and the "system" of which he is a part. In crisis situations he is apt to engage in self-revealing forms of competition which violate the official norms of organizational etiquette; if he fails in his struggle and is still young enough, this may be the occasion he chooses to move to another job. If, however, he lacks avenues of "escape," he is less likely to express dissatisfaction openly, even in extreme situations. His approach then is more likely to be one of maintaining a passive acceptance of public norms while minimizing his active involvement in the constructive games of mobility, and to be accessible at private levels to descriptions of his firm or organization in personal or psychological terms, rather than in the constructive rhetoric of the organization. Publicly, he leaves the impression of being the obedient, disciplined bureaucratic clod whose work is no longer a source of meaning or engagement. His nonwork life then takes on new meanings and becomes the source of his satisfactions and gratifications.

At precisely this point he is likely to rediscover meaningful activities —hobbies, sports, intellectual pursuits, flowers, music, and other interests that lie outside the scope of the organization. For those so disabused, earlier college training then inadvertently becomes of much greater "use" than had been imagined. The college course in music appreciation, Ibsen, tennis, sailing, flower arrangement, and so on can be resurrected and used as a reserve of "useless" interests to fall back on. Whatever the interest, whether connected to the collegiate past or newly discovered, it provides this individual with a set of identifications which are not connected to the public life of the organization. He finds a set of meanings in the private sphere which makes his job situation more tolerable and endurable.

This change in world outlook from job aspiration to private meanings has an effect on participation within the organizational bureaucracy. Paralleling his dis-identification from the official culture of organization rhetoric, the individual begins to identify downward with groups and cliques lower in the organization than himself. Some of these lower-rung people will still be striving for mobility, others may be resisting dominance by the organizational mentality. In either case, the "dropout" tries to socialize the upcoming generation to the "realities" of bureaucracy, to help disabuse them, to make them allies, and, by so doing, to use them to legitimate his own occupational failure to himself. In one sense he helps the organization by helping to socialize future failures in the way that he was once socialized to accept failure. If his efforts are misdirected on those who become successes, he suffers the fate of being regarded as a cynic, pessimist, and sour-grapes artist. Apart from the results of his underground sabotage, however, these "defenses" are the means he uses to "fight" the constructive mobiles who work at his own and higher levels. He proves, at least, that there is gratification in expressing sublimated hostility and resentment.

PSYCHOLOGICAL RESPONSES TO BUREAUCRATIZATION

All of the foregoing implies that the stable organizational man devotes less than his full capacity to achieving organizational goals which are the instruments of his personal mobility. This problem has become aggravated since the late sixties. Youth failures in high school, college, and on jobs frequently drop out of the competition altogether. Lack of a commitment to mobility thus becomes a problem for the organization, a fact which older administrative and production specialists are well aware of. A mechanical commitment leads to routinization of work, underwork, pleasurable sabotage of efficiency, gamelike good-soldier schweikism, and the perversion of organizational ends. The end in this line of development is a purely noninstrumental sociability at work. The bureaucratic job becomes a place where one goes to "relax" from his other more engaging and meaningful activities. But the term *relax* is not quite appropriate, because no matter how deep the state of disaffection and disengagement, the bureaucrat must involve himself sufficiently to maintain the "flow" of work. In spite of his extra-curricular activities, he cannot *not* be involved because his living depends upon acceptable job performance. In the need to affirm a nonexistent success, the moderately successful individual will overstate his commitment to the traditional public values of his organization. So, in spite of all of the noninstrumental games that are characteristic of bureaucracy, the participants, whether committed or not, do the work demanded of them.

Professional sociologists and students of management have pointed to the clique structures in bureaucracy, to its internal warfare, to the personal and informal quality of interpersonal relations in bureaucracy, and to its complex internal politics to show that the formal structure of bureaucracy does not really operate as intended. The informal group and its social gratifications, the social and political cliques, claques, and cabals, are offered as evidence to show that the formal patterns of organization do not in fact prevail. To the extent that it can be shown that an informal and disaffected viewpoint exists, it has been said that the Weberian description of bureaucracy is not accurate—that the model of Prussian compulsiveness and anality is not general. In these terms American bureaucracy has been seen as a generous, open, non-anal, get-things-done enterprise. By this argument Weber can be shown to apply to imperial Germany but not to the United States.

Yet, for all the differences, it would be a mistake to make this distinction. The Weberian description remains operative precisely because the "nonbureaucratic" responses in the American system of bureaucracy are often a reaction against the official climate, the bureaucratic manual, and the formal table of organization. The informal groups thus respond to and are created in opposition to the official organization. In this negative sense, bureaucracy breeds its own opposition. Some of this opposition exists to affirm the structure of bureaucracy by providing outlets within which disaffection and disaffiliation can be expressed and contained. Other opposition, at least in the ideal, attacks the very structure of social order contained in the bureaucracy or, for that matter, any organized activity; but even this opposition has learned to use bureaucratic techniques and devices to oppose bureaucratic and nonbureaucratic organizations. Success in such opposition, as we shall see in Chapter 13, may well lead to the dominance of new bureaucratic structures or to institutional chaos.

Those individuals who fully embrace their occupational organization make a psychological transvaluation and henceforward identify with its objectives. Their personalities are no longer oriented toward their own personal values but, in transvaluation, become oriented toward the ends of the organization. These are the other-directed organization men at all levels. Those who *cannot* identify, respond instead to the impersonality, the powerlessness, and the sense of isolation that all bureaucracy produces among those who "cannot cope" with the system. These latter attempt to counteract their sense of disaffection by building a life of social and human creativity within the bureaucracy. They make friends of competitors and refuse to engage in cutthroat competition; they try to make a way of life for themselves by civilizing the brutal warfare of bureaucratic politics. No doubt these mild types do lend a civilizing quality to bureaucracy. Yet in spite of their apparent opposition to bureaucracy, they respond to the bureaucratic framework even in their opposition. Their negative response can exist only in relation to what bureaucracy gives them to fight against. In all cases of life within the large organization, bureaucracy sets the framework for action and the terms under which personality is expressed and created.

II.

Political and economic frameworks of the new society

4. *Economic class and personality*

Over the past thirty years American sociologists have made social classes a central dimension of their work. But as they have done so, the economic components of class have become less and less important to theory and research. More and more in American sociology, class has come to mean *social* class. Robert MacIver, W. Lloyd Warner, August Hollingshead, Harold Kaufman, and Richard Centers, to mention only a few analysts, have emphasized the prestige and associational character of class, and by the implication of neglect have reduced the importance of the economic dimension.*

On the other hand, economists who have concerned themselves with social analysis have tended to emphasize the close relationship between social and economic aspects of class. Among these are Thorstein Veblen and all those who have followed the German tradition of political economy. Such figures as Marx, Weber, Sombart, Schumpeter, Tawney, Michels, and Halbwachs have incorporated social, economic, and historical perspectives into their class theories.

Throughout the recent literature on class, attention has been paid

* The work of E. Digby Baltzell, the Lipset and Bendix study *Social Mobility in Industrial Society,* as well as other authors previously mentioned, have, however, dealt with the economic dimensions of class.

only infrequently to the specific relationships between social and economic class, despite the fact that this discussion has covered a wide range of historical periods and almost all points in the social structure.

Here we wish to discuss in a relatively abstract and general way the central themes of economic analysis that appear to underlie most theories of social class. By making these themes explicit in this chapter, we hope to set the framework for a subsequent analysis of changes in social and economic class in American society, especially as they relate to class life styles, the cultures of various classes, personality in relationship to class, politics in relationship to class, and to overall changes in the "class system" as a separate entity. In order to do this we must first specify the basic economic dimensions of class. We have chosen to focus on:

1. The business cycle as a measure of economic opportunity, noting particularly how the movements of the cycle are related to the political and social psychology of classes.
2. The business cycle in relation to the underlying historical-secular trend. Here we wish to note how the cyclic movement and the long-term trend relate to changes in classes and class systems.

This analysis does not offer a new theory. Rather, we wish to state for present purposes what is implied by several older theorists such as Schumpeter, Veblen, Selig Perlman, and Mannheim, and certain contemporaries such as Gerth and Mills who have worked in this tradition. From this statement we hope, in Chapters 7 and 8, to draw a portrait of established and emerging status and class structures.

NONECONOMIC MEANINGS OF BUSINESS CYCLES

Any measure of the business cycle, no matter how it is determined or specifically calculated, can be viewed also as a measure of existing income opportunity in the society as a whole. Upward movements of the cycle are characterized by investment and expansion. Corresponding with rises in investment and expansion is a range of economic opportunities more or less directly connected to the rise. These opportunities exist in the form of

1. Possibilities for employment in previously nonexistent jobs.
2. Greater income for existing jobs.

3. Overtime employment at existing jobs.
4. Greater availability of existing jobs.
5. Greater possibilities for mobility from job to job.
6. Enhanced income possibilities through capital investment and technological change.
7. Greater possibilities for the expansion of businesses.
8. Increased chances for the accumulation of capital.
9. Chances for greater return on invested capital.
10. Profits from the sales of inventories due to rises in prices.

In a downward movement of the economy these forms of opportunity are reversed and become so many losses in opportunity. The lack of, or availability of, opportunity in these terms is a description of the movement of the whole society rather than a description of the opportunity chances of particular individuals, and in this sense is an economic statement rather than a statement about class.

The description of the business cycle as a series of different types of income opportunity and loss of opportunity is only one way of viewing the noneconomic meanings of economic movements. In a complex money economy, one man's opportunity can be another man's loss. When it is understood that a major correlate of business upturn is an increase in prices and price levels, the operation of the business cycle can be viewed not simply as a set of increased or decreased opportunities but also as a set of increased or decreased costs to members of the society. Moreover, the movement of business is not a unitary phenomenon affecting all groups and individuals equally. The effects of both the upward and downward movement on different groups and individuals depend on their relationship to the direction of change. There are, of course, leads and lags in price and cost levels which arise out of "premature" and "delayed" price rises, inventory conditions, time spreads between production and sale, the incurring and liquidating of debts, and similar phenomena. The cumulative effect of such factors prevents a direct and equal reflection of economic trends in the income distribution and the relative class position of individuals.

The relationship of groups and individuals to these somewhat irregular changes in income opportunities and costs can nevertheless be stated in a clear enough manner to enable us to see their economic and social consequences. The position of an individual or a group in the economic structure can be defined by the relations of that individual or group to changes in the average net income of the total economy or, conversely, to changes in average net costs of the total economy. The average net income of the individual or group may rise or fall in phase with changes in average net income, and at faster or slower rates. This can be expressed in the ratio of the percentage change in average net *group* income to the percentage change in average net *total* income. This we label the *income elasticity* of a group in a market relationship. The same may be done for the relations of a group to changes in total average costs. This ratio is the *cost elasticity* of a group. The consequences of these changes on a particular group become apparent when it is realized that *changes in income elasticity do not necessarily coincide with changes in cost elasticity*. For this reason, various individuals and groups are differently affected by changes in the opportunity and cost structure of the total economy. For some groups, income opportunities may expand faster than costs, whereas for others, costs may rise faster than income. Put simply, an aged person with a fixed income has no income elasticity, and a nonunionized producer who has no inventory carryovers has enormous cost elasticity.

The relationship among costs, prices, and time in an upward movement of the economy leads to three different situations:

1. A rise in income at a faster rate than a rise in costs results in an accumulation of "unearned" increment due to the increasing difference between income and costs.
2. The reverse is a cost rise at a more rapid rate than an income rise, a situation that leads to an accumulation of losses.
3. Income and costs can rise at equal rates and in an upward movement sustain a fixed relationship to each other.

The same relationships are possible in a downward movement of the economy wherein the relationships between costs and income are simply reversed. Thus there may be gainers and losers in both inflationary and deflationary periods, depending on the relationship of their income and cost elasticity.

The three situations described for the upward and downward movements actually describe three general cases wherein, theoretically, the social effect resulting from the movement will be the same whether the movement is upward or downward. Movement in either direction will place individuals and groups in one of the following three situations:

1. The movement of the business cycle is favorable to the economic position of a specific group. This group moves upward at a faster rate than the average upward movement or moves downward at a slower rate than the average downward movement. In either case, the class or individual experiences an above-average success. In subsequent discussion we will refer to these groups as *ascendant* groups.
2. The movement of the cycle is unfavorable to a specific group. This group moves upward at a slower rate than the average or moves downward at a faster rate. Such groups will be referred to as *descendant* groups.
3. The individual or group in question remains unaffected because the cost-income ratio remains the same in spite of the movement of the cycle. This group moves in phase with the total average movement of prices and costs. These groups will be referred to as the economically *unaffected*.

Each of the above situations is a theoretically possible relationship between an individual or group and cyclical movement in the economy as a whole. In each of these typical economic situations there develop correlative social and psychological attitudes that reflect the economic position of the individual or group in the movement as a whole.

The business cycle is so important to the underlying dynamic of personality that its movements can be directly related to the individual's conception of himself, of others, of the future, and of the world. The relationships between economic movement and personality will be especially marked for those individuals who are prone to construct a definition of who and what they are by comparing themselves with others to whom they are socially related and whose response they consider socially significant. This whole matter can be put in another terminology: because of differences in income and cost elasticity, business cycles affect individuals and groups differently, and therefore their social relationships, self-definition, expectations of the future, and world views are continuously altered by inflationary and deflationary economic movements. The invidious comparison of one's self with others and with one's previous states provides a psychological framework for defining one's self.

THE BUSINESS CYCLE AND THE PSYCHOLOGY OF CLASSES

These economic and psychological relationships can be illustrated with examples for each of the typical situations. To the extent that we deal with typical situations, our examples are deliberately heightened for illustrative purposes. Whether the examples are markedly accurate depends on the rapidity of change in the class's comparative economic position and the length of time covered during the upward or downward movement. Short-term economic advantages and disadvantages for a given group are more likely to cause only immediate buoyancy or depression in the group without affecting its overall ideology; long-term movements will shape the personality and political psychology of classes.

While short-term economic gains and losses are less likely to produce stabilized norms for a class, sharp gains or losses in individual cases often produce highly dramatic consequences. Major losses like those of the 1929 depression may result in idiosyncratic suicides. Major unanticipated gains may result in *la folie du succès,* and wild spending sprees resulting in economic irrationalities and the appearance of joyous narcissism. Apart from such dramatic examples, wide fluctuations in gains and losses in the short run can result in feelings of elation or depression, illusions of persecution or godly selection, feelings of real or imagined rejection by former peers or ridicule by former inferiors. Thus what appear to be symptoms of individual pathology are social and economic in origin.

Short-term fluctuations especially, however normal, are likely to be important for another reason: they accentuate and dramatize the long-term trend. Thus a group which has been losing ground slowly and undramatically over a long period of time may suddenly perceive the erosion of its economic position only during a downturn of the business cycle. Or, it may discover its overall decline only when it fails to make a recovery proportionate to that of the whole economy during a subsequent recovery. Thus the expansion and contraction of business levels may serve to heighten the awareness of individuals and classes of their relative positions, not only in respect to the short term but also in respect to the long-term trend. Unstylized short-run responses are likely to be replaced in the long run by stylized ideological responses which become a stable part of the personality and life plan of a class.

TYPES OF RELATIONSHIPS TO ECONOMIC MOVEMENTS

Type 1. Ascent in relation to the average movement of the economy. The individual whose income opportunity expands at a faster rate than the general price level (whether advancing or declining) experiences "unearned" increments of success. That is, the price movement itself, apart from his direct efforts, is working in his favor. Because of his unexpected success, this individual is likely to be optimistic, aggressive, self-assured, and oriented to a future which he envisages as holding possibilities for ever greater success. This is the classical psychology of the *parvenu* who, because he is favorably situated in relation to the economic drift, sees himself—usually unconsciously—as fulfilled and justified by his actions. "Making it" with the upward movement means not looking at the past, or redefining the past to make it more attractive.

Illustrations of this type are Henry Ford, Sr. ("History is bunk"), the Texas oil barons, insurance executives, advertising, radio, and TV executives, and, until recently, the missile industry including inventors, manufacturers, scientists, and technicians. For these groups the projection of the present into the future leads to an expectation of ultimate self-fulfillment. This future-mindedness de-emphasizes qualities such as introspection, self-awareness, or disinterested intellectual pursuit. Such successful groups will be committed to the established scheme of society which they will identify with their own success. They will characteristically be without resentment, except for a resentment they may hold against those groups that had achieved and sustained a predominance over them and had previously denied them social recognition. Thus, for example, the Texas oil barons can resent the Wall Street financiers and Eastern upper-class socialites and yet be quite untouched by any other feeling of resentment. Within their psychological purview, there is no one else available for them to compete with. Ascendant groups will tend to be uncritical and affirmative.

Ascendant groups are also likely to assert the functional value of their current economic activity. According to type, this means pointing out, for example, the decisive role of oil in comparison with coal (its importance to the national income, welfare, defenses, and so forth); the indispensability of advertising for the continued successful operation of the total economy; the humanitarian and welfare functions of insurance, and the functional necessity of upper-level management in all expanding bureaucracies. In their institutional and self-legitimations, ascendant groups hold that the price and salary mechanism is a true measure of social utility, and that all other yardsticks for measuring it—such as intelligence, pietistic selflessness, or humanitarianism —disguise the operation of true social value. In the last analysis, they would say, "Preachers as well as professors have to be paid by somebody." Life and all its codes are committed to the current direction of the movement that accounts for their above-average success. The entire world is pulled into their buoyant psychological vortex.

Where ascendancy rests upon large but short-run gains, the immediate response is likely to be unstylized and vulgar conspicuous consumption and a ritualistic pursuit of pleasure. Frequently such "unexpected" short-run gains are likely to surprise the individual himself. He finds it hard to believe in his own good fortune. If it persists, he is likely to discover objective bases for his success, and the emotional quality surrounding it will be transformed from one of being surprised at his own good luck to accepting success as if it were earned. Should the advantage accrue from a downward price movement, the person may rediscover or reconstruct the virtues of those habits of mind—lack of venturesomeness, parsimoniousness, cost-consciousness, high liquidity preference—that are rewarded by a declining market. In this case the group or individual in question feels vindicated for upholding time-honored virtues. Such a hoarding mentality was rewarded in the early years of the depression in the thirties when cautiousness with cash paid off. Never since that time have these virtues been rewarded —a cause of deep resentment among groups deriving their income from nonexpanding sections of the economy.

Type 2. Descent in relation to the average movement of the economy. In some cases the income opportunities of individuals or groups expand at a slower rate than the general movement of prices and wages. This would be the case of the worker whose wages do not automatically escalate with price rises. Some persons, such as the pensioner, the Negro, and the unorganized worker with a relatively inelastic income, may experience relative or absolute decline in income due to an inflationary movement. Groups whose income expands at a slower rate than the general price movement find themselves in an invidious position with respect to both their previous position and to those who have not experienced a similar decline. These persons' response to their descendance is determined by the social and economic *level* they occupied before the movement that resulted in their decline.

Compared with other groups, their economic and psychological starting point in the earlier period could have been favorable or unfavorable. The *starting point* of a descending group is crucial, so much so that it affects its entire subsequent response. Two typical starting points and responses are:

1. Groups that earlier were in *favored* economic positions, but now find themselves displaced by other ascendant groups, tend, in the short run, to develop a psychology of status defensiveness. In an effort to defend their status, despite the erosion of their economic underpinnings, they tend to justify themselves on grounds other than economic function or wealth. Like Warner's upper upper class in Yankee City, such a group asserts its heredity, the dignity and source of its income rather than its absolute size, or any of the higher functional values whose carriers they can claim to be. They discover the superiority of their morality, breeding, blood, taste, dress, and other consumption styles. They assert the superior value of such social functions as political qualifications and personal leadership rather than economic skills and activities. The classic example of this type is the English landed aristocracy, which historically moved from lordly and manorial roles to political ones in phase with the encroachment of industrial predominance.* In post–Civil War America, the Southern landed aristocracy followed a similar path, attempting to uphold its way of life well into the twentieth century to the point where it was sustained only by a compulsive enactment of hollow social rituals, as described in the works of Tennessee Williams. In contemporary times this drama of

* A substantial portion of the English landed aristocracy, as pointed out by Barrington Moore in *Social Origins of Dictatorship and Democracy,* were able to survive because they shifted the basis of their investment from land to trade and later to industry. In doing so, however, much of their character as a landed aristocracy was lost.

social "face-saving" is enacted wherever landed wealth is losing predominance to industrial and commercial wealth. A comparative case in point is the tendency of the older landed Spanish elements in Latin America to control political positions while the newer groups, of European and North American origin, are increasingly taking over the economic sphere.*

An identical psychological situation occurs in periods of prolonged inflation. The rapid devaluation of currency brings to the foreground a range of social types who, at least for the period of inflation, win out in the competition. Germany in the 1920's, as described by Erich Maria Remarque in *The Black Obelisk,* is a case in point. A good current example is Chile, where the landed aristocratic and traditional upper-class groups have been all but disfranchised economically by the duration and intensity of the inflation.

The social and time perspective of descending groups is toward the past and its hallowed traditions. The relevance of the current social drift is denied by the psychological device of refusing to recognize the movement of time and social change. Because their commitment is to the past, groups like this are resentful of anyone who denies the past, particularly the *parvenu,* the "vulgar mob," the social climber, and all other ascendant types and groups such as the "uppity" Negro in the South. Because of these dynamics, descendant groups attempt to attach themselves to archaic styles of consumption which cannot easily be emulated. They use or display heirlooms, antiques, or other consumption items not easily available on the market or unattainable by cash purchases; they make much of the old school emblem, the white shoe, peculiarities of linguistic usage, and other quaint or archaic prestige symbols. If the economic pressures are persistent and failure looms, these defensive tactics eventually lead them to withdraw into small social enclaves which deny admission to newcomers, with the result that they become more and more removed from the main feeling and tone of the society as a whole. In their final defense they give oth-

* In this chapter we offer a comparative method which uses illustrations worldwide. In our application of this analysis in subsequent chapters, we focus our analysis on American class structures. Where, however, American upper classes become part of a worldwide international upper class, we have noted such developments.

ers the impression of being quaint relics of the past, if not queer. On the plane of social action they will attempt to use political methods* to prevent ascendant economic groups from achieving the full social and economic return from their economic rise. In sum, they make major claims to prestige on the basis of past performance and noneconomic functions.

If one focuses on the very short-run effects rather than on the long-run trends, one finds that the descendant group tends to develop a psychology of grumbling and dissatisfaction, and to postpone expenditures for durable goods. Individuals within the group, generally speaking, experience idiosyncratic "personal" moods of depression. This is likely to be the case for certain groups during periods of temporary recession, as in 1949 or 1954 or 1970, or for any fixed-income groups in an inflationary war economy without wage and price controls. The idiosyncratic nature of such moods is most pronounced when economic misfortune affects only an individual or a relatively small group.

The pattern of resentment elected by this group always centers on one common device; namely, any group that threatens its particular area of ascendancy will be resented. The resentful groups as well as the objects of resentment can exist at different levels in the social structure, and the objects selected can be composed of quite disparate groups whose minimum qualification for selection is their measure of social visibility. Thus a white-collar group in the United States may resent highly paid industrial workers in a manner similar to the ways that a landowning group in the nineteenth century resented manufacturers. Only moderately successful children of Italian and Irish immigrants resent strongly even the physical mobility of Negroes and Puerto Ricans into their environs, and Negroes, whatever their sense of injustice about their own position, have been intolerant of Puerto Ricans and of Jews who have been more mobile than themselves in their own environment. The Jews in Europe and America, after leaving the ghettos as they scaled the pyramids of society, have been the object of re-

* The Protestant upper classes have thus attempted to exclude newer immigrant groups from political and economic leadership as long as possible. This process has been documented by E. Digby Baltzell in *The Protestant Establishment* (New York, 1964).

sentment by successively higher social classes in phase with their own ascent. One can define social mobility by locating the class groups that resent one's ascendancy.

2. The second kind of descendant group is that in an economically *unfavored* position before an upward phase of the economy. Such persons find themselves further disadvantaged, and their psychological responses are quite different from those who began in a favored position. Their decline is a decline from nadir, and so is experienced in a quite different way from a decline that allows more favorable memories of the past.

Because of their unfavorable memories of the past they are less likely to be committed to it. In a psychological sense they have no past because they do not care to remember it. For a different reason they are as fully uncommitted to the present as the descending group described above whose commitments were totally to the past. This is because relative to their previous situation they have nothing to lose. Theirs, then, is a psychology of noncommitment to both present and past, of resenting and rejecting the total framework of society. When such groups act (the Townsendites in the 1930's and some radical movements in the United States, and, in general, communists who lack an economically secure past), it is to seek political solutions for economic problems and to make broad attacks on the framework of constituted society. Even when not politically radical, their fundamental psyche is one of resentment. Their perception, intelligence, and attention are directed to discovering flaws and weaknesses in the character and morality of the system and in the individuals who symbolize it. Profane and irreverent attitudes toward society's most cherished and hallowed institutions and symbols can be held without compunction.

In some cases the rejection of the present constitutes a total rejection of the dominant materialistic system and all its sustaining values. Such total forms of rejection can lead to the construction of imaginary alternative worlds which may take the form of a projected religious ordering of the world. Forms of total rejection can involve images of future other worlds, hopes for divine intervention or miraculous universal revelations, or, finally, as recently illustrated by the Jehovah's Witnesses, the hope for a total apocalypse. Only this imagined future is real and alive. The sublimation of current resentments thus may have the respectability of the religious; religion absorbs and disguises what would otherwise be a radical dissatisfaction and a potential threat to the equanimity of the established scheme of society.* This psychology need not be limited to absolutely marginal groups. It can also be characteristic of relatively marginal groups such as intellectuals and various segments of the middle class.†

The marginality of middle-class youth is structural in character, in the sense that youth increasingly have been kept off the labor market well past the teen-age stage. What with graduate education, scholarships, and remittances, many have not appeared on the labor scene until well into their thirties. This structural marginality results in a lack of commitment to the economic institutions and to an increased anxiety about accepting these commitments. Anxieties about failure and an inability to compete increase as one approaches the age when it appears that he must begin to compete. Entry into the labor market at the higher ages undoubtedly increases the anxiety. The result may be forms of rebellion which are based on fears of deprivations that the youth as yet has not experienced.

The absolutely marginal groups need not seek their solution in apocalypse or otherworldliness. The range of secular institutions and activities that permit the expression of resentment or vicarious feelings of superiority is broad, as one would expect in a secular society. The mass media, with its parade of villains, bestiality, and sadism, serves the purpose for those who do not find the "religious" way. The orgy and the public display of the nude and the provocative Hollywood, Swedish, or Italian star, and so forth, allow each according to his needs

* This is the classic psychology of the slave, the disfranchised, and the marginal, particularly in epochs of institutional intractability. The original and essentially slave morality of Christianity has asserted itself repeatedly. The Jehovah's Witnesses at a recent convention in New York cheered enthusiastically for a prediction of the imminent apocalypse and total destruction of the world. Similar psychological phenomena have been widely noted in lower-class American Negroes and Puerto Ricans. Also see Sigmund Freud, *The Future of an Illusion* (New York, 1949).

† The rate of production of intellectuals in the United States until the postwar years appears to have been greater than the ability of bureaucratic expansion to absorb it. The expansion of advertising, the mass media, and "researching" in the postwar years has provided major areas of intellectual opportunity. Thus the marginality of intellectuals has until recently been more a product of secular trends than of cyclical movements.

to sublimate his hostility, resentment, and masochism in a vicarious playing of his sexual role in relation to the particular object in view. A major form of secular escape has become drug usage, ranging from the quasi-religiously defined usage associated with Zen to the withdrawal and retreat from the world associated with other drugs. Intensive escape from routine is associated with amphetamine and other "highs." According to this theory, these forms of secular escape become all the more socially necessary and all the more intensely displayed and employed during expansive phases of business, when the failure of the unsuccessful is accentuated. It is a truly modern phenomenon that responses to movements of the economy can be expressed by the ingestion of modern and not so modern chemicals.

Type 3. Economically unaffected groups. The situation for economically unaffected groups is one in which income position roughly corresponds to the movement of the total economy. This group's response to the economic movement is not easily predictable. This is because much of the response will be determined not only by the group's position before the latest business movement but also by the movement of other socially visible groups whose movement does not parallel its own. In other words, this group's own position, while remaining stationary relative to the movement of business, is drastically altered in comparison with other groups which move out of phase with the general movement. The group's response is conditioned by its relative lack of movement. An apt illustration of this is the case of almost any white-collar group whose income has kept pace with price rises since 1936, but which has experienced a decline relative to the enormous advance of skilled workmen who moved from no employment to high-wage full employment in the same period.

This category of the economically unaffected contains several possibilities:

1. If the individual or group was relatively well favored in the previous phase and continues to be relatively well favored in the present, while the group nearest to it in the previous phase achieves greater gains in the present one, it will tend to respond like the descendant groups mentioned earlier. The response will be the same in spite of the fact that the group's position will not be directly affected by its own

relationship to the economy. The similar response in this case is evoked by the invidious comparison which the group makes between itself and socially visible and competitive groups. Members of this group differ from those of a descendant group in that they are less likely to be deeply emotionally involved in their comparative failure, since their loss is relative and not absolute. It is easier for them to sustain favorable self-images and perhaps even to retain high expectations. Their specific experiences will mainly define the structure of their resentments.

2. A group that, while remaining in a largely unchanged position relative to the total movement of prices and opportunity, sees other groups that were previously higher descending to its own position, presents an entirely new possibility. The stationary group may achieve some degree of vindication for prior defeats, and may have opportunities to express resentments which were previously unexpressed, as did professors and intellectuals vis-à-vis businessmen in the 1930's. It may also see in the descending group opportunities for establishing social contacts which would not have been feasible in the past; the economically ascendant group now finds itself in the position of being able to associate with groups which were previously above it. For example, any portrait of the postbellum South (as described by Faulkner, among others) shows this reversal of roles. For the descendant group, however, social meetings on the downward slope tend to make the descent a little more unbearable; the result is to stimulate defensive action of a political and social nature by the descendant group.

Type 4. Psychologically unaffected groups. There are, finally, groups that may experience no shifts in psychological tone and attitude, even in the face of extreme changes in the business cycle. These groups do not fall into clear-cut categories, but if classified along economic lines there are three of them.

1. Market-oriented groups which are protected from the vicissitudes of the business cycle by virtue of their capital and income sources are not psychologically affected by a relative decline in their position. That is, their access to wealth is so steady that a relative decline does not affect their image of their present or future expectations. An example would be the hoarder with vast cash reserves or highly mobile noncur-

rency investments (jewels, valued works of art, and so forth).* Perhaps the best example, however, is that of the leading families of wealth with highly diversified investment portfolios.

2. Groups that are partially or completely protected from the fluctuations of the market because of the public or semipublic nature of their sources of income are similarly psychologically unaffected. One example would be groups whose investments are in large portfolios of government bonds, or in industries that are publicly subsidized in phase with price movements, such as utilities or atomic weapons. In the current phase, another example would be such bureaucratic groups as the armed services, the intelligence corps, and groups in advanced weapons research, testing, and manufacturing, whose work serves higher military purposes not subject to price-cost fluctuations. The market affects these groups only insofar as state income is drastically altered by business movements. As a rule, the average military man (excluding perhaps the top military leaders) has anxieties only about the appropriation and does not concern himself with business conditions. The conception of self, future, and world is apt to be given by participation in the totally encompassing and psychologically monopolistic institution. In such total institutions, the rest of the world is conceived of as the "outside."

3. Finally, there are the economically submarginal groups who are unaffected psychologically by market fluctuations because they do not participate at any time in the market system. The subsistence farmer in the market economy who does not orient himself to the market is unaffected by movements of business. He subsists at all price levels.† The most obvious examples, perhaps, are individuals more or less permanently incarcerated in mental institutions and prisons, a not insub-

* The small-time hoarder is a different case. In an inflationary phase he sees his hoard (his life work) evaporate; bitterness results. In a deflationary phase his hoard expands in value; he beats his chest with pride and self-satisfaction.

† The pure type, of course, is possible only in squatting and marginal rural areas, where land taxes are very low or where poaching is possible. To the extent that such groups orient themselves to cash income, no matter how peripherally or marginally or no matter how sporadically, they will be affected if only minimally by the availability of opportunity in inflationary and deflationary periods, e.g., the competition for manual unskilled and menial positions increases sharply during depressions.

stantial portion of the population. But this is not the only case of being completely removed from economic participation. Bums, hoboes, tramps, transients, scavengers, gypsies, the habitués of Skid Row, and the newer dropouts, provided they do not graduate out of the ranks in periods of prosperity, can all be immunized from business fluctuations. Since they are not economically committed to the society in any phase, there is little possibility for induced resentment,* and little expectation of anything but immediate survival and gratification in terms of values and standards outside the framework of the dominant social order.

SECULAR TRENDS, CHANGES IN CLASS STRUCTURE, AND ALTERATIONS IN WORLD VIEWS

While the analysis given above may explain the successes and failures of groups in relation to the total economy and in relation to other groups during short- and long-run economic movements, it does not explain the social consequences of secular trends which span long periods of time.

Beyond a single cycle of inflation and deflation, one can see class history as a series of responses to such cycles. The effects of a succession of cycles we call a short-term trend. When social history is viewed from the perspective of the short-term trend, we can see another set of implications from business movements. The secular trend may continuously work against a group, which thereby suffers a historic decline, irrespective of temporary gains and losses. If such a group loses continuously for a long enough period of time, it may in time virtually drop out of existence, as happened with the old Southern aristocracy. Another possibility is that a group will recoup losses suffered in a previous phase; for such a group the intermediate phases are a kind of equilibrium wherein gains and losses occur only to a minor extent. As an example of such differential effects, we can note that small business, which lost ground in the 1930's, regained it in the 1950's; but in the long run it appears to be placed in a more and more defensive position in comparison with big business. The same has been true of the family-sized farmer who, however, has been largely displaced already by cor-

* Although all sorts of idiosyncratic resentment may persist throughout and despite all economic movements.

porate industrialized agriculture. On the other hand, top businessmen and managerial executives in both of these phases did not lose their power, influence, or prestige.*

Over even longer periods of time, other factors operate which are independent of any particular phase of the business cycle and which radically reconstitute both the economic and the social structure in ways that are impossible to predict in advance. The long-range secular trend, while it is related in its consequences to the consequences of business cycles, leads to more basic changes in the organization of the economy and its technological structure.

The significant factors in the long-range secular trend are (1) changes in the rate of accumulation of capital, and (2) changes in the dominant forms of capital in the society.

1. Rate changes in capital accumulation. The rate of capital accumulation affects the structure of the entire class system and sets the larger framework of economic opportunity.

If accumulation increases at an increasing rate, the society is likely to be expansive at almost all levels. This is the classic image of the frontier society in a state of accelerating expansion. In this situation the invidious "comparison with others" is less likely to prevail as a basic psychological dimension of social life, because all groups share in the expanding opportunities. Opportunity is a continuously growing pie with larger and larger slices for each man. So long as the size of his slice increases, the individual's attention is directed inward to his success as it relates to his own past; he does not develop a sharp consciousness of external competition. In the United States in the nineteenth century, for example, immigrants who came with nothing willingly accepted what they got because it was more than what they had had. They compared their life in America with their life in the past in the "old country," and so long as they were "getting ahead" in America they did not resent those older Americans who had already achieved success. The immigrant is the pure case, but the same psychology applied to the westward movement of "Yankee" Americans

* The defensive psychology of businessmen in the 1930's is best described in the Lynds' *Middletown in Transition* (New York, 1937), which presents a description of businessmen's attitudes toward self and world at the point where their conception of the universe has been drastically challenged by the failure of the market.

who entered on the ground floor of that economic expansion. Slavery and, to a large extent, segregation and discrimination prevented the American Negro until recently from sharing in such opportunity. In a long-term period of economic expansion, when opportunity is broadly available, defensive invidious comparison is not likely to be used.

In a capital expansive age, the dominant tone of society is likely to be optimistic, future-oriented, and self-confident. The image of the future appears so golden that the past is rarely noticed. Tensions between classes tend to be reduced; the success of one person does not appear to be contingent on another's loss. A general emphasis is placed upon individual opportunity, individualism, individual initiative, and entrepreneurship rather than on collective class corporatism. The system of mobility is more likely to be an open class system with technical competence and achieved status likely to be rewarded. In the United States this was the age of Horatio Alger and the Great American Dream.

If capital accumulation occurs at a decreasing rate, on the other hand, this is experienced by individuals as a shrinkage of opportunity. From the point of view of "society," individual assertiveness and aggressiveness decline in value. Society tends to focus less on individuals and more on classes and groups. The psychological tone of the society as a whole is apt to be a defensive one in which past accomplishments and historical heroes are favorably reassessed. The traditions of the past are accentuated and glorified. Paralleling a return to the past is an accentuation of class conflict; class comes to be recognized as a social phenomenon and is experienced as a psychological milieu. The class conflict, however, may occur at a legal rather than at a revolutionary level; or the personal tensions arising from the visibility of class differences may be wholly internalized and expressed in idiosyncrasies of individual behavior, including neuroses and psychoses. For many members of the society, adaptations and adjustments between the values of the earlier age—emphasizing equality, individualism, and status achievement—and the newer values of group identity and collective corporatism will have to be made. Individuals, or more probably generations, that are psychologically caught between the two periods will often experience identity crises. David Riesman in his book *The Lonely Crowd* and William H. Whyte in his book *The Organization Man* together depicted the identity crises and corporate aspects of this stage in American history. Individualism as an ideology is being replaced only with difficulty by group, corporate, or status categories of identification. Contemporary class psychology is most closely related to this stage.

A third possibility arises where capital accumulation does *not* occur.* In this case all major accumulation has taken place and the plant is merely sustained. In the history of Western capitalistic countries, this would be the stage following the previous ones of increasing rates of accumulation and increasing accumulation at decreasing rates. When no accumulation takes place, opportunity ends in all but the traditionally established spheres, and a psychology of defending established gains and privileges sets in. In this case the society is likely to take on a caste character, where opportunity is rigidly allocated on the basis of ritual, legal, and religious sanctions. Status rather than class becomes a dominant organizing principle. Class conflict is minimal, and individuals exist not as legal entities but only as members of a corporate class. Psychologically there is a loss of self in the external rhythm and ritual of prescribed codes of behavior which are intolerant of both individualism and of sensitive awareness of pasts and futures. The transition to this state, when it occurs to the individual who spans a decisively important stretch of the secularization process, is apt to be

* The failure of a society to maintain past levels of expansion can have a variety of causes. In some cases external and internal exploitation (Czechoslovakia, for example) can both cause past capital to be disinvested (that is, used up without replacement) or expropriated and exported. In other cases the effect of a depression can demoralize the capital-accumulating classes, so that their economic approach is to hoard or preserve past wealth rather than accumulate new wealth. In underdeveloped countries a combination of political instability and economic immaturity causes the new elites either to deposit profits from capital investments in foreign banks or to dissipate wealth in extravagant living. Economic inefficiency can cause the simple erosion of capital. This is especially true after a revolution, when a new political elite begins to exercise investment functions according to political criteria.

Finally, a successful business class, after having accumulated capital, can shift its economic interest from industrial investment and expansion to investments in real estate, foreign investment, trade, banking, and shipping, neglecting in doing so the internal industry of the country. At the same time the scions of Protestant buccaneers become gentlemen who restrict their economic activity and become interested in politics, the arts, culture, sports, or gentleman farming. This latter process does not impede capital accumulation if the resources diverted to such activities are not too great, or if a new class of business buccaneers who stimulate investment replaces the old investors.

fraught with internal crises and upheaval. England would be an example of a country where the rate of capital accumulation has fallen sharply and where much of social policy is an attempt to maintain international standards and advantages, despite the lower rate of accumulation.*

China is in an early frontier stage where individualism takes the form of competitive and brutal devotion to party and factional demands, and Russia is in a stage of late frontier. The underdeveloped world, now undergoing the initial stages of accumulation, experiences the frontier psychology at least in those of the traditional strata who are given access to participation in the new opportunities. But any application of this model to the underdeveloped world must be done with great caution, since accumulation in these cases is frequently only a secondary effect of primary accumulation in the world's metropolitan centers.

2. *Changes in the form of capital.* Long-term changes in the rate of capital accumulation primarily affect the rigidity and flexibility of the class system; or, to state the matter differently, the measure for the secular trend would be a measure for class flexibility or inflexibility. The content of the class system itself is still another matter. The content of the class system—which groups and individuals come to predominate and which lose ground—is determined by the shifts in the kinds of capital wealth, emerging technologies, and forms of institutional organization that become the basis of society. Capital can be based on land, mining, plant, inventory, contracts, brand names, reputation, and so forth. Different forms of capital and technology gain ascendance in different periods, just as different forms of capital are accumulated at different rates. Class predominance in the overall structure of society, then, is a function of the ascendance of forms of capital and differences in the rates of accumulation of the different forms.

Each form of capital, wealth, or organization is accompanied by different sets of skills, education, personality characteristics, and oc-

* This is not to say that the English economy has ceased to expand or that it is at a zero rate of investment as it was in 1930. Moreover, in the case of England the decline in the rate of expansion was, at least until 1945, partly compensated for by the opportunity offered by the empire. For France, on the other hand, such factors as a stable population and an early retirement age acted to offset the effects on opportunity caused by the decline in the rate of expansion.

cupations. The growth of a given form of capital, wealth, or organization thus results in a reconstitution of the characteristics of the labor force as well as the educational system, personality formation, and class institutions. Thus changes in the form of capital result in premiums being placed on individuals who possess the skills and characteristics appropriate to the expanding sector. Conversely, previously favored groups are devalued by such forms of social change. When this phenomenon occurs, the individual responds as described earlier in this chapter.

Seen in these terms, the decline of feudalism, for example, can be stated simply as a decrease in the relative importance of land as a form of capital and an increase in the relative rate of growth of commercial and, later, industrial capital. The decline of feudalism came about because the expansion of a particular form of capital brought with it new classes—new economic actors who collected around the new possibilities, techniques, and opportunities. In due course social, economic, and political interests arose to defend and to further the legal establishment of what had been only socially recognized economic interests and positions.

The success of a class or an economic group, while based upon economic and political power, has consequences for more than the economic and political organization of a society. When a predominant class has distinctive ideologies, skills, and personality traits, its success results in the legitimation of these personal and cultural characteristics. They become incorporated in the predominant personality models of the society and become the object of emulation, education, and reward in many sectors of the society. Thus every change in the structure of the class system results in a change in the distribution of personalities within the society. Weber's classic studies on China and India stress precisely this point. The dominance of the political bureaucrat in Russia and the business bureaucrat in the West are current examples. The "scientific" businessman, the Ph.D. in mathematics or physics who enters the missile-hardware or electronics business, or the computer-minded organization man, are emergent examples.

Such transformations of capital from land and commercial bases to industrial and scientific bases at the present time in the underdeveloped world constitute a major revision and reorganization of the class structure of underdeveloped societies. The process is not necessarily a repetition of the earlier shift from feudalism to capitalism as experienced in the Western world, since the major sources of investment for economic development are external to the underdeveloped world.

Industries whose form of capital accumulates at a slower rate, or not at all, provide little opportunity to the ambitious and competent. At the same time slowly accumulating forms of capital fail to attract the best personnel in the society. The vested interests, irrevocably committed to a form of capital or technology which declines or which has a relatively slower rate of growth, find their past superiority increasingly threatened by individuals attached to newer and faster-growing industries. The "establishment" is apt to seek government intervention to protect its income and status position; thus, for example, mineral resources industries such as copper and petroleum have sought government support to prevent the decline of their capital investment. A still better example is the railroad industry, which has been threatened since the twenties by more highly mobile and direct forms of transportation such as trucks and aircraft—that is, forms of capital which bring a much higher return per unit invested. Again, in such cases, attempts are made to dip into the public treasury to protect previous capital. The military and economic indispensability of the firm to the society as a whole justifies claims for such subsidies. When a sufficient number of defensive groups arise—usually in a stage of decreasing rates of accumulation—competition for protective legislation and fiscal favors can become intense. This is approximately the case in the United States at the present time in connection with railroads, steel, petroleum, automobiles, airframes, and coal. Increasingly, political rather than market decisions determine the distribution of gains and advantages. Thus political brokers and officials may be in a position to make crucial societal decisions. When this occurs in a bureaucratic environment, phenomena such as influence peddling, lobbying, bribery, blackmail, payoffs, and other such activities are apt to become the basis of honorable professions, without which the economic decisions in the bureaucratic marketplace would be hard to make. Conflicts for hegemony between such groups determine the subsequent structure of society, and in a basic sense determine the relationships between social class and economic opportunity.

In the bureaucratic state, military and foreign policy require huge governmental investments and expenditures in the building of industries or in the transferring of investments and expenditures from previously favored industries to other industries. Thus missile-building and the military hardware industry, as well as electronic and specialized scientific, instrument, and chemical industries, may expand at previously unanticipated rates, producing new subclasses and new prestige, power, and income for those classes. At the same time, relative loss of government subsidies may devalue the past claims and standing of all other groups relative to the new groups, and especially those groups whose skills, abilities, and position were due to subsidies which have been cut or replaced by those of the new groups. Government policy, always important in the past, now increasingly affects the total character of the class system within American society.

5. *The coordination of organizations*

CLASS AND THE POWER CLIQUES

The direct relationship between class and political power as postulated by Marx has been denied by almost all uncommitted thinkers. Moreover, Marx's formulation that economic classes are the chief agents in political and social action presumes that classes have a corporate character and are active agents. Actually, even under Marxist analysis, classes are a distributive phenomenon—that is, collections of individuals responding roughly in the same ways to the same economic situation—and not corporate entities as were the medieval estates.

Even if one were to assume with Marx that economic interests are a major basis for political action, there must be intervening agencies to channel the actions of the individuals who make up the classes. Political parties have, with some justification, been singled out as a major channeling agency. It is easy to note, however, that the same economic interests organize a number of different political parties, that many class interests are organized in the same party, and that some class interests remain unorganized by any political party. These points are particularly well illustrated in the United States, and they indicate that political parties are both more and less than the sum total of class agencies.

With the development of the bureaucratic administrative state, major decisions are also made by nonelective executive agencies and by individuals who are relatively anonymous to the public at large. Such decisions are based on highly legalistic and technical documents that do not appear to be substantive in nature, but may result in individual and group advantages and disadvantages involving billions of dollars —without appearing to be political. Reaching and influencing the key anonymous individuals making such decisions do not require the complex operations of mass political parties, nor even formally organized pressure groups and associations which by virtue of their formal organization tend to become conspicuous. Reaching and influencing these key decision-makers may, rather, rest on the exercise of personal influence. In this sense personal influence is a major concept in the understanding of modern society.

The power clique is one major mechanism by which specialized class interests get translated into social and political action. The conception of a power clique does not provide a complete answer to the relationship between class and power, nor does it encompass an understanding of the public life of political parties. These are separate problems which can be investigated in their own right. Rather, in a centralized bureaucratic society in which all institutions are typified by centralized administrations, the relationships between class, power, and party are significantly mediated by an intervening dimension of conduct that we subsume under the term *power clique.*

C. Wright Mills suggested that there are three power elites that make the effective decisions concerning the national destiny of the United States. In concentrating his attention on the top power elites, Mills, perhaps for the sake of his central argument, overlooked the existence at every level of society, not just at the top, of similar interlocking cliques which attempt to influence actions in social spheres that are relevant to the position of their members. E. Digby Baltzell, in *Philadelphia Gentlemen,* highlighted the clique nature of a regional elite, and David Riesman, through his largely negative conception of power as expressed in the "veto" group, came close to specifying cliques as organized around particular interests. Since the publication of Floyd Hunter's *Community Power Structure,* which largely ignores the party and electoral apparatus in decision-making, several studies have appeared which point to the central role of personal influence and power cliques.

Power cliques cut across various institutional boundaries. The membership of any specific clique is apt to be composed of representatives from different economic, political, military, social, prestige, or communications institutions. The vast majority of these membership institutions are bureaucratic and, at a legal level, stress the formal and procedural aspects of organization. Cliques that cut across bureaucratic and organizational jurisdictions are, almost ironically, the coordinators of these legal organizational entities. We use the term "interinstitutional power clique" to describe this phenomenon.

When one adds up all the individual firms, corporations, government bureaus, educational and religious agencies, and so on, in all areas of life, it is clear that bureaucracy is the common mode for the formal organization of all these institutions. The interrelations between bureaucracies are part of the bureaucratization of the organization of society itself.

Most modern theorists of bureaucracy have been more interested in examining problems of administration and management than in examining the implications of bureaucracy for society as a whole. Modern apologists have argued that the superabundance of bureaucracies actually provides degrees of freedom for the individual which were not possible in a more loosely organized society. This freedom is said to exist in the interstices between and within giant organizations which, because they are too large, cannot control the detailed actions of individuals. In the fact that the organization makes specific but limited demands on the bureaucrat, the same apologists see an opportunity for the individual to develop a rich private life independent of his work in the bureaucracy: discussions on the uses and problems of leisure are a by-product of this observation.* Moreover, they would argue that American society is so large, so sprawling, and composed of so many unrelated and antagonistic organizations that no one group, unit, or institution can dominate its life. This is some-

* We will note later the ways in which we think these problems can be resolved.

times called organizational pluralism or, in negative terms, veto power (Riesman) or countervailing power (Galbraith). In this perspective, organizations become units of representation, and though the older notion of individual representation is lost, the idea of democratic representation is retained.

Opposed to this conception of pluralistic neutralization, C. Wright Mills developed the image of coordinated bureaucratic elites who operate the society in a relatively informal but total way. The military, business, and governmental elites affiliate with the great American financial families and segments of international society and politics. Through a system of relatively informal coordination, the leaders of the political, economic, and military orders constitute an informal governing board for the whole society. From his book *The Power Elite* one could draw the inference from Mills that there is a settled and stable arrangement by which all political actions are well organized and clearly formulated by an organized elite. To the extent that Mills left this impression, one could argue strongly against it. Certainly he presented no evidence for systematic and coordinated control. We would argue that Mills overdrew his point, but that, nevertheless, at several levels in American politics a kind of informal coordination is achieved.

The distinctive feature of the American system is a kind of political coordination that takes place without the existence of a governing board or a central unifying figure. The question raised but not answered by Mills and by Hunter is: What are the specific mechanisms by which societal coordination takes place? Although this is an old question in political studies, we think there is an almost primitive solution to the problem of the coordination of modern bureaucratic society. At its simplest level we would argue that societal coordination is achieved through the *personal relations* at all levels of the middle and upper managerial classes and the top owners and directors in all types of bureaucracies—business, financial, industrial, labor, religious, educational, mass communications, and so on. This would suggest that some of the older notions (especially Marxist ones) of the relationship between social and economic classes and political power are no longer adequate to explain politics in a bureaucratic world. Thus the precise relationship between social and economic classes and political power is still an open question in our society.

CHARACTERISTICS OF INTER-INSTITUTIONAL POWER CLIQUES

The major coordinators and organizers of society's decision-making activities at any level are the inter-institutional power cliques.

Allison Davis and his co-authors, in their book *Deep South,* describe the operation of inter-institutional cliques in classic terms (though they do not use the term) when they show the operation of a clique to be an informal, self-selected grouping of like-minded men and women who by the nature of their association try to monopolize prestige within a community. The authors' description is almost a description of the power clique, except that they describe it only as related to sociability, social status, and prestige. Essentially the same categories broadened to include (a) power and (b) inter-institutional decision-making would describe the basic ingredients of the inter-institutional power clique. The latter's essential characteristics are these:

1. There is no formal definition of membership, but rather a subliminal recognition of likemindedness based either on personal attraction or recognition of common personal or institutional interests.
2. There is no precise definition of the limits of membership, but, rather, as Hunter has indicated, there are star members and peripheral members who have interlocking memberships in other cliques surrounding other star members. In this respect they resemble Lewis Yablonsky's "near" groups in the delinquent juvenile gang.
3. For our present discussion we exclude cliques that operate only within one organization, not because these are not power cliques but rather because study of them is best suited to studies of industrial organizations and large-scale administration, and not to the coordination of American society.
4. The specific characteristic of inter-institutional cliques is that their membership is drawn from a variety of agencies, organizations, and institutions, and that the origins of the clique members' loyalties lie largely outside the framework of institutional participation.

The specific origins of these loyalties underpinning the individual clique are diverse:

1. The clique may include the common members of a graduating class in a college who retain personal friendships or reinvoke them as they follow their careers in distinct and different fields. This is the old-school-tie notion that ranges in degree from the brotherhood of the fraternity to simply having graduated from the same school, even if in different years. In England this is described as "the Establishment."
2. The clique may include an earlier common friendship in a given community from which members have migrated to the same city of opportunity.
3. It may include members of a group of graduate students who secured their major training and perspective from the same professor or group of professors.
4. It may be made up of a number of people who previously, in an earlier career stage, worked in the same office or organization, but later branched off into different industries and different institutional orders.
5. It may rest on common descent or extended kinship ties.
6. It may rest on common wartime experience in combat, in victory, in defeat, in participation in the same military unit at the same or different times, or in a memory of the common real or symbolic bloodletting of war.
7. It may be based on common ties to social, fraternal, or business lodges and associations.
8. It may be based on the invocation of an image of common ethnic, migrant, or religious communities.
9. It may be created "rationally" when individuals in similar or parallel positions seek each other out to discuss common problems, or to settle at a personal level problems that would be extremely difficult to solve at a formal level. Mutual attractiveness, based on similarity in position, perspective, and talent, provides the basis for enduring social relationships that go far beyond the occasion of the initial contact.

Regardless of where these common starting points originate for any individual (and he may have clique contacts arising from more than one of the sources mentioned above), his subsequent life experiences place him in positions to become a member of other cliques. This he does by simply introducing friends whom he knows from different areas in the life stages of his career. For example, the old "army buddy" may be introduced to the classmate or the friend from the home town. Consequently, over time a multiplicity of cliques emerge, dissolve, and fade into one another; thus one's personal relations serve as a point of coordination of an infinite interlocking of friendship patterns. *What appear to be overlapping sets of friendship patterns, however, are much more than this when one sees them acted out in the context of institutional participation.*

On the basis of one's institutional position, one can offer institutional rewards to members of one's clique who are not members of his institution. And, conversely, to the extent that he is identified by other clique members, one is in a position to make a claim on these others for the institutional opportunities they can offer him. In the context of institutional participation, the clique member acts to further the interests of other clique members in other institutions by distributing to them such rewards and resources as he may command.

These rewards can include:

1. *Jobs.* Individuals who have jobs to offer will tend to seek out their clique members for prospects, and, if they are peers, employ one another's protégés. Hence a powerful clique may monopolize all jobs in a given area. Thus prior acquaintance or relationship, direct or through marriage with a Kennedy, resulted in a new type of official in the Kennedy administration. This particular inter-institutional power clique was called, rather incorrectly, the Irish Mafia.

2. *Budgets.* Individuals who have at their disposal the disbursement of funds will tend to distribute such funds to other clique members who are in a position to supply the necessary goods and services. This is not to imply fraud; rather, the clique member suppliers are known and are regarded as "trustworthy," though at times well-qualified suppliers of goods and services may wonder why they did not receive a contract.

3. *Policy.* Each individual in a clique, when he confronts his own organization or the community at large, can call on members of his clique to provide him with essential information—sometimes confidential information that would otherwise not be available to him. He

can also rely on the direct and vocal support of other clique members, or can count on a clique member who is not directly involved in the issue to apply personal pressure, persuasion, and influence on a third party. When clique members include members of the press or mass media, an issue may be made salient through publicity, to present favorable aspects of one's case and to suppress its unfavorable aspects.

4. *Third-Party Influence.* When a proposal involves securing the approval of a distant or personally unknown institutional decision-maker, a clique member who has direct and personal relations with the decision-maker may be used to secure a favorable decision.

5. *Support in Depth.* One core clique may be used to mobilize all of the indirect clique brothers in support of a proposition or proposal, so that an entire group may be mobilized behind an issue.

CLIQUE FUNCTIONING AND BUREAUCRATIC CONFLICT

Up to this point we have talked as if institutional power cliques operate from the standpoint of one person or one clique. It must be recognized that at any given time there are an infinite number of cliques whose planes of action may conflict and cut across one another—or they may be totally unrelated to one another. Membership in one clique may be recognized by others and may therefore disqualify one from membership in other cross-purpose cliques.

Each clique tends to develop an inner structure of loyalties and a rewarding of respective members, so that fulfillment of the obligation to one clique means an inability to fulfill obligations to others. Moreover, prestige within a clique is largely based on the actual or potential power to provide more rewards to fellow clique members than one takes. Prestige and power, therefore, are a transaction in which support is exchanged for more concrete benefits, regardless of personal friendship. The individual who always seeks favors and never reciprocates may be accepted as a clique member, but he tends only to be tolerated. And startling reversals in positions of "pecking orders" occur in a clique when a low-level member secures a position that suddenly gives him patronage, disposable funds, and an opportunity to affect policy or the life chances of others.

Because of the requirement that prestige and power be based on an ability to bestow these forms of patronage, each member of the clique seeks to enlarge his status by enlarging the areas that ultimately come under the control of the clique. As a result, there is an inherent tendency of cliques to expand until they reach limits placed upon them either by (a) the counter-expansive action of other cliques, or by (b) institutional officers who in their roles must protect the integrity of their office and their organization from their use as sources of opportunities for the cliques. Short of these limits, the institution becomes the happy hunting ground for rival cliques.

In his theory of bureaucracy Weber implies that the integrity of the formal organization is the essential characteristic of the bureaucracy. In principle, bureaucratic rules maintain that the official cannot have personal, informal, or work-related connections with officials in outside organizations or other agencies. Whenever bureaucrats allow informal or personal ties to influence their actions, they deviate from strict legality. The fact that such deviation occurs with frequency is not startling. But it does mean that bureaucratic leaders themselves can at times ignore the rules. At other times, especially when organizations are the scene of clique rivalries, they insist on the integrity of the organization and its rules.

When conflicts between cliques within bureaucracies come to a head and a victory of one clique over another results, it is often followed by a liquidation of those defeated clique members who have not made their peace in time; they are replaced by clique members of the victorious officials who must be rewarded. For this reason, after a power struggle a bureaucracy may seem to be inundated by swarms of locusts —new position holders with new styles of thought, language, and action—who give a completely new tone and color to an old organization. Thus President Johnson, to all intents and purposes, eliminated the "Irish Mafia" and replaced it with the old party professionals, reflecting his Senate and Texas background. President Nixon, on the other hand, selected his administrative "team" from among individuals whose lives intersected with his at a number of different points in his personal and political career. This included Robert Finch and Murray Chotiner from his early senatorial campaigns; old congressional associates such as Melvin R. Laird; staff members and allies such as William P. Rogers and Warren Burger from his vice-presidential days; and former law firm associates such as John N. Mitchell. Yet Nixon has been less inclined toward cronyism than other Presidents in the recent past. Many of his appointments have reflected convention promises, necessary measures to unify the party, and repayment of political obligations to campaign supporters. The changeover of personnel between any two administrations results in a change in the tone and complexion of government, and affects even nonpolitical civil service appointees.

In his effort to achieve personal and political loyalty, the head of an organization faces a major obstacle in those high-ranking bureaucratic specialists who feel they can wield power on the basis of their technical expertise and specialized knowledge. Leaders above the bureaucratic level, in order to secure loyalty and control, quite often must purge such technically qualified bureaucrats. When such purges are successful, specialized skills, knowledge, and efficiency are sacrificed for political loyalty and dependability. Inexperienced and "unqualified" replacements for old-line bureaucrats in a long period of transition will lack not only the necessary technical and administrative knowledge but the knowledge of ongoing arrangements and commitments entered into by their predecessors. In such periods of transition, old-line bureaucrats will engage in "guerrilla warfare" with the new political appointees. In the long run the nonpolitical bureaucrat is ultimately defeated.

The individual clique member, if he wishes to survive the transition period, must be sensitive to balances of power within his institution, and must wait to see if his clique will look after him if it loses an institutional struggle. Or else he must be prepared to jump if necessary to other institutions or job areas before a defeat.

If a star clique member in an institutional conflict has a second line of defense because of *other* jobs and budgets that he can make available to his protégés, he can command greater loyalties in his battles within the institution. The star member of a given clique may occupy an institutional position that is not the center of battle. But the success of *his* clique members in the institution of battle may result in one institution being dominated by another despite there being no official connection between the two. At times, when the star member appears to be particularly successful not so much in his own institution but in the efforts of his clique members in other institutions, it may appear that his power is growing at cancerous rates.

True, as one's success increases, the number of victims of his success also increases, but this does not mean that success generates its own limitations. Rather, as one's successes multiply, the problem of manpower for the clique becomes greater. One must provide personnel who are at least nominally capable of fulfilling the positions created by success, and one must provide the patronage to keep one's clique members loyal. To a certain extent success itself generates the means of fulfilling these requirements, for each success means that more budgets and jobs are at the disposal of the clique, and disaffected members of defeated cliques become allies.

A real limitation on the growth of the clique rests on the ability of individuals who are irrevocably committed to several defeated cliques to merge and find resources which will enable them to organize and provide patronage for newly emerging counter-cliques. This is by no means assured. If the membership of a clique is organized around special abilities to handle technological or institutional processes, the counter-cliques may be irrevocably defeated. The most general way that a triumphant clique can otherwise be defeated is by the weakening of its interpersonal ties by the extension of its lines. Individual clique members may become star members of smaller cliques and fractionate the former victorious clique. It is in this sense that in the fully bureaucratized society there is some check on the absolute control of the absolute horde.

Finally, a limitation on the success of a clique may occur when a successful clique member, by virtue of his success, begins to identify more with his organization than with his clique. He may value the integrity of the organization more than his status within the clique. In such cases he will limit clique participation or modify it so that it does not interfere with his formal position.

Regardless of the outcome of clique struggles, recognition of the concept of the inter-institutional clique indicates (a) continuous tension between formal position and wider status groups, on the one hand, and (b) the interpersonal basis of greater coordination between organizations and institutions than can be inferred from the study of their formal connections.

COORDINATION AT THE LEVEL OF TOP LEADERSHIP

The preceding discussion has examined the mechanisms of interbureaucratic coordination at the level of the upper managerial classes. Except for the examples of presidential appointments, it did not include a consideration of top leadership at either the political or economic levels. It would seem nonetheless that coordination at the very top in both politics and corporate family dynasties involves not only the same principles but the further recognition by the leaders that they hold decisive power in their hands. This recognition makes a critical difference at top levels of societal coordination in both the political and economic orders.

"Political" leaders of economic, government, and military bureaucracies have an awareness of their power positions apart from formal administrative and legal restrictions. They understand the need to take extra-legal initiatives to maintain order, and they are especially conscious of respecting the limits and restrictions imposed upon their matching members in other institutions. So to speak, top powerholders are capable of developing a sense of empathy for their counterparts in competing institutions. This results partly from the fact that as leaders they are separated from their own organizational membership whom they must lead, discipline, and control. Lacking "understanding" from their own world, they are more likely to gain a sense of understanding from their organizational equals in competitive bureaucracies. Top leaders in this sense are part of an informal club based on a mutual understanding of one another's problems. Such clubs, based on organizationally diverse personnel in similar top positions, are normally designated *organizational and political elites*. The elite need not be formally organized; rather, it is defined by a mutual awareness and similarity in the use of power and attitudes toward political and organizational problems. Members of such clubs can appreciate and respect the craft of leadership which is frequently demonstrated by their own competitors.

Top leaders must necessarily work and negotiate with their equivalents in other bureaucracies, organizations, and leadership circles. On crucial issues which affect their personal and organizational positions and responsibility, these top leaders seek out those organization counterparts who become for the moment their allies, or their opposition with whom they must negotiate because they represent the relevant opposing institution. The model for this theory is to be found in military practice during war: victorious and defeated generals observe the etiquette of recognizing each others' dignity and status. The time-honored military example is particularly instructive because competing armies are pure examples of bureaucracies negotiating with each other. In this respect the military codes illustrate types of interbureaucratic communication between top leaders, though these codes are not so well formalized in civilian institutions, except for the diplomatic corps.

In looking at top-level coordination among organizations in the United States, it is easy to see that even the President, despite his vast powers, cannot act unilaterally. John F. Kennedy, albeit through his minions, had to negotiate with the steel industry when he wanted to hold the line on steel prices in 1961. From the *New York Times* report it was clear that Roger Blough of U. S. Steel negotiated with the administration with the assurance of a general commanding a large army that had suffered only a temporary defeat. This same drama was repeated several years later when Lyndon Johnson negotiated in the same way with the heads of the copper and aluminum industries. Negotiations between the White House and the dominant branches of government (Pentagon, FBI, CIA, Supreme Court, and so on) and the business corporations, labor unions, and other vested interest groups of America have become an everyday commonplace. Society is coordinated through the institutional leaders who head the dominant institutions of society.

It is one of the ambiguities of American politics that no one leader or institutional area has been able to dominate all of the political life of the society. So far, at least, the United States has not opted for a totalitarian solution. If there is any genius in American politics, as Daniel Boorstin claims in his *Genius of American Politics,* it is not in its democratic ethos but rather in its unwillingness to accept totalitarian solutions.

But totalitarianism must be distinguished from the centralized concentration of power. It is clear that political power is now centralized and coordinated at the highest levels by informal methods, even when the parties involved are formally in conflict. The drama of politics is now played for a national and international audience. All older notions of grass-roots democracy and lower-level political pluralism are obsolete. The causes of this change have been the new role of the corporation in American society, the growth of the federal bureaucracy, and the size and importance of the federal budget in politicizing economic decisions.

6. *Coordination and competition among elites*

THE DECLINE OF COMMUNITY POLITICS

The "coordination" of society by heads of major institutions and agencies parallels at a national level a general phenomenon that in an earlier period occurred at the local level. Earlier in American history, up to the end of the nineteenth century and perhaps into the first decades of the twentieth, the pattern of local politics was one in which one group of leaders dominated all levels of public life in the local community.

During the period from 1860 to 1910 the population of the United States grew from 31 million to 92 million, while the number of people living in incorporated cities of 2,500 or more increased from 6 million to 44 million. Yet up to 1900 the United States was still a largely rural society, a country of small towns and what we would now regard as medium-sized cities. These small towns and cities were dominated by businessmen who controlled the churches, schools, charity, and civic organizations. "Eastern culture" had not yet penetrated the country. More than half the population was foreign born and did not fully participate in the civic life of the community. Therefore, for the most part the cultural tone of the community was set by white Protestant small businessmen in small towns—Sinclair Lewis' *Main Street.*

Usually one family, one clique, or one group controlled Main Street.

In the Lynds' study of Middletown, this was the "X" family; in Springdale it was Jones, and in Hunter's study of Atlanta it was the Banker. In company towns like Hershey, Pennsylvania, or Kohler, Wisconsin, to name only two, the pattern of dominance by a single family owning the major industry of the community was especially clear. According to Warner, in Yankee City, which was studied during a period of transition, the middle upper class tended to control the community through its leadership over the active middle class. The upper upper class entered politics only when a vital issue was at stake, and on those occasions was capable of disciplining the middle upper class. From available evidence there is a long and strong tradition of community political coordination by dominant businessmen.

The autonomy of the local community and local business leaders was substantially altered when big business entered American towns and cities. In Yankee City this occurred when the locally owned shoe industry was absorbed by national corporations. When big business entered local communities through factory managers and local supervisors, the political tendency was to use local leaders as a screen to conceal the power and influence of the corporation on local life. As American society has grown and become more centralized, big business has abandoned much of its attempt to control the local community, not because it has met resistance from local leaders but because its interest is focused more exclusively on national policies and budgets. Big business tends to be active in the local community only when a specific interest such as real estate assessments, water supply, or disposal of industrial waste is involved.

Except for specific interests, local government possesses little that is worth controlling, whereas the federal government may be all important to the life and success of a big business. For example, a minor change in the tax laws pertaining to depreciation allowances may result in millions of dollars of savings to a national corporation. This can also be true of tariff legislation, labor law, monetary policy, credit policies, foreign aid, military spending, and so on. As corporations become larger, their fate is more directly linked to decisions made at a national political level. Thus as the local community declines in relative importance it begins to enjoy a degree of freedom from the direct concern of giant corporations. The freedom thus gained, however, leaves the local community in a powerless position. A decision to relocate a plant based on national considerations can convert any particular community into virtually a ghost town. Thus even the minimal but necessary concern of the giant corporation may be decisive in determining the prosperity, the way of life, and the future of a community; but such losses for the community are minor issues for the corporate giant.

CORPORATE AND FEDERAL POWER

In the influence and control of national policy, and in the coordination of its own effort, American business has had a changing history. Before the enactment of federal anti-trust legislation, American business firms tried to organize themselves and minimize competition through various types of mutually acceptable agreements, sometimes secret and sometimes open. They included a wide range of mechanisms such as price-fixing, rebates and kickbacks, restriction of competition, and allocations of markets. For the most part, such agreements were unsuccessful because of generally low business ethics and the absence of an agency to act as referee—with the result that agreements were broken by the first firm that saw an opportunity to gain an advantage by abrogating them.

Where business agreements did not work, alternative methods were employed, such as absorption of competition through amicable arrangements or by means of business wars. With continued competition and growth in size, the unit and cost of warfare grew larger. Before the turn of the century the cost of business warfare became exorbitantly high. When the trust movement was started to reduce these costs, it appeared to be an ideal solution. But trusts soon came to be held illegal. After this the method employed was one of direct combinations and mergers of large-scale enterprises. These mergers, begun after the anti-trust legislation, have resulted in what are now our giant corporations. But even these corporate giants have in the past been plagued by a whole series of anti-trust actions which have revealed that the corporate structure is still supported by informal agreements, price leadership, and outright conspiratorial actions to set prices, allocate markets, and assign "rights" to win "competitive" bidding, as in the electrical industry's turbine scandal, to mention one example. Since the enactment of anti-trust laws, the attack on business giantism and on restriction of competition has been as continuous as the growth in size of business units, the reduction of competition, and price uniformity. All the while big business was expanding, it was being attacked by government, by farmers, by labor, by muckrakers, and by smaller businesses which were being squeezed out. These attacks no doubt heightened the conspiratorial inclinations of American businessmen, but they also revealed to these businessmen the need for something more than conspiratorial action.

In the early 1920's American business began to be conscious of its public relations. A whole genus of business organizations like the U.S. Chamber of Commerce, the National Association of Manufacturers (NAM), and hundreds of trade associations became the public relations branches of American business. The largest of these was and is the U.S. Chamber of Commerce, a national organization of Main Streeters who have played the role of fronting for big business. Local chambers of commerce have been quite willing to play this role in exchange for the psychic pleasure of being associated with representatives of big business.

On the political side, the Republican party, after the Civil War and up through the 1930's, appeared to be the special vehicle of both big and small business interests. So conspicuously identified with business was the Republican party that it appeared to be dominated by conservative economic interests and as a result could be easily attacked by all anti-business groups. It was easy to equate the Republican party with the Chamber of Commerce and the National Association of Manufacturers.

During the 1930's depression-type muckrakers, radicals, communists, and left-wing New Dealers saw the Republican party, the Chamber of Commerce, the NAM, and the trade associations as a united front of business against the rest of society. There is little doubt that these critics overestimated the power of business organizations. When Roosevelt pointed to the "economic royalists," he played to an audience that was disenchanted with business because of its failure to maintain prosperity. For the most part the Chamber of Commerce, the NAM, and other business organizations were primarily public relations enterprises which attempted to create a favorable climate of opinion for business. In some cases these organizations functioned as clubs where businessmen could meet with one another and with government officials to make deals which affected their mutual futures. There is no evidence, however, to suggest that these public relations branches of American business acted to create a unified line of action for the entire business community. American business has always been much too suspicious and competitive to be able to unite.

The movement toward overall business coordination in the United States never came to fruition. This was the case up to the 1930's, partly because the power of the federal government was primarily negative and partly because business itself lacked the administrative machinery to control such a heterogeneous assemblage. Thus American business, although certainly possessed of enormous power, was always characterized by factionalism, regional competition, and an innate tendency to destroy or dominate competitors. The predatory instincts of the businessman have no doubt been America's greatest safeguard against a unified business domination of the country. The image of a single-minded, coordinated conspiracy by American business has been more an image necessary to sustain anti-business propaganda and reform legislation than it has been a reality. At least until the 1930's, the evils of business were more a matter of irresponsibility and overcompetition than conspiratorial coordination.

It was precisely during the thirties, when American business was clearly on the defensive, that it found a new role in American life. When the New Deal introduced the idea of the giant federal budget, for the first time the federal government became a major market for business. The large federal budget redefined the role of the federal agency. Now the administrative rulings of regulative agencies, procurement agencies, and budgetary departments could create opportunities for particular firms. Business began to depend on winning the award for the contract. Because of this, as H. L. Nieburg has shown in his book *In the Name of Science,* it became necessary for the giant corporation acting as an individual unit to deal directly with a specific government department, legislator, or official whose decisions or policies would affect the critical allocation of millions or billions of dollars.

The size of the federal budget increased still more dramatically during World War II, but now, from the vantage point of the seventies, even these war budgets were small. The expansion of government spending has resulted in unprecedented opportunities for business: for many firms the government budget may be the only market, and even doctrinaire businessmen can approach government independently of a particular political ideology or philosophy. It does not matter if the legislator or official is pro- or anti-business in his overall philosophy; a firm can still make large amounts of money by getting a favorable hearing or contract from him or his committee. At times it appears that some producers, regions, cities, and congressional districts are especially favored in the allocation of federal funds. Some critics of this new system have raised questions concerning the ethics of the federal systems of contracts and income redistribution.

THE LOBBYIST AS A POLITICAL AND ETHICAL FIGURE

As the federal budget became larger, the role of the lobbyist became greater. In his expanded role the lobbyist became an immediate gatekeeper or liaison man between the individual firm and the government department. In addition to his efforts to influence the design of legislation, he now began to play an active role in the writing of it. As the size of federal budgets increased through the fifties and sixties, the single professional lobbyist, or even the legal representative of the firm, proved to be insufficient. With increases in scale, lobbying lost its craftlike quality.

Lobbying has now become so legalistic, so complex, so intricate that it can no longer be carried out by individual agents. It is now necessary for large firms, organizations, and other vested interests to maintain their own "Washington office." The Washington office is staffed by a range of specialists whose duties include keeping abreast of administrative decisions, reading relevant technical bulletins, and picking up inside information on legislative and budgetary opportunities. In his older form, the individual professional lobbyist hardly exists. Where he has managed to stay in business, he can now exist only as the agent of numerous smaller businesses which cannot afford a full-time professional staff.

Professional lobbying has become such a fundamental institution that congressmen, too, often depend on the lobbyist. The idea of the congressman's constituency used to be that of citizen-voters, but today this is an old-fashioned notion. In most congressional districts the citizen-voter's interests lie with the industrial base of his community. The congressman who does not at least claim credit for a government contract, a new highway, or a new military appropriation is thought not to be doing his job. The constituency will not tolerate the congressman who does not get a share of federal expenditures for the folks back home. Congressmen must thus reflect industrial interests, some of which extend over larger geographic boundaries than their congressional districts. They do this through the medium of the lobbyist, who is the paid representative of the firm, corporation, state, city, professional organization, and so on.

The congressman finds himself in a unique relationship with the lobbyist. Frequently the latter writes the legislation that is to be submitted by the congressman. In an immediate sense this represents a savings to the taxpayer. Meanwhile, the congressman is in a position to take favors from his friends whose legislation he introduces and supports—though this is not to say that congressmen are necessarily corrupted by these new opportunities to supplement their incomes.

In part, the definition of what constitutes corruption has changed. Thus the Sherman Adams–Bernard Goldfine scandal during the Eisenhower years, which focused on a vicuna coat, involved a very small amount of money received from a small businessman for relatively small favors; but it was sufficiently explosive to cost Adams his job, even though a President was trying to protect him. Bobby Baker's activities in the Senate, when they were exposed, were regarded as highly irregular; there seems to be little doubt that many officials and elected representatives were involved with Baker's activities. But these cases, as well as those of someone like Senator Thomas Dodd of Connecticut, represent relatively minor violations of the norms, and the sums of money involved are almost trifling. Compared with these publicized cases, one can point to the normal activities of congressmen and senators in, let us say, the case of the TFX-11, of the National Science Foundation, and of the Mohole project, or of the research and development costs of the supersonic transport plane. All of these cases involved hundreds of millions or even billions of dollars, major elective officials, major industries, and intensive lobbying, but none apparently involved illegal or "unethical" action. The ethical structure of the relations between business and government has undergone major revision since the days of the muckrakers.

The normalizing of what used to be regarded as "unethical" has occurred without a corresponding change in symbolic ethical standards. This poses no problem in the case of the cheap chiseler, the five-percenter, the shakedown artist, or the influence peddler in high circles who can be cast in the role of a vulgar, crude, overweaningly ambitious operator. The arrest of "cheap" types—Bobby Baker, Billie Sol Estes, Bernard Goldfine—and their public exposure and punishment provide an outlet for the expression of resentment and moral indignation on the part of the masses, including the liberal sector of the middle class. Because the chiseler is caught and exposed in a nationally televised morality drama, the more conventional opportunities for using influence and connections seem even more respectable and legitimate. Thus the enforcement of justice in the extreme cases makes for tacit approval of more polished and subtle—and more serious—forms of influence and favoritism. When the cheap chiselers get caught, the rest of us can maintain our sense of righteousness by vicariously participating in a national morality play in which we celebrate our civic virtue without altering fundamental business and political processes.

This morality play, until the mid-sixties, appeared to be a recurrent necessity in American public life. It helped to sustain the self-image of the American as honest, moral, ethical, and civically upright. This scenario works to its logical conclusion so long as the villain can be clearly defined and is not "respectable." When a respectable business leader is caught in conspiratorial behavior, as in the case of price-fixing in the electrical industry, or in industrial espionage, as in the case of automobile safety, traditional values are betrayed. But now the new mass culture rescues the errant businessman by portraying established society as a moral cesspool where all public life, economic as well as political, is corrupt. Success in society, according to the media, depends on mastering the techniques of fraud and deception. The cynical nature of the mass media makes the public atmosphere an object of satire and burlesque and defines the fool as someone who holds to the older morality. Humor replaces moral indignation as a means of affirming the older morality.* Thus we are still unable to respond appropriately to the illegal activities of respectable businessmen whose illegal activities are part of the normal exercise of their business situation.

By now the institutionalization of lobbying and influence peddling has proceeded to such a degree that major decisions on government contracts affecting billions of dollars are made as a matter of course by methods which once might have required cruder and more direct forms of bribery and collusion. Small business has, for the most part, been left out of this process. Lacking information resources, institutional power, and trained technical and political staffs, small business has resorted to shoddy and obviously illegal means to gain petty favors. In their desperation small businessmen are more apt to hire marginal types to represent them in Washington, so that the character of small-business lobbying is one of cheapness and meanness. While small business appears to be grasping and greedy in laying claims to small shares, professionalized big business gets the grants, the contracts, and the concessions on a business-as-usual basis.

The techniques of big-business lobbying have been rationalized far beyond what would have been imaginable thirty years ago. These techniques include not only the use of specialized market- and opinion-research departments, lawyers and legal firms, and the entertainment of administrative officials and elected representatives, but more significantly the employment of retired military officers and government officials, and the luring away of other officials from relatively low-paid government jobs. This easy flow of personnel from major government agencies to business has two major implications:

1. The high-ranking military officer or professional administrator has an intimate familiarity with the agency he left, and has friends and contacts in the agency. His knowledge of the inside operations of government is immediately translatable into an economic opportunity for himself in industry and for the firm in its relations with government.

2. Once the government official is aware of his potential value to industry, business opportunities can be determined in advance. By establishing friendly contacts with the potential employer-contractor, the

* In this respect contemporary mass media emulate some of the oldest themes in the serious arts. Don Quixote, Candide, Simplicimus, Gargantua, and Pantagruel portrayed themes similar to those now appearing in the mass media.

government official can establish his value to his would-be employer. He makes his future career in business by carrying out his official duties as a government official. In sociological terms, this would be known as a special case of anticipatory socialization: the official proves his value to his would-be employer in advance of his employment.

THE FAILURE OF POLITICAL UNITY AMONG BUSINESSMEN

The tremendous potential of government contracts for the individual firm has destroyed the character of interbusiness cooperation. Where previously collusion and restraint of competition implied business unity, even this form of unity no longer seems to be necessary. Now individual firms compete to influence government decisions, because these firms are like states unto themselves and because the rewards of any one government decision can be so great. As the TFX case has shown, the giant airframe and engine producers will compete ruthlessly against each other to secure a decisive $10 billion contract. What is different from the past is that (1) big business does not compete in an "open" market against hundreds of other businesses, and (2) the size of the unit of competition has grown tremendously.

Thus monolithic unity of business is not as necessary as it might have seemed to be in the 1920's or the 1930's. Looking at the matter from a slightly different angle, business in the thirties tended to unite in an attack on the New Deal, especially in and through business organizations surrounding the Republican party. But as the budgetary implications of the New Deal and World War II became apparent, it became more difficult for American business to regard the Democrats as enemies. Even to businessmen it became clear that the Democrats had saved them from the American system they sought to uphold. As a result, big business has been weaned away from much of its ideological conservatism. It is clear, after all, that the welfare state has provided—if indeed it has for anyone—for the welfare of business.

It took business almost twenty years to realize these truths, but by the 1950's almost all major segments of the American business community had become aware of these facts of business life. This awareness produced an interesting result within the business community.

Business has split into two "factions," which are reflected in the split within the Republican party.* The so-called Eastern wing has become a partisan of the welfare state and has willingly accepted all that welfare means. This faction espouses (sometimes through Wall Street statesmen) welfarism and internationalism without much regard to party. The *older* Republican ideology has become reserved largely for the partisans of small business in smaller communities and for bigger businessmen in areas not as directly affected by specific federal budget policy—a case in point of the latter being Fort Worth and Dallas bankers who are linked to oil-drilling speculations. The right wing of the Republican party reflects to some degree an older, more authentic Republicanism, in part gone mad by its inability to maintain earlier American traditions of Main Street business and Babbittry.

Ironically, as right-wing Republicanism has become more ideologically passionate, big business has become more ideologically neutral. The Democratic party under both John F. Kennedy and Lyndon Johnson attracted a great deal of support from big business. Richard Nixon's major political asset before his election seemed to be that he was the only person who could unite both factions of his party. Having been elected, he apparently provides an acceptable political rhetoric for the right wing, and some freedom from federal administrative restraints for big business, while avoiding a change in the major commitment of the federal government to Keynesian budgetary and monetary policy. Despite changes in federal administration, we are in the midst of evolving a new form of interrelationship between business and federal power.

THE COALESCENCE OF ECONOMIC AND POLITICAL JURISDICTIONS

Given the new circumstances of political and economic decision-making in the United States, it is hard to draw a firm line, at either the national or the regional level, between where political jurisdictions or even institutional areas begin and end. As John Kenneth Galbraith, in his book *The New Industrial State,* has cogently noted, it is no longer possible to separate economic from political jurisdictions. For exam-

* The beginnings of this split occurred in the thirties and resulted finally in an open confrontation during the campaign for the Republican nomination in 1964.

ple, a congressman may at times represent a private interest (a large firm with a plant in his area) and at other times represent the public. The public itself may be capable of confusing its interests with those of the firm on which it depends; thus it is hard to say which constituency, for example, a representative from the Detroit area actually represents.

In much the same way, leaders of business are coopted into the administrative area: such men as Nelson Rockefeller, Robert McNamara, Charles E. Wilson, Douglas Dillon, Henry Cabot Lodge, Averell Harriman, and Ellsworth Bunker have made the shift from one administration to another without wholly abandoning their long-term business affiliations. At other times businessmen will use their role as business leaders to make significant statements on national policy which are primarily of a political character. Thus, for example, Henry Ford II, in the Johnson administration, had a major role of selling government policy to the business community, and vice versa. At other times David Rockefeller has had this role in the banking community, while Laurence Rockefeller has been a spokesman in the area of natural resources. Nelson Rockefeller frequently has had this role with respect to Latin American relations. John J. McCloy and, to a lesser extent, Douglas Dillon played this role with respect to diplomatic and fiscal policy in Europe, while Eugene Black and, to a much lesser extent, David Lilienthal have been key figures for the underdeveloped world. This list could be extended indefinitely for all major areas of political, economic, military, and ideological jurisdictions. It is becoming increasingly difficult to distinguish the interests that officials represent.

The overlapping of roles and interests makes it difficult to find a simple paradigm for American politics. Various stars, public spokesmen, and public or private officials become the representatives of various combinations of governmental, industrial, and military networks. At times these "networks" of interconnected "leaders" deal exclusively in one area and can cooperate with each other. At other times these same leaders compete with each other in their attempts to gain contracts, define policy, and affect budgets. Moreover, the individuals, firms, and governmental agencies involved are themselves not constant. They realign themselves on specific issues. Some combinations or groups in the combination become inactive as issues change. On another issue, new combinations of competing groups arise with perhaps some of the same as well as different participating members. Depending on the issue and the political and economic stakes involved, previous allies become enemies, and vice versa.

The one constant in this shifting pattern of alliances and rivalries is that entry into the game requires that its participants have sufficiently great resources, influence, or discretion to be "qualified" to take part in the making of these decisions. To the extent that all participants are sufficiently powerful to enter the game, there is a power elite; but this power elite is not a permanent unified alliance of the powerful against the powerless, as some specific cases prove:

1. The steel industry's price hike in 1962 and its revocation under pressure from the Kennedy administration. Kennedy was able to prevail by fragmenting the steel industry through personal contacts located in and out of the industry and on several continents.

2. The Suez crisis of 1956 and the split in U.S. oil and financial factions on that issue. Domestic and Latin American producers saw prospects for gaining while the Pentagon, the State Department, and oil producers primarily based in the Middle East came in conflict with each other over American policy. The same concern for business revenues derived from oil has plagued American Presidents with respect to Israeli-Arab conflicts. The State Department, sensitive to American oil companies, has tended to delay pro-Israeli actions by elected political leaders who respond more in terms of political constituencies. The situation is further complicated by the attempt to respond to Russia's military presence in the Mediterranean.

3. The development of atomic energy as opposed to conventional sources of power. Conflicts in this area have involved the advocates of public and private power, the Atomic Energy Commission and factions within the AEC, the coal industry (and coal-producing states and their congressmen), the manufacturers of atomic reactors, and the manufacturers of conventional electric-generating equipment. Banking and financial interests who see electric-power generation primarily as an opportunity for investment align themselves on the basis of past and present investments and investment opportunities. State governments compete with federal jurisdictions for the right to allocate monopolies

over the development of atomic energy, and to allocate these monopolies between public and private agencies, thus to determine which interests shall benefit from their development.

4. The relation of the Communications Satellite Corporation to conventional communications industries. Characteristically, COMSAT became an independent private corporation partly subsidized by federal research and development funds, and bestowing benefits to those private communications agencies that collectively are its customers.

5. The allocation of contracts for research and development and for production of the TFX fighter, the supersonic transport, the antiballistic missile, and the combat helicopter. These projects involve billions of dollars in contracts and, in the case of some, enormous subsidies to "private" producers. Each has involved titanic power struggles between combinations of airframe and engine firms, missile producers, the Defense Department, congressional, state, and regional groups, and divisions within the executive department. Such struggles concern the attempt to control and receive the benefits of a significant part of the federal budget. They have also involved reviews, recriminations, and charges of waste, incompetence, overcharge, profiteering, contract-fixing, and Defense Department collusion and misrepresentation of defense needs. Beyond this, they have involved conflicts over the control and content of American military and foreign policy.

In all of the above cases, different assortments of military, business, industrial, banking, fiscal, and government interests entered a complicated "mix" to determine who would win the spoils. There was no way to determine in advance what the outcome might be, but in any one of these situations it is entirely possible that groups and firms which cooperated on one issue might find themselves aligned against one another in other situations.

In most cases, however, each inter-institutional complex focuses on the area of its central concern and does not—at least publicly—find itself directly at odds with another. To the extent this is true, the political system may gain some stability from the stability of factions. But the participants in any one complex (faction) who collaborate around a specific issue may be involved in other complexes with respect to other issues. Thus the allies of a complex in one area may be simultaneously its enemies in another area. In this image, domestic politics resembles international diplomacy—that is, a continuously shifting system of alliances where the overall structure is defined only by the immediate interests of the participants in the game. If there is a stabilizing force in such a system of national politics, it rests in the fact that the parties to the conflicts (and cooperation) must limit their victories over each other in *specific* cases in order to be able to claim as allies the same parties who, on other issues, were enemies. Self-restraint and a willingness to achieve less than total victory account for political coordination short of monolithic control. In this sense political pluralism is an important factor.

The inter-institutional system rests on informal agreements among competitors. Such agreements can be the most effective regulators of competition so long as all parties to the competition share a favorable position at the public trough. Agreement is possible because all parties to the contract see some possibilities for future gain, even though they may suffer short-run losses. These terms exclude all groups who have nothing to gain by making short-term compromises. Outright resentment, disengagement, and attacks on the entire structure of society are reserved for those who have no hopes of participating in the spoils.

Resentment by the relatively powerless may well serve to organize, coordinate, and discipline the dominant elites. So long as these elites must concern themselves with the potential power of groups that are at present relatively powerless, they are forced to limit the intensity of their own competition. It is for this reason that the various elites need not be unified. They struggle, they compete, they align and realign—but usually they exercise restraint in their conflicts with each other.

III.

Emerging life styles and the new classes

7. *Changes in the life styles of American classes*

THE CREATION OF LIFE STYLES.

As Max Weber noted many years ago in his essay "Class Status and Power," capital, wealth, and income are not by themselves sufficient as indices for specifying the life styles of classes. Within given income levels, the way in which income is spent involves elements of choice. Life styles may thus take a variety of forms within the same income categories, depending upon the character of consumption choices.*

In considering the problem of the life styles of classes in the United States, we have found it useful to refer to Harold Finestone's seminal essay on "cat" culture. In that essay called "Cats, Kicks, and Color," Finestone, using Johan Huizinga's theory of play, pointed out that one of the major characteristics of the Negro's "cat" culture is its artificiality. The cat literally invented his own language, his own morality, his own dress styles, and his own codes of interpersonal conduct. He used

* In dealing with "class" and especially the life styles of classes, we are primarily concerned with the distributive behavior of individuals and families who are roughly in the same economic situation. We are not here concerned with behavior that is collectively organized and expressed through such institutions as parties, associations, groups, and other collectivities. The agencies that direct and organize the activities of the members of one or more classes have in part been treated in earlier chapters; we will treat new institutions and collectivities in subsequent chapters.

all of these inventions to frame a total way of life for himself. The cat who was denied access to the life styles of the dominant culture could borrow directly from that culture to construct his own way of life. Reacting to rejection by the dominant culture, the cat insulated himself by developing a unique life style. At least within his own self-selected group he thus achieved a basis for dignity, self-respect, and status competition.

The artifice of cat culture was maintained by the conscious effort of those involved in it. Black youth in the cat culture deliberately cultivated a style of living and playfully changed and restyled, elaborated and extended it. The cat, even while creating and enacting his life style, knew that it was an artificial convention which could not be lived completely within the embrace of the dominant culture. As Finestone noted, "He has to make place in his scheme of life for police, lock-ups, jails and penitentiaries, to say nothing of the agonies of withdrawal distress." Always there were occasions when the cat was forced to suspend his play, to look consciously at himself with a sense of irony and satire. When he did so, he faced the fact that there was nothing left in life for him. When his play collapsed, the cat stepped outside of himself and became a bemused spectator of his own play without having any other basis for a viable self.

Finestone's essay is only one of a series of analyses of the artificiality of Negro culture in the United States. St. Clair Drake and Horace Cayton, in their book *Black Metropolis,* described the extensive emulation of middle- and upper-class white life styles by Negroes at almost all levels of the Negro class hierarchy. Perhaps more than anyone else, E. Franklin Frazier, in his revealing and bitter analysis of the *Black Bourgeoisie,* described the enormous psychological and social cost for Negroes of their attempt to emulate a nonexistent, white, upper-middle-class life style. All of these studies have pointed to the attempts of Negroes who, lacking a tradition with which they are able to identify, try to find life styles by emulating a dominant white culture which has rejected them. This effort to copy what is alien to its emulators has resulted in a parody of white styles. The Negro overacts selected themes from white life to the point of satirizing them and, in most cases, unlike the "cat," is not aware that he is doing so. For the lower-middle-class, middle-class, and upper-class Negro, to recognize his inadequate emulation would be too difficult to bear because such an admission would reveal the artificiality of his entire way of life and would leave no basis for living with himself.

Apart from Negro culture, the Finestone essay, in pointing out the conscious and artificial play of cat culture, permits us once again to raise the general question of the authenticity and spuriousness of life styles and class "cultures."* The existence of artificial life styles, self-consciously created as if they were works of art, suggests a lack of inevitability in the living patterns that classes adopt. The stages of class experience through which the individual passes in the course of the life cycle do not present an easy succession of life patterns which the individual can accept as "natural" or "authentic." It would rather seem that each stage in the class history of the individual presents a problem of learning new class patterns. The greater the individual's mobility, the greater the amount of flexibility and "learning" necessary for each stage. The greater the mobility, the greater will be the consciousness of adopting new patterns of conduct demanded by each change in status. Instances of rapid mobility are thus psychological equivalents of the predominant Negro experience in American society. In both instances life styles are artificial creations or adoptions. The bearer himself is aware of the fact that the style can be donned and discarded at will and, therefore, it can be acted out with some degree of self-irony and self-satire. The irony and satire express a certain degree of discomfort which the individual experiences when behaving in a way that he does not see as "natural," or "authentic," or ordinary.

In our terms, an "authentic" life style is one that exists as part of the "natural" and "inevitable" environment of the individual. The individual, without reflection, assumes that he has been destined for the way of life which in fact is his. He takes his way of life for granted and acts it out without self-consciousness, defensiveness, or irony.

While there is an abundant literature on the artificial nature of Negro life styles and on the adaptive capacities of mobility-minded whites,

* This is an issue first raised by Edward Sapir in his essay "Culture, Genuine and Spurious," *American Journal of Sociology,* XXIX (1924), 401–429, and continued by Melvin Tumin, "Culture, Genuine and Spurious: A Re-evaluation," *American Sociological Review,* X, No. 2 (April 1945). We have dealt with this theme in *Small Town in Mass Society,* chap. 4, "Springdale and the Mass Society" (Princeton, 1958), pp. 80–107.

the same kind of reporting is not available for white middle-, upper-middle-, and upper-class life styles. One significant exception is Seeley, Sim, and Loosely's *Crestwood Heights,* as it is discussed in *The Eclipse of Community,* in which Maurice Stein points out the ironic element in the life style of the upper middle class of Toronto. The subjects of that study displayed a capacity to talk about themselves and their participation in the community objectively and analytically. Thus they could consciously analyze what one had to do in order to "get along" in Crestwood Heights. They worked at behaving appropriately and understood the consequences of alternative lines of conduct. Newcomers to the community displayed a facility for picking up the cues and quickly adjusted themselves to the Crestwood Heights style. In all of this there was a quality of both ironic self-detachment and self-rationalization not dissimilar to the self-rationalization of the bureaucratic personality.

While *Crestwood Heights* most clearly expresses the theme of self-irony, similar themes have been expressed for the metropolitan New York City upper middle class in A. C. Spectorsky's book *The Exurbanites,* and for the aspiring middle-class Levittown dweller in John Keats's book *The Crack in the Picture Window.* On another plane, the element of ironic self-detachment is the basic theme of Jules Fieffer's cartoons, whose contents appeal precisely to those who are the objects of his satire. We are not dealing here only with intellectual sophisticates and beats, since magazines like *Playboy, Esquire,* and the *New Yorker,* in their overall tone, make similar appeals to their respective readers. The existence of a market for satire on middle- and upper-middle-class life styles suggests that the phenomenon of ironic self-detachment is a generalized feature of a number of life styles in American society.

It is our contention that present American life styles are predominantly self-conscious creations which permeate almost all aspects of American life, with a few exceptions to be noted. Lacking the sanction of tradition, these patterns are not lived with the comfort that comes from being taken for granted, but are rather known to be artificial. The major traditional life styles of the nineteenth century are now defunct and have been replaced by new sets of living patterns unique to American history.

THE DECLINE OF OLDER LIFE STYLES

The literature on class points to the dominance of several distinct traditional life styles in the United States.

1. The historically dominant life style tradition is perhaps best defined as Babbittry—the aggressive, social, uncultured, energetic, optimistic way of life of the late frontier. In many respects Babbittry is a secularization of life styles associated with those of the fundamentalist Protestant "bible belt" as they emerged out of the revival of Methodist and Baptist movements in the early and mid-nineteenth century. This style is stereotyped in the small-town, churchgoing Protestant moralism of the Midwest, especially in the Iowa of Grant Wood, who depicts the parsimonious, taciturn upholders of public propriety.

2. The urban aristocracy of the late nineteenth century best illustrates traditional upper-class life styles. Brahmin culture on Boston's Beacon Hill (which itself, in its indigenous elements, was a dilution of earlier New England transcendentalism) suggests this style. Gramercy Square intellectualism in New York City was a similar phenomenon. In both these instances there were social, cultural, and intellectual affiliations with European, especially English, elements, reflecting the absence of an American tradition upon which to draw. These European affiliations were frequently with aristocratic and intellectual culture as was the case, for example, with Henry Adams. Such imitation can, of course, be looked upon as a continuation of a process already begun within the European upper classes themselves. Throughout the seventeenth and eighteenth centuries the landed aristocracy of Europe was penetrated by newly wealthy bourgeoisie who adopted this life style. By the time the Americans began to imitate the Europeans, their model was largely an imitation itself. As Georg Simmel and Huizinga have pointed out, the life style of the European aristocracy, having been cut off from its historical roots in the Middle Ages, especially in the religious brotherhoods of knights, by the time of the *ancien régime* had become but a shadow of its former self. Such artificial mummification was imitated and continued in the upper-class style of the American South, which emphasized elegance, leisure, *noblesse oblige,* high etiquette, and slavery. The Civil War rent this class asunder, but its style remained as a model for would-be Southern belles and aristocrats.

Like those of European aristocrats before them, American upper-class life styles underwent a continuous process of dilution. In the nineteenth century the entrance of the robber barons into this class provided an infusion of healthy vulgarity. With newly gained wealth from newly formed industries, they added gaudiness and garrishness to American upper-class culture. Both these styles were described by Veblen, Edith Wharton, and Gustavus Myers.

There is clear evidence that these upper-class life styles have declined and all but disappeared. Certainly there are no more Southern aristocrats who can be taken seriously. Senator Claghorn, the mint-julep-drinking Southern colonel, and Blanche DuBois, the deluded postbellum belle in *A Streetcar Named Desire,* caricature a dead epoch. A few aged dowagers on Beacon Hill represent a living connection to the nineteenth century, but that tradition has been effectively broken by the industrialization of Boston's Route 128. Gramercy Square, now in the jet age, qualifies as an historical monument. The Babbittry of Iowa and Minnesota has given way to the vacation-minded, Cadillac-driving farmer who may still go to church but takes his Bermuda trip more seriously. Whether their economic basis was destroyed or not, that these life styles have not been able to sustain themselves requires some explanation.

Between 1880 and 1924 hundreds of thousands of immigrants from southern and eastern Europe entered the United States. They entered the society beneath the Anglo-Saxons and northern Europeans who had come earlier to set the tone of traditional American life styles. The new immigrants thought the streets of America were paved with gold, and in trying to make their dream come true they absorbed many elements of American culture while bolstering authentic American vulgarity. The sociologists and social philosophers of the twenties and thirties, calling this "assimilation," tried to show how the southern and eastern European Catholic and Jewish immigrants were becoming Americanized by absorbing the cultural patterns of American life—patterns which these sociologists were never able to define.* In fact,

* Some sociologists defined these cultural styles in terms of Anglo-Saxon Protestant and north European criteria. Others developed an image of a "melting pot," which by its very nature was not definable.

the immigrants absorbed American culture, and enriched it, by over-affirming the American dream.

The end of immigration in the 1920's halted the process by which American cultural patterns were continuously reinforced by the support of new adherents. For the first time in American history, American culture was left with the problem of supporting itself with the cultural resources of a population born and bred within it. Through all of American history, Europe and its immigrants had provided examples, models, and styles that served as tradition for a society without a history. These infusions provided a succession of accretions that supported life styles not capable of supporting themselves indigenously. It is quite apparent that without new immigrants after 1924, the older styles of American culture have not been able to support themselves. All the historic forms of American life styles are on the verge of collapse and, especially in the last twenty years, have succumbed to a series of new trends. The evidence for these new trends is suggested by the following:

1. A "cultural revolution" has occurred which makes possible the life of the sophisticated consumer of the arts. The "arts explosion" supported by foundation expenditures now has a solid economic and fiscal basis for careers, markets, and consumers. Consumption of the arts in their old classic and ultramodern forms has become a basic way of life in suburbia, in middle-class urban developments, and in Iowa, where farmers' wives can now purchase "original" oil paintings directly from Sears, Roebuck. It is clear that artistic cultivation, sophistication, and consumption serve as a new basis for status and life styles in the broad middle sector. No matter how dependent on the Old World cultural tradition America may continue to be, this is a wholly new development and one which has replaced small-town, middle-class, bourgeoisie Babbittry, not to mention the Protestant church itself.

2. For the upper class it appears that a new international society dominated by "international aristocrats" has emerged. This is a class composed of multimillionaire international businessmen, Greek shipping magnates, Latin-American aristocrats, Southeast Asian politicians, Spanish nobility, world political leaders, movie stars, artistic

heroes, models, fashion designers, and party girls. Their style of life became immediately recognizable when it was presented as La Dolce Vita. The movie by that name emphasized the moral and cultural degeneracy of a style which includes jet travel, leisure, international partying, Swiss boarding schools, swimming off yachts in the Mediterranean, and residences and apartments on several continents.

These life-style themes presented in the cultural explosion and in the behavior of the international upper class have become the models for most other life styles in the United States. As a result, a new set of styles has emerged, replacing the older forms indigenous to the nineteenth century. The older forms now exist only at the fringes of American life, where exposure to society's central tendencies is weak. The survivals of nineteenth-century life styles still practiced in limited ways include the following:

1. The culture of Appalachia (wherever it may be found, if and when it has not degenerated into a roadside culture of neon lights, pinball machines, juke boxes, and Lolita-ism), the Swamp Yankee culture of New England, the marginal dirt-farmer culture of upper Wisconsin and Michigan, ghost mining towns in the Far West, and Tennessee hillbillies—all represent survivals of this unhallowed past. Rural poverty programs, their workers and their literary spokesmen, have rediscovered this America and are in the process of bringing it into the modern world.

2. There are pockets of Negro revivalist culture in the South and in the urban North, but frequently they have been contaminated by black bourgeoisie, cat, or poverty cultures, all of which directly or indirectly reflect the middle class. The civil rights movement and black nationalism have made major inroads into revivalism. Martin Luther King, Jr., as a Protestant, bible-oriented minister, stood as a symbol which bridged the gap between the older religion of passive hymn-singing-supplication-for-redemption-from-a-white-god and the newer passion for civil disobedience and militant activism associated with black nationalism and separatism. The new secular redemption consists either of an admission into a black version of the American way of life or a re-creation of it under black leadership. These movements will put an end to the historic tradition of Negro revivalism which was part of a once-dominant American tradition connected to slavery. Black na-

tionalism rejects the idea of admission to white society, but so far has offered no ideal of a life other than that of permanent revolt. The idea of Negritude, French-African in origin, is a proposed alternative. To the extent that Negritude glorifies the African past, it is acceptable only to a minority of militants, most of whom are young; but it has had revolutionary effects upon both black and white styles of dress and grooming.

3. An authentic American way of life which parallels Negro revivalism is the old Southern redneck culture of the county courthouse and the cotton-and-tobacco-warehouse town, best symbolized by the Ku Klux Klan. Klan redneck culture emerged out of the Southern defeat in the Civil War and has survived and maintained its dignity at the expense of the Southern black. It appears that the civil rights movement, the FBI, and the federal government have put this tradition on the defensive; but under the increased pressures of civil rights and black nationalist movements, and federal programs, redneck racism has become increasingly politicized and diffused throughout America. Politicized racism, even under George Wallace and Lester Maddox, has been fairly weak and largely confined to the South until now. To the extent that the militant Southern movement can merge or ally itself with other groups or movements which oppose the militant black and radical white student movements in our society, it represents the greatest threat to the highest traditional ideals of American society.

4. In those small towns of the North that have survived the population declines caused by the industrialization of agriculture since World War II, there still exist innumerable Babbittlike businessmen, conventional and philistine in their tastes and ultra-conservative in their politics. We have described the type in our book *Small Town in Mass Society*. *Peyton Place* portrays the direction this style takes when it decides to move.

5. The last major residue of tradition is the older generation of immigrants. Traditional cultures are relished and relived by these immigrants acting within their own age and ethnic groups. Thus it is still possible to find the authentic enactment of Jewish traditions in Brooklyn when a group of old *shtetl* cronies meet for a social or ritual evening. To some extent, a different form of *shtetl* culture was propagated by the influx of Hasidic Jews from Poland and Hungary after World

War II. As described by Solomon Poll in his book *The Hasidic Community of Williamsburg,* these Jews settled in Brooklyn and in other outlying areas of metropolitan New York City and contributed a new dimension to immigrant culture, at times to the embarrassment of more acculturated Jewish groups. Postwar Puerto Ricans and Latin American groups tended to repeat the pattern in which village and church organizations provide the forms for "old country" culture and mutual aid in conflict with the attractiveness of their new surroundings. In a manner almost parallel to the description of the Polish peasant given by W. I. Thomas and Florian Znaniecki, these organizations fight to retain their hold over their members in the face of the homogenizing process of American life. Older immigrant groups such as the Slovenes retain their organizations, and when they meet at an annual lodge picnic will act more like Slovenes than "Americans." But the ethnic cultures of the older immigrants exist side by side with the mass consumption of television. In old age, after a lifetime of "hard work and struggle," the immigrant wishes to indulge and enjoy himself, and does so by allowing himself to be embraced by mass culture. The older immigrant exists culturally between a Lawrence Welk–Art Linkletter–Peyton Place syndrome and selected styles and tastes reminiscent of his European past. With the passing of this last generation of foreign born, all direct connections to European peasant, ghetto, and rural poor culture will end.

Needless to say, there remain some groups—the children and grandchildren of immigrants—who have not completely "made it" out of their ethnic cultures and who are not secure in their Americanism. These groups eagerly embrace the visible and obvious symbols of Americanism: they are attentive to mass culture and ardent in their purchase of consumer durables such as automobiles, homes, televisions, and stereos. They voice a strident overaffirmation of Americanism, such as they see it, patriotism, and a virulent opposition to those who have not "made it" yet—the blacks and the Spanish—and toward those who have but do not appreciate it, namely white, middle-class college youths.

CAUSES FOR THE DISAPPEARANCE OF OLDER LIFE STYLES

How can we account for the disappearance of the dominant forms of culture and life styles of the late nineteenth and early twentieth centuries? Four factors seem to be at work.

1. One factor, already noted, was the stopping of immigration in 1924, which ended the mass cultural transfusions off which American culture had been living for more than a hundred years. The culture of the immigrant has always been at odds with that of the dominant society, and it has always been defensive. Because their cultural tradition was defensive, the American-born children of the immigrant disidentified with their parents and the immigrant past, which was the process of Americanization. But before 1924 the process was never completely successful. As long as there were continuous waves of new immigrants, acculturation could never be complete. After 1924, however, the psychology of second-generation disidentification proved to be the decisive factor in the break with all immigrant culture.

2. Up to the end of World War II rural American culture, partly immigrant itself, was in a situation similar to that of the immigrant. The culture of the dominant urban society was not directly accessible to the sons and daughters of rural Americans throughout the years of the rapid contraction of rural society (particularly the years 1890 to 1950), when the cities achieved overwhelming dominance in American life. Like immigrant culture, rural culture was not attractive to its youth. The lure of the big city for rural youth has been endlessly documented. After World War II rural youth left their homes for the blandishments of urban and metropolitan life and identified with an urban culture which they did not know except as a stereotype learned from exposure to the mass media. Thus, though they had no clear-cut models of life styles with which they could identify in advance of migration, rural youth forsook their tradition in spite of all its wholesomeness and Babbittry.

3. Before World War II the crucial factor leading to the decline of traditional upper-class life styles was the end of the opportunity for making new fortunes. America's great established industrial and fiscal families rationalized the processes of reinvestment, expansion, capital growth, and horizontal and vertical monopoly. By retaining control even while decentralizing through the use of professional managers (whose loyalties they obtained by a liberal sharing of profits), the great wealth holders of the late nineteenth and early twentieth cen-

turies became stabilized. This meant that the second, third, and fourth generations of the stabilized wealthy families became accustomed to their wealth, did not have to spend all their time making money, had time to develop new tastes, and, finally, became conscious of the vulgarity of their robber-baron ancestors and parents. These wealthy descendants began to seek social and civic respectability, following the usual processes of cleaning money by techniques such as commissioning biographers or historians to etch new portraits that transformed robber barons into industrial statesmen, burying old scandals, gaining college educations at prestigious institutions, establishing universities and colleges, collecting art, setting up philanthropies under the family name, and holding dignified cotillion and debutante ceremonies. They linked themselves through marriage to the European nobility and the earlier respectable, but declining, landed wealth. Newport, Arlington County, Beacon Hill, Upper Park Avenue, Grosse Point, Lake Placid, and similar places have been centers for their activities.

In an effort to find alternative points of identification, later generations continued and intensified the practice of importing models of conduct based upon those of European nobility (the old saga of the American heiress and the Italian Duke). While this was an established American upper-class practice, after World War I it took a different form. This was exactly the time when the European nobility had declined and degenerated through the loss of its functions, a process brought about by the democratic or totalitarian movements that replaced remnants of feudal society in England and on the Continent. What was then emulated was a style that had no social or economic basis and was, at the time of emulation, inauthentic. But the "aristocratic" model still looked good to newly wealthy Americans. Its slow attrition did not matter, particularly since a new connection had been established between Europe and Hollywood. This link to the Hollywood celebrity added the glamour and excitement of international immorality, a combination which provided a solution for the quest for a meaningful use of economically enforced leisure by the American upper class.

Traditionally, the European nobility have welcomed the infusions of money and support given by American Maecenases, though it should be noted that the Americans have not been unique in patronizing the defunct European nobility. American benefactors have their counterparts in the Orient, the Middle East, and especially in Latin America. Weber, though perhaps not Schumpeter, would have been impressed by the capacity of Europeans to make a highly profitable industry out of their ability simply to act out a style completely lacking an economic, political, or social base. In one of its more obviously commercial forms, this style involved the sale of fake antiques by the titled but impoverished owners of authentic antiques to newly rich and impressed Americans. This process of making capital out of nothing represents the higher artistry of the magician.

Since the development of jet air travel, pursuit of the new international, European-focused upper-class life style no longer requires residence in any given country. The world becomes the stage for international play, fun, and excitement. Segments of this new class have embraced the new sophistication of the jet-set and discotheque life. They have successively embraced La Dolce Vita, op, pop, camp, the multi-media, drug and counter cultures, and sophisticated Black Panther and white SDS radical movements. This should not be surprising, for historically the upper classes have always produced more than their share of liberated individuals. What is remarkable is the fantastic speed at which these cultural movements have been accepted and abandoned by, among others, upper-class adherents.

Membership in the international set is drawn from all parts of the world. Money, titles, sexual attractiveness, and reputation are the major qualifications for entry. A new upper-class model without a national base has emerged and provides something to emulate in place of the older American upper-class gaudiness and vulgarity.

4. There have been drastic changes in the occupational structure of the Western world, especially in the United States, which have resulted in a new middle class of college-bred administrators, professionals, and managers. The members of this class, emerging especially since World War II and to a large extent based on America's new world position, have achieved a prosperity far beyond their youthful expectations for success. They have experienced a sense of self-esteem in their new positions of responsibility in business, industry, bureaucracy, and academia. But for all its economic success and sense of self-esteem, this class is new to the American scene and lacks an established tradition

to fall back upon. It finds itself in the position of having to create a life style which will somehow express its newfound sense of dignity and social self-esteem. At the same time this new life style has had to organize a leisure created by reduced hours of work. In its quest this class has provided a seminal solution for the problem of defining new life styles for the rest of American society in the post–World War II period.

NEW WHITE-COLLAR LIFE STYLES

In finding themselves inordinately successful and prosperous by their own standards, the members of the higher managerial, administrative, professional, intellectual, and bureaucratic class have been forced to live off a past which did not prepare them for these positions. A large number of the members of this class are descendants of ethnic and rural parents whose cultures they have rejected. Almost all of them are college educated. Though it is difficult to prove, it is likely that their college experience was the source from which their new life style could be built.

Having rejected its own past, this generation was in a particularly impressionable position in regard to its college experience, so that what it saw and did in college provided it with its first alternative to the rejected ethnic and rural culture. Thus the culture of the American university and the bearers of this culture, the university professors, are of critical importance as models for shaping the new middle-class life styles.

To the rural and ethnic youth who went to college in the thirties and forties, college culture and the professorial life style appeared to be the epitome of refinement, sophistication, and gentility. The generation of G.I.-Bill World War II veterans who went to college from 1945 to 1952 was the largest contingent to be so exposed and impressed. In their experience, campus life involved the use of literature, art, music, theater, and museums as major supports to leisure. These patterns, once seen, became a reservoir of life-style models which the college graduate could take with him when he entered the occupational world, especially during the fifties when he moved to the suburbs and embraced a way of life for which he had no role models.

Under the stress of having to adopt new leisure models for which his family background left him unprepared, the new suburbanite, and especially his wife, could revert to these college-diffused but skin-deep patterns of cultivated, genteel leisure. Since most of the new suburbanites' neighbors were in the same position, each helped the other in affirming the new suburban patterns, and all were provided encouragement, direction, and assistance by women's, household, and gardening magazines and Sunday supplements as well as by sophisticated magazines like *Esquire, Playboy,* and the *New Yorker.*

In all of this the university professor has played a special role. As the bearer of a genteel campus culture, he had the advantage that his interest in art, literature, poetry, music, and drama was part of his professional qualifications for office. It was not that he was cultured per se but that cultural dissemination was his job, and he had an almost exclusive monopoly on conventional culture. The bearers of this campus culture at that time, in the twenties, thirties, and forties, though including some intellectual refugees from Europe, were mainly white, Anglo-Saxon Protestants. And almost every campus had at least one tweedy, pipe-smoking, casual, unhurried, unbusinesslike "Eastern" professor who had, if not a family tie, at least a school tie to "Eastern Culture." Through the image of Eastern culture a model of upper-middle-class, cultivated gentility was broadly diffused to several generations of aspiring second-generation ethnic and rural immigrants. For these latter groups, which later became the suburban middle class, the campus experience left an indelible impression which was later reinvoked in the suburban setting. It is for this reason that the upper-middle-class suburb resembles, especially on weekends, a campuslike setting.

After World War II the American university entered a phase of large-scale expansion which required the recruitment of new staff from the ranks of educated second-generation ethnic and rural immigrants. These immigrant sons formed a new strata of university officials and professors, and in their new roles on the campus adopted a life style reminiscent of the one they had only observed earlier. In the fifties and sixties their enactment of the style validated their own mobility. They were also able to impress the style on their less-cultivated students, who were now exposing themselves to the process of acquiring middle-class gentility.

The university now became the major center for the production of culture and for setting new styles of cultural consumption and leisure. Poets in residence, sports celebrities, writers' conferences, foundation-supported theaters, encounter groups, businessmen's retreats, and avant-garde anti-culture became part of the campus cultural scene. Today the university has a major function in supporting the life-style patterns of a newly ascendant middle class and its youth.

While the campus became a major source of cultural consumption and leisure models, it has not been the only one. Paralleling developments in the university, European and English literature presented a model of upper-middle-class life that was sophisticated, casual, carefree, bland, and slightly immoral. This too was a way of life of genteel cultural consumption. As described by Noel Coward, Evelyn Waugh, and many others, the inhabitants of this world seemed never to work at jobs, taking endless delight in pursuing a lightheaded existence of interpersonal repartee and pleasure based on a moral code that bore no relationship to Babbittry and its Protestant morality.

Later, as it developed, television and its commercial advertisements presented still another variation of "fun" morality. Cigarette ads specialized in romantic scenes in sporting environments—menthol cigarettes and canoes in cool water, suggestively romantic scenes of single women in sports cars, with hair tints, at carefree sandy beaches—in all a highly active, social, fun-loving, expensive, smiling, sporty, physically fit, sweet-smelling, and romantic way of life, with no suggestion of seriousness. This model was fabricated by the exurbanite copywriter and TV producer and was in fact a portrayal of their own idealized self-image projected onto a public seeking consumption styles and life patterns to organize their own leisure.

As the cultural revolution moved on, TV and TV commercials found it harder to stay ahead of the trends. Commercials flirted with the new pornography, go-go girls, the sexually liberated woman (Virginia Slims), op and psychedelic artwork, camp cartoons, and soul. Television programs have mirrored for their audiences all of the problems of inadequate parents and revolutionary youth, but television producers have found it difficult to develop either moral or ethical criteria for the resolution of these problems. They would like to identify with both youth and parents, radicals and conservatives; but value conflicts run deeply, and television declines to offend. Continuous compromise leaves all issues unresolved.

The themes developed between the late thirties and the early fifties on campus, in literary portrayals, and by mass media were the basic raw materials out of which post–World War II middle-class and suburban life styles were constructed. If these styles or segments of them had been thoroughly and fully absorbed, they might have provided a basis for an authentic way of life. By authentic we mean no more than an unself-conscious acceptance of one's way of life. Its validation would rest in its self-confident acceptance. But this did not happen. Perhaps the creation of new models has occurred so rapidly that the individuals who seek these styles cannot absorb them in one generation; or perhaps the speed of middle-class success and mobility since World War II offered too many opportunities to don and discard a succession of ways of life. As a result, each *stage* in the life cycle of the new middle class has posed the problem: How shall I live?

Above all, the emphasis has been upon consciousness of choice. But this consciousness itself reveals the fact that the individual has no past to which he cares to refer as a guide for conduct in his new status. Instead he looks around to see what others are doing, just as others are watching him. Since the new middle class has nothing of its own upon which to draw, models are ultimately absorbed from the other major sources we have mentioned. The result of all this is that the individual emulator is uncomfortable. There is always a slight self-conscious defensiveness in his attitude about himself. He tries to play down his success if it exceeds that of his neighbors. He may retain an interior decorator to style his home and then apologetically mock himself for the luxury of his tastes, acting as if he were a detached stranger in his own home. Or, again, he may complain of his children's high styles of taste and their expense, comparing their charmed life with his struggle for success, at the same time taking pride when possible in youth's ability to openly and blatantly enjoy itself in a self-satisfied upper-middle-class style. No wonder Fieffer and Spectorsky, the satirists of this class, are embraced by its members. And no wonder a good deal of humor within such circles consists of self-satire, self-mockery, and invidious comparisons of those who have not sufficiently absorbed the canons of taste appropriate to a given income and life stage, and those whose income is not adequate to maintain an idealized life style. At such psychological points there is an awareness of the self-conscious manner of the life style. But this awareness is also an affirmation of the style, because no alternative is available to the individual. In this sense the upper middle class is in the same psychological situation as Finestone's cats.

PROSPECTS FOR STABILITY IN LIFE STYLES

It is theoretically possible to imagine that with the passage of time, over a period of several generations, the life styles from cat to swinger currently evolving may become so accepted that the irony and self-consciousness associated with them will disappear. With time they could become traditional and assume a measure of dignity. While this is conceivable, there are several limitations and restrictions on this process in the United States.

Each new recruit or group (if one sees the process as involving a progression of ethnic and other ascendant groups) entering these forms of status competition tends to absorb the current styles of prestige and competition at a higher and more perfected level than the older and more established groups which they are emulating. Thus the Irish upper class has gone beyond the upper-crust Episcopalians and Presbyterians in their acting out of upper-class styles; the Kennedys would be a perfect example. Upper-class Jews, in their efforts to catch up, have exceeded Episcopalian codes of sedateness, social ritual, and dignified public service. On another upper-class level, shipping merchants, opera stars, and cinema celebrities have gone far beyond the upper class in exhibiting upper-class styles of degeneracy and immorality. In upper-middle-class suburbia it is a common joke that the *nouveau riche* Jewish lady collects New England antiques, wash basins, pine bureaus, and other objects for which she is practically the only market. Yet another example is the university professor who was a Methodist or Baptist, but now, trying to perfect the campus life style, joins a middle-class Episcopalian church, thereby creating a new Episcopalian manner in the community. Because the emulator is not fully cognizant of what it is he is emulating, he frequently caricatures his models and in so doing creates a new style. But the drama of emulation also affects the emulated, who views with anxiety the too perfect competition of the emulator. Thus both the emulated and the emulator add new dimensions to existing life styles. So long as there is mobility, which creates such needs for emulation, it will be difficult to stabilize life styles and give them the legitimacy of tradition.

A second source of strain derives from within the family structure of the mobile middle classes. Children, particularly in the new middle class, easily perceive their parents' mobility patterns because each change of income and each change of residence associated with it call forth demands from parents to behave in new ways more appropriate to their new status level. The parental lecture goes something like this: "This is not Madison [or Brooklyn], it is Concord [or Babylon] and that sort of thing isn't done here." These children are victims of their parents' aspirations for the children to be more successful than themselves in conforming to the new life styles. They pressure their children to exhibit the preferred life styles more perfectly than the parents themselves have been able to. John Seeley, Alexander Sim, and Elizabeth Loosely, in their study *Crestwood Heights,* describe the parental anxieties which are expressed in excessive demands on the children for artistic, social, intellectual, or other such performances. When performance falls short, there is ready recourse to reading specialists, tutoring, and psychiatrists. Eric Erikson, in *Childhood and Society,* has not noted this phenomenon in his examination of the early life stages, but we would argue that it is a major factor in shaping the consciousness of middle-class youth to an awareness of the fictions on which their lives rest. Thus these children are even more aware than their parents of the artificiality, superficiality, and inauthenticity of their parents' and their own way of life.

One result, for at least some middle-class youth, is to resent what they regard as the hypocrisy of their parents and, if their parents insist upon imposing their styles, to seek alternative styles of their own, a search which is supported by elderly radical youth leaders, disc jockeys, psychedelic religious leaders, campus radical professors, exponents of new pop, op, multimedia communications, and perpetually youthful senators, mayors, and governors. Thus the children's resentment may lead directly to middle-class juvenile delinquency or to other forms of rebellion against gentility. In carrying out their rebellion, middle-class youth adopt life styles that are beat, existentially honest or hippy, politically radical, anti-mobility-minded, contemptuous of the rational, bureaucratic world as they experience it in the universities, and, finally, emulative of the cat who is himself a grotesque emulation of the life styles of parents of the middle-class youth.

It is perhaps too soon to ascertain the outcome of this intergenerational process, since the percentages of youth who ultimately rebel as opposed to those who choose their parents' life styles are not fully known. More important, it is not known to what extent such rebellion results in the creation of a new life style. The rebellious styles may be nothing more than passing stages in the process of socialization to the middle-class way of life.

From another point of view, the attack on the new middle classes and their life styles—an attack by radical youths, militant black nationalists, and white, racist anti-intellectuals—may eliminate a great deal of the ironic self-detachment of the new middle classes. Some succumb to anti-intellectualism, and others discover that their way of life has great value precisely because it is under attack. Adherence to this way of life will become self-consciously defensive.

Let us assume, however, that there are few alternatives to the newly emerging life styles, whose major themes we have described. If the social pressures in support of these styles take on the forms of a major social movement sanctioned by the mass media and supported by American economic and political institutions, these new life styles may become a permanent part of American culture, and in several generations may become authentic. In the following chapter we suggest what the class structure would look like if these styles were to become stabilized.

8. *The new class system and its life styles*

If one took the characteristic life styles now visible in American society and assumed that they were to become the basis for forming the future life-style traditions of the different classes, what would the American class structure look like? Of course, classes do not simply disappear. As we indicated in Chapter 4, even with changes in their economic basis classes remain, though their psychology may be drastically altered. The same is true of life styles. New life styles may replace older ones even while the economic basis of both styles remains the same. More likely, however, new life styles will not completely replace old ones, but will simply become accretions on them. Any innovations in life styles thus increase the complexity of the class system because older classes and styles coexist with the new ones. Recognizing this, we can foresee not only new classes and styles but also a wide range of different life styles within each strata.

THE UPPER CLASSES

The upper classes include the older industrial aristocrats whose wealth was accumulated after the Civil War and sustained up to the depression of the 1930's. The investments of this class were in banking, chemicals, railroads, steel, shipping, petroleum, and automobiles.

Some of the familiar names are du Pont, Whitney, Adams, Harriman, Eaton, Rockefeller, Mellon, Duke, Pew, Manville, and Ford. These "groups" have survived a number of economic cycles over a variety of industrial phases and have remained at the top. Now that they are stable in their economic positions, they can afford a certain amount of patrician restraint and *noblesse oblige*. In both business and philanthropic activities they have sufficient confidence in their own social and economic positions to be able to allow paid professionals to manage their wealth. E. Digby Baltzell has been the major sociological chronicler of their mentality and life style, and the historian Gabriel Kolko has most carefully analyzed the mechanisms by which they have protected and maintained their wealth. In modern times no one has analyzed the administrative and legal structures by which the families making up this group are organized, though Robert Brady, in his book *Business as a System of Power,* suggested how this might be done.

This segment of the upper class has a long and continuing tradition of social intercourse with European nobility, Eastern Ivy League schools, and the exclusive New York City social and debutante life. Because both their social and economic activities have an international flavor, upper-class individuals tend to be internationally minded, and they occasionally come in contact with and "use" world-minded intellectuals as spokesmen for projects consistent with worldwide business interests.

Since the twenties, new sets of investment opportunities have accounted for additions to this upper class. These opportunities include Texas oil, space industries, electronics, communications, real estate, air transport, and the entire industrial expansion of the West. Names like Hunt, Murchison, Getty, Hughes, Giovanini, Kaiser, and Kennedy are most closely associated with these opportunities. The older industrial aristocracy regards these groups as *nouveau riche* and for this reason the newer wealth has not been admitted into this class nor has it accepted the patrician style. In being excluded the new groups have tried to invent their own styles, which include massive purchases of art, establishing universities and other monuments, subsidizing sons in political and journalistic enterprises, overcompeting in conspicuous philanthropy, and, above all, linking themselves to the international life of the jet and celebrity sets. These styles of living and pleasure go beyond the patrician style. For example, Howard Hughes distinguished himself by his investments in Hollywood starlets (Jane Russell) and Las Vegas real estate, and J. Paul Getty bought an English manorial estate. Grace Kelly married Prince Rainier and upheld a principality, rejuvenated by this transfusion of American beauty, aspiration, and *nouveau* wealth.

But not all these *nouveaux riches* have been internationally successful. Where this wealth is not internationally minded or not successful enough to become so, it will attempt to join older regional elites from previous periods. In cities like St. Louis, Cleveland, and Milwaukee, post–World War II real estate speculators may hobnob with old German brewery families. Out of such regional elites new national and international elites may emerge, depending upon the future potential of the industrial base off which they live. It is difficult to foresee who from this group will rise to the top, because capital growth patterns are difficult to predict.

In addition to the older industrial aristocrats and the *nouveaux riches,* there is a type of wealth based on a wholly new kind of economic opportunity in American society. As we have noted before, the federal bureaucracy and the elite managerial class in modern industry are now in a position to command important investment and political decisions. These people have the power to determine the distribution of contracts, subcontracts, and great expenditures of money. These upper-level bureaucrats and managers, whose positions are based on talent, hold key positions in the society and are indispensable to its functioning. It is "natural" that they should receive a disproportionate share of the social wealth. Through processes like stock options, "kickbacks," "marrying the boss's daughter," "taking over the firm," "salvaging a declining corporation," and so on, the managers can acquire wealth. We have in mind men such as McNamara of Ford, the Defense Department, and the World Bank; Gruenwalt of du Pont, who married the boss's daughter; Litchfield, a professor whose consulting activities gained him control of a corporation and who later became president of a university; Theodore Sorensen, now with a New York law firm; and Leonard Bernstein, Sol Linowitz, Abe Fortas, Billie Sol Estes, and Bobbie Baker, the latter two having failed in mid-course. Though these men have not necessarily acquired massive wealth, they have established themselves in positions from which they may build substantial "equity." It is difficult to say which of them will accumulate the successful "portfolios," but, in the long run, wealth-holding follows the key positions to which they have access.

Insofar as the successful bureaucrats and managers aspire to upper-class social status, they are unique in that they constitute a new strata for recruitment into the upper class. As *potential* recruits, however, they face the problem of whose styles to emulate, and thus they have a choice. The choices available include the styles of the older social aristocracy, the *nouveau riche* style of the oil-electronics-space-industry types, the style of politically ascendant wealthy groups, or that of the socially minded international set. Specific choices will determine specific future fates, and the heirs of this generation of successes may or may not emerge at the top, depending on social and fiscal decisions made by the principals during this generation.

Related to the higher managerial and bureaucratic expert is the Ph.D. *nouveau riche*. The former Cal Tech, Columbia, MIT, Harvard, Berkeley, or Chicago academic or scientist-technician turned entrepreneur is a special case of a single idea related to space, electronics, data-control systems, or atomic energy being used to inaugurate an industry. These Ph.D. technicians add a wholly new dimension to potential upper-class life styles. Because their major life experience was in the university, they have an intellectual and literary bent which historically has not been characteristic of the American upper class. While the Ph.D. technicians are bookish and literary, they can also follow the stock market with mathematical precision. They have a talent which is highly remunerative, so they are appreciated even by old-style, upper-class business vulgarians. To the extent that they are admired by their economic superiors, they may be both accepted and emulated by them. Where that is the case, they may influence the future conventions of upper-class life styles.

All these groups—based on old wealth, massive wealth, vulgar wealth, intellectual wealth, and managerial-bureaucratic wealth—are joined by the international class of movie stars, sports heroes, artistic heroes, space heroes, and dramatized political heroes who through personal effort, skill, and talent have distinguished themselves in a special line of human endeavor. They are recognized because they are active, exciting, and proficient. Personal, physical, intellectual, or technical performance is impressive especially to old-line *rentier* wealth, which, because it has never been asked to do anything (after the first and second moneymaking generations), is overly impressed by any achievement. This provides the link between the old-line wealth and the celebrity.*

It seems likely that two dominant themes will be added to the styles of the traditional American upper class. One is the expansiveness of the Texas tycoon, whether oil businessman or political manipulator: in either case he steps out in a big way unself-consciously, confident that his manner will produce results because it has done so in the past in Texas. The gall of the Texan will continue to help shape in the future, as it has in the past, the leadership style of the United States on the world scene.

The other theme is provided by the Ph.D. intellectual-entrepreneur of space, science, and data-processing, who in his narrow instrumental rationality thinks of himself as an educated man. He is literate, reads and writes books, and thinks the problems of the world can be solved by his methods without knowing that once upon a time St. Simon, Comte, and Marx had similar visions. In the meantime, he has brought intellectuality to the life style of the American upper classes. The new technically based industries and Washington, with its big federal budgets, provide the basis for this emergent class. In its major outlines this class parallels emergent managerial, technical, and bureaucratic upper-class patterns that appear to be characteristic of modern Russia.

A major innovation in the United States, though not in Europe, has appeared among both new members of the upper class and the scions of the older upper class. This is upper-class radicalism. Not only is it appropriate for the upper class to engage in the degenerate sexuality described by Robert Graves in his Claudian novels, by Choderlos de Laclos in *Les Liaisons Dangereuses,* and by Federico Fellini in *La Dolce Vita,* but also in the use of drugs, as illustrated in De Quincey's *Anatomy of Melancholia.* Various forms of gambling and alcoholism

* The relatively simple, dull Babbittry of traditional business leadership has been reasserted in the public prominence given to it by the appointment of representatives of this class to major offices in the Nixon administration. It is not unusual that a leadership class may lag behind social and cultural elites in the same society. Differences in such styles, as we shall see, are increasing.

are not new to the upper class, but "radical chic" in politics is. It involves an identification with the political movements of the lowest classes through social affairs which become prestigeful events designed to raise political funds for the downtrodden, the oppressed, and revolutionaries. To be sure, not all of this new politics comes from the old upper classes. Increasingly it is a means by which artistic social climbers demonstrate their liberalism, their modness—not madness—and their in-ness. Frequently they are so "in" that they are ahead of all others who by definition must be out. Of course, "radical politics," whether it represents new or old wealth, provides an ideology for personal liberation beyond politics. It may be sexual, personal, or cultural. It seeks to escape from the bonds of classes, but is usually enacted in the form of a class-based arrogance which justifies itself in the right of the individual to such stylized behavior.* The best description of this in European society is in Dostoevsky's *The Possessed* or Turgenev's *Fathers and Sons*. Such behavior can be found in the old upper class in all societies, and at times in new classes where the acquisition of wealth is so great in a short time that the group has not had time to learn to be degenerate in more sophisticated ways.

The new "radical chic" includes, then, the sons and daughters of America's wealthiest families, some of whom financed the Students for a Democratic Society (SDS), the Weathermen, and the Columbia and Harvard riots. It also includes radical "think tanks" and journalistic ventures which have had the misfortune of being economically successful, though it is hard to determine whether this was an intention

* See Renato Poggioli, *The Theory of the Avant-Garde* (Cambridge, Mass., 1968). Poggioli makes this point with respect to the avant-garde in the arts. Some of his illustrations suggest that by the nineteenth century prestigeful modernism included experimentation with many contemporary forms of drugs: "And from the more or less conscious sense of that relationship there originated among romantic avant-garde artists the illusory hope of being able to attain aesthetic ecstasy, a mystic state of grace, by means of certain physiological and psychological stimulants: opium in the cases of DeQuincey, Coleridge, Novalis, and Nerval; alcohol in the case of Poe; hashish in Baudelaire's case; absinthe in Verlaine's and Rimbaud's—in short, those drugs which give easy access to the 'artificial paradises' found in other heavens than that of art" (pp. 194–195).

To complete the comparisons between classes, we would add that drugs are instrumental to the overworked and underfed lower classes in that they provide a release from pain, especially from hunger. For the upper class, their "pain" is the emptiness of existence; their stylized vices serve to fill such emptiness.

or a result.* As the new upper-class political style emerges, it becomes apparent that the new styles can be profitable and appropriate to all classes. One of the great virtues of commercial capitalism is that its market mentality and its permissiveness permit profit-making from all forms of self-destruction, whether political, narcotic, or alcoholic. Herbert Marcuse would argue that the promiscuity of such permissiveness is actually a permissive repression. We would disagree, arguing that such permissiveness represents the destruction of the older repressive culture and is really the new culture.

THE UPPER MIDDLE CLASS

The upper middle class historically has been the responsible backbone of the community because of its civic participation and its support of cultural affairs. All large and medium-sized cities can point to the older and distinguished residential suburbs (Westchester, Shaker Heights, West Hartford, The Main Line, Brookline, Scarsdale, Harrison, The North Shore) which date to the twenties and earlier. In some cities this upper middle class may be regarded as the upper crust, but this is true only from a local perspective. When this local upper crust is compared to the national and international upper class, it is clearly only an urban and regional upper middle class with an economic base in upper middle management—proprietors and executives in retailing and distribution, the more successful of the fee professionals, and so on. Since World War II, however, this older upper middle class has been joined by newcomers who have deviated from the older suburban style. The new segments of the upper middle class located in the greatly expanded suburbia and exurbia have added new dimensions to upper-middle-class life styles.

In the more sophisticated and advanced regional, suburban, and university centers, upper-class styles have penetrated the class system. With the development of mass media and mass communications, patterns of emulation have been diffused culturally and geographically throughout the society. The density of the new culture is determined by previous class position, social and cultural mobility and sensitivity,

* See Dennis H. Wrong, "The Case of the New York Review," *Commentary*, November 1970.

and access to the mass media. Radical chic, now an emerging style, will compete with and be partially absorbed by the following styles, some of which are themselves relatively new and unstabilized.

1. The style of the Country Gentleman includes the image of the serious-minded sportsman or the nautical devotee, or some combination of these. During leisure hours the advocate of this style retreats into his chosen pleasure and invests substantial portions of his earnings to maintain it. The country gentleman emphasizes the estate-like quality of his residence with elaborate gardens, swimming pools, and other yard facilities. The nautical gentleman builds his life around a boat, nautical dress styles, and involvement in cup races. This sporting life is combined with fashionable, elaborate entertainment and membership in country or golf clubs which incorporate all members of the family into their activities. This outdoor, healthy, casual, and sophisticated approach carries with it only a minimum emphasis on culture, urban sophistication, and avant-gardism. Fresh air and sun are preferred to books and intellectually taxing activities, and so these groups are less likely to orient themselves to the city in their recreational patterns.

2. The style of the Culture-Vulture intellectual, as opposed to that of the Country Gentleman, emphasizes cultural consumption and quasi-avant-garde cultural sophistication. Books, talk, theater, music, and museum-going are standard fare. This group has been in the vanguard of the cultural revolution for the past fifteen years. It has embraced the avant-garde arts, the emphasis on movies as an art form, the theater of the absurd, multimedia experiments, new forms of music, pop and op art, and the new pornography. The publishing industry, book and record clubs, music groups, Broadway and off-Broadway theater, and the dance have all depended on the cultural demand created by this segment of the upper middle class. Authentic cultural producers frequently resent this group because they have destroyed the exclusivity of the arts. This group lives in the suburbs but closer to the city, in luxury apartments bordering the city; or in the city itself, in upper-middle-class apartments if the children have gone to college or have not yet been born. Here we find studied bohemianism and the cocktail party circuit attended by artists or intellectuals in temporary captivity. Among this group are many people who, though they grad-

uated from the university, have psychologically never left it. A high percentage of them, especially around the larger cities, are Jews.

3. The Cultured Academic may not be a professor, but he aspires to be both cultural and gentlemanly in a pastoral environment that finds the university setting to be the ideal place of residence. Thus businessmen, upper-level managers, and professionals have chosen to live in the vicinity of places like Cambridge, MIT, Princeton, Ann Arbor, UCLA, Berkeley, and almost any other major university environment. Princeton, New Jersey, as described in *Fortune,* is populated by upper-echelon Wall Street professionals who own reconstructed early-model luxury cars, attempt to participate in university-connected cultural events, maintain old school ties, and, in general, tone down their affluence in order to leave the impression of established, secure, genteel solidity. The Ph.D. *nouveau riche* contributes substantially to this style, for it offers a convenient compromise between an intellectual past and newly acquired economic success.

4. The Fun-Lover specializes in active social participation—sports, indoor and outdoor parties, dancing, discotheque, world travel, hunting safaris, flying, and skiing. This group in its focus on "fun" most obviously models itself on the jet set and is primarily concerned with movement, gaiety, and remaining eternally young. Though it may occasionally evidence a mild interest in culture, it does not take culture seriously because it does not wish to sit in any one place for too long.

A special, primarily occupational variant of this active group are the young men who specialize in being on the move and who convey the impression of being "in"—influential in science, technology, and administration. The type is exemplified in the world-traveling junior executive, the dashing astronaut, or the youthful college president. They appear to be in a hurry to get somewhere to solve some complex problem which is partially secret and very important, and their manner is always slightly boastful. Although they are likely to be quite a distance from the men at the very top, their life consists in advancing their contacts. Occasionally the right contact may pay off. These men, who are highly elastic to opportunity, represent the middle ranks of government and large-scale business.

5. Lastly there is the old-upper-middle-class Vulgarian who be-

lieves in conspicuous consumption. In the postwar period he is unable to crystallize a pattern of consumption because there is no single style he can understand. For the most part these are people who own their own businesses and who, not without diligence and hard work, have risen far beyond their expectations. They are ready to enjoy the benefits of their business success, but lack both a model to imitate and the sophistication to create their own style. They are left holding a bundle of money, without knowing exactly what to do with it. Thus the plethora of Thunderbirds, Cadillacs, and Lincolns among middle-aged and older Iowa farmers, merchants, and small-town bankers, who, also, in the winter months take the two-week Caribbean cruise. The urban businessman in construction, retailing, or insurance, who invests in conspicuous consumption, is another example. For the most part, the necessity for hard work isolates this group from the life styles that would validate their small business successes.

THE LOWER MIDDLE CLASS

The lower middle class follows the themes indicated for the upper middle class, but it does so from a different historical base. Going to church, taking pride in property, being neat and orderly, and showing a capacity for moral indignation against corruption are the chief elements of the lower-middle-class legacy. These traditional lower-middle-class virtues are in conflict with modern upper-middle-class and university-bred sophistication, and are declining under the pressure of the new patterns.

This conflict in class values can be seen clearly in the older lower-middle-class and middle-class religious groups, for example, the Baptists, Methodists, Congregationalists, and the Church of the Latter Day Saints. The older generation which has lived through the moral epoch and into the modern epoch still wishes to uphold the older bible-loving Christian virtues. Yet in their older age and retirement they also wish to loosen up a bit and enjoy themselves—so perhaps some drinking may be condoned, and perhaps even a trip to a wicked place like Las Vegas, a night on the town, a sexy movie, or a lascivious thought. The older moralists have relaxed their morality on the grounds of a deserved self-indulgence.

But they differ from the upper middle classes because they have not yet absorbed the newer life styles. This lack of acceptance of the new tone of the classes above them expresses itself in attitudes of resentment and moral indignation against the immorality of society. The older moralists point to the political and economic corruption of establishment leaders and to the degeneracy of the international celebrity set. Though they may still be actively religious in the old sense and, in their view, pursuing the way of Jesus, their moral indignation has largely been secularized. Now it is expressed in political protest and reform movements such as the John Birch Society, or organizations espousing such virtues as integrity, honesty, public service, citizenship, and opposition to corruption. Their resentments focus upon the Negro and upon white radical college students, whom they believe to be not only lacking in all of the traditional American virtues but actively attacking such virtues while expecting rewards for their vices. This group has sometimes been called the silent majority; it includes Southern Baptists such as Bobbie Baker and Billie Sol Estes (who was a lay preacher), who are at once exponents of the old virtues and examples of the fall from grace into secular corruption. No doubt this is one of the reasons why they played their roles as anti-heroes so successfully. The combination of middle-class fraud and Puritan righteous indignation is, of course, one of the basic elements of the American tradition.

The younger generation in the lower middle class presents a different problem. Although those in small towns and medium-sized cities may have been exposed to the morality and religiosity of their parents, they have been more thoroughly exposed to upper-middle-class patterns in youth magazines, television, and the cinema. Unlike their parents, this group will have had direct exposure to the new sophistication at the state university or city college, which is their instrument of mobility. The conflicts expressed by these youth are different from those of their parents.

The residues of virtue and morality which they carry with them are at odds with the secular world they live in. Their parents, in their view, have submitted to the system and show no concern for the world. The children point to flaws and weaknesses at all levels of society and see bureaucracy robbing them of their freedom and dignity. Like that of their parents, their moral indignation has been secularized, but in their case it is expressed as disgust with their parents, their elders, and with dehumanized bureaucracy. At present these youth often express themselves in protest, reform, peace, youth, religious revival, rock-festival revival, existentialist, or radical activities to save the world. If they are not liberated, they may join the hard-hats and express their resentment by attacking those who have succeeded in "liberating" themselves. In the lives of these young people, "liberation" can produce total reversals and inversions of social character in short periods of time.

For the youth of the lower middle class, especially those who go to college, the culturally stylized life of the upper middle class always represents an example if not an option. Their desire to go to college is itself an affirmation of a desire to ascend; but going to college delays the real issues of life for four years, and so for these years it is still possible to protest, reject, and remain morally uprighteous. The protest, criticism, and political activities of these youth are alternatives to the styles of life and morality displayed by the upper middle class. As these youth end their college careers, get married, have children, acquire mortgages, and hold down jobs, they may be forced to shed protest politics, civil rights and reform movements. It would appear that the protests of these youth groups represent the last measure of rebellion against their own cooptation into the upper middle class. Much of politics on the campus, then, is not politics in the usual sense at all, but only an expression for or against cooptation into the affluent middle class.

To carry the point one step further, once coopted the issue of cooptation and depoliticization is not wholly resolved. The education of the middle class often leads to unexpected success within the establishment. The largess of the corporate, publishing, and banking worlds as well as of universities and philanthropic institutions may lead to impressive incomes which the individual may find reprehensible in terms of his earlier rebellion. He must find a way to live with both his older radical idealism and his new success.

The resolution of this problem seems to lie in the pursuit of culture in such a way that radical ideals can be expressed without threatening the job. Thus a substantial radical political literature exists and a great number of morally, religiously, and sexually irreverent books and periodicals are published. Radical idealism and politics easily become intellectualized. Politics can become a cultural activity, like listening to fine music. In this way political intellectualism and cultural aspiration operate in the same direction. Culture becomes the opiate of the aspiring educated classes.

THE WORKING CLASSES

The working classes are in the most difficult position of all in American society. They do not have access to a university education, nor do they receive any training in the higher cultural forms. They are therefore cut off from the mainstream of the new culture. When they are exposed to the new culture, it is primarily through the mass media or casual personal contacts. Thus they are not able to emulate the new styles accurately, and when they try, their efforts result in caricatures. Only in small communities and in rural areas are members of the working classes coopted into middle-class activities. In those marginal areas the working classes may exhibit some of the middle-class styles, but this is only at the small-town level. For the most part the working-class style always falls short of providing an independent basis for a working-class life style. Some authors have talked about a working-class or lower-class subculture as if it were independent from the rest of society and its classes. These authors have failed to notice that the poverty of lower-class culture is a result of its failure to be sufficiently emulative *because* it is outside the mainstream of society, and not because it has created something on its own.

To the extent that the working classes are aware of new life styles of which they are not a part, they are desperately conscious of their personal educational disadvantages. They resent the educated unless they are their own children. They become aware of the error of not having finished high school or of not having gone to college. Thousands of degree-giving institutes, including adult and evening education courses in universities, cater to this specific desperation.

Their awareness of their own educational deficiencies accentuates their desire to educate their children, some of whom will go to a city college or a state university. Those who are successful will enter the middle class and thus affirm the American dream. The continuous expansion of the higher educational institutions in providing for an avenue of mobility keeps alive the older American equalitarian and success ethic. The working classes, though they are unsuccessful themselves, can feel vindicated if their children get an education.

Life for the working classes is not wholly dismal. They are offered a broad fare of engaging and distracting involvements: the mass media (Ed Sullivan, football and baseball games, space shots, "Hogan's Heroes," and so on); fishing, hunting, and camping; unlimited home improvements by the do-it-yourself method; and Catholic religiosity, Protestant self-satisfaction, beer, and compulsiveness as outlets that allow them to make their compromise with life in an increasingly middle-class world to which they feel they do not belong. They can strive to belong, and even though their children do not go to college, they can get jobs and help in the acquisition of the American symbols of success: automobiles, garden tractors, houses, modern furniture, outboard motors, color TV sets, camping trailers, and a million other objects from American industry.

All of this is possible because for skilled and semiskilled white union members, life in America has not been at all bad. America has not suffered a major depression since World War II, and the recessions have been of short duration. Wage raises have remained reasonably in line with the rising cost of living, and there have been opportunities for overtime, moonlighting, and jobs for wives and unmarried children. Since most of these opportunities are, for the older generation, greater than they had expected in their depression-bound youth, they have some grounds for satisfaction. The new chances for consumption have given them a stake in American society. As union members they remain loyal insofar as the unions serve as bargaining agents; otherwise they are not much interested in labor's traditional causes. Their stake in society, protected by seniority and virtual job monopolies, makes them hostile to the aspirations of less-favored groups who seek economic and social equality. Organized workers, favored by the relatively benign labor legislation and economic policies of the Kennedy and Johnson administrations, have become increasingly conservative. They have developed vested interests, and resist those below who would challenge their new prosperity and their claims to having made it in America. Some of them become adherents of racist arguments.

On issues of bread-and-butter unionism, they remain liberal. They are forced to use the rhetoric of patriotism and superpatriotism, especially in their reaction to the rebellion of middle-class college youth and the draft deferments these youth have received while their own children have been drafted. Perhaps part of their resentment is due to the fact that they lack both the psychological and verbal resources to protect their own children. If given the opportunity to express anonymously their attitude to the war in Vietnam, their identification with their children becomes apparent.*

THE SUBWORKING CLASSES

Subworking classes are committed to almost nothing except immediate pleasure. The original members of this class (hoboes, tramps, and bums) have been joined by cats, hippies, opouts, copouts, dropouts, surf bums, communards, and other economically marginal groups. Narcotics, alcohol, sex, or some other inarticulate activity short of suicide is used to absorb time, attention, and energy. Oddly, this style is itself an emulation of the jet-set and upper-middle-class fun and immorality ethic which in part derives from a kind of emulation of this same subworking-class style of life. Radical chic culture appears to be the common ground for these two extremes, allowing the upper and lower classes to have fun together *en passant*. Earlier forms of radical chic were the weekend meeting of the Vassar coed and the Negro cat, or the NYU Bronx bagel and the Tomcat, who could exploit each other in the name of civil rights. But such relationships can exist only in a make-believe world. The upper-discotheque and Ivy League girl can maintain the fiction (temporarily) much more easily than the cat or other outcast who after the weekend must go on living without a future. Of course, if she wishes, the Ivy League girl (or boy) can also drop out.

The major problem of pursuing such a life style is the need to accept the total inaccessibility of success as defined in the society at large, and the accompanying feeling of failure. No matter how much contact these subclasses have with the "slumming" coed, the well-intentioned civil rights worker, the Northern white liberal, the Jewish college radical, the well-meaning Protestant minister or Catholic priest, they have almost no way out of their situation. No matter how extensive the

* Harlan Hahn, "Dove Sentiments Among Blue-Collar Workers," *Dissent*, May–June 1970, pp. 202–205.

poverty programs, this class is stalemated. This is why violence and aggressiveness in such groups are erratic, unpredictable, and imperfectly contained. Violence is always possible, especially when triggered by community action programs and the emulation of peaceful civil rights demonstrations.

Protest movements, civil rights programs, and community action solutions are not simple attempts to deal with this uncontained aggression. Their meaning differs for two different groups of the subworking class:

1. There is, first, the traditional-minded subworking class which depends upon religion and religious ecstasy to provide a controlled release for emotion and resentment. The Southern Negro and the Harlem store-front minister are prime examples. Historically, since the time of the Romans, Christianity has served this function more efficiently than most have been willing to recognize. Religion in its Protestant variation has accomplished a similar function for the Negro in America, though lately the Catholics have seen that they too have an audience. Both the Protestant and the Catholic churches now offer themselves as a point of attachment for those members of the subworking class who would like to avoid descending to the very bottom of the social heap.

Yet religion, whether Catholic or Protestant, in its very nature a symbolic activity, is never wholly successful in pacifying the people. Martin Luther King, Jr., up to 1966, seems to have swayed the mass with his message of Christian nonviolence and to have prevented more civil violence than otherwise would have occurred. His assassination may have removed a major brake on potentially violent civil and political action among both organized and unorganized blacks. But extreme deprivation, provocation, or social contagion can always evoke hostility and aggression as a response to long-term, institutionally based deprivation. Nowadays among the subworking class, even the religious are not wholly predictable.

2. The older Christian ethic attempted to justify slavery and to reconcile the slave to his lot. It also justified and reconciled lower-class positions by emphasizing that the social world reflects God's will. The new wrinkle in this ethic is the secular politicizing of the subworking class, particularly urban blacks and Puerto Ricans. These new nation-

alist and protest groups have begun to accept the implications of direct action. Through movements of black nationalism, riots, urban guerilla warfare, and other forms of group assertion, their actions stand opposed to the religious forms of sublimation that until recently have controlled them.

The major issue for these secularized and politically prodded subworking classes is whether they can develop a leadership with the political skills and abilities to organize and sustain the process of politicization. This remains to be seen. If the process follows the classic American pattern, responsible Negro leadership will be coopted as it has been in the past, leaving the masses of blacks to their own devices. At best this means having to produce a continuous succession of new leaders, each of whom after five or ten years of struggle decides he too must think of himself and the needs of his family. All other ethnic groups in the American past have been bought off in this way, so it is not unreasonable to assume that the blacks and the Puerto Ricans can suffer or enjoy a similar fate. If this happens, the aggressiveness and violence of the subworking-class movement will be turned against itself, with intermittent periods of crisis and disorder, particularly in the cities. On the other hand, if a measure of leadership stability can be achieved, a major new political force will have entered the scene of American politics, and no one can predict what the consequences might be. All in all, these pressures from below offer both creative and destructive possibilities for American society.

LIFE STYLES IN THE HISTORICAL PROCESS

If the above analysis is correct, it is obvious that throughout American history there has been no life style capable of sustaining and reinforcing itself from the resources provided by its bearers' children. The great traditional life styles have been sustained primarily by immigrants from foreign shores, by internal immigrants mainly from rural areas, and by ascendant groups. All of these "immigrants," as strangers who lack confidence in their own past, have emulated upper classes and by so doing have given the emulated style a new vitality until their own children or grandchildren abandoned it. Why has this been so?

Throughout American history, and more recently in Europe as well, the rate of economic and political change has been so great that new patterns have been imposed on whole populations before those populations have had an opportunity to absorb and consolidate older life styles. An instability of life style appears in any period of fundamental institutional change, the case of Europe in its emergence from feudalism to capitalism being a prime example. (Veblen, in his *Imperial Germany and the Industrial Revolution,* made this a central point in his analysis of Germany and Japan.) If the United States, as a world model, fails to stabilize any single set of styles, there will likely be no permanent replacements in Europe and in the underdeveloped world for the traditional life styles now being forgotten and destroyed.

In much of our analysis there has been little evidence of total innovation in the creation of new life styles. In almost all cases where there has been some creation, it arises out of imperfect or overperfect emulation. Aspiring classes emulate the stereotyped life styles of distant and not directly observed groups, and thus introduce the possibility of distortion. Only selected elements of a total life style are emulated, enhanced, caricatured, and elaborated in the process of stereotyping. In this way meanings are introduced which were only minimally present. For example, the cultural patterns of the English urban middle classes are emphasized and exaggerated by aspirants who emulate that style: selected aspects of the original style take on a quality of completeness and totality they never had. In just this way the culture of the English upper classes has been fractionated into four dimensions of emulation by Americans. As we have described them, these are the gentlemanly style, the search for culture, the fun and immorality theme, and the diversions of the late aristocracy. Each of these dimensions has been the object of emulation by a different group in American society, and each of these groups in turn polarizes the given style and creates a total way of life from it.

When the life style being emulated is distant, there is also the possibility that only a given historical stage of a life style may become the object of emulation. Thus an American elite will emulate the life style of European aristocracies at the exact point when that life style might collapse if it were not for the emulation. Neither group has a basis for its style, except for the fact that the style is validated by emulation. In this mirroring process the parties to the emulation validate each other, where otherwise the style would die.

This same process of emulation, accentuation, and distortion also takes place domestically. In periods of cultural revolution, the amount of distortion in the emulating process is almost unimaginable; but this distortion results in intense innovation and creativity. The rate of change within the last ten years accounts for what otherwise appear to be discontinuities in cultural traditions and life styles. It is for this reason that a book like *Catch-22* becomes understandable. For example, lower-class blacks, when attempting to emulate nonblack styles, caricature selective aspects of middle-class culture, both broadening them and investing them with a comic playfulness which in other situations is a "put-on." In so doing they suggest new and unanticipated possibilities for the middle-class fun morality, which in turn is emulated by the very groups who may have been the original source of that emulation. These circulating patterns of emulation add new and unanticipated dimensions to a life style, revitalize it, and change its characteristics.

The only limit to this ebb and flow of emulation is the social and psychological needs of those groups who do the emulating. These needs, as we have tried to indicate, are based on the collapse of older life styles and the ability of newer ones to give expression to the changes in the life position of the people involved. In the evolution of society, there would seem to be no end to this process.

IV.

New social structures and political forces in American life

9. The politics of the new middle class in the local community

CULTURAL PERSPECTIVES AND POLITICAL CONTROL

The development of the service professions, the bureaucratization of business with its proliferation of managers and paid executives, and the growth in numbers of the academic intellectuals have revamped the structure of the middle class. In some degree these new segments of the middle class all operate in the direction suggested by such pluralist political analysts as Robert Dahl and Aaron Wildavsky. A significant percentage of the new population of articulate and culture-minded higher white-collar workers, professionals, business managers, industrial executives, and academicians are not likely to have the perspective of the traditional small-town businessman. In towns and cities where the classical business perspective is still alive in local small-scale business, the new middle classes are likely to oppose it. Their opposition rests specifically on their interest in education, in cultural consumption, and in their commitment to liberal planning institutions for local affairs, all of which traditional business opposed when it dominated the small town. Traditionally, businessmen imposed upon the community an ideology that was realized in low taxes.

THE NEW MIDDLE CLASSES AND SUBURBAN POLITICS

University towns and university sections of larger cities are the extreme cases of the new middle-class community. Since the end of World War II a major portion of the new professional, managerial, and executive classes has been located in the suburbs. Descriptions of upper-middle-class communities suggest that the social and cultural climate of the university is imitated in the suburban community. Suburbanites emphasize the arts, cultural consumption, partying, books, and education in much the same way they experienced these things while they were in college. Suburbanites also like to concern themselves with local politics, in which they have their greatest opportunity to engage in participatory democracy. Pluralist theorists have not noted the similarity in class composition of the university town, the suburb, and the urban middle-class enclave.

Since World War II one of the standard political dramas in the new suburbs has been a battle between older small-town (mainly Republican) residents and new suburban commuters. The older residents who have not been connected to the newer sources of income have reflected a small-business scarcity perspective expressed as a low-tax ideology. Commuters, they believe, have no concern for fiscal stability, the sanctity of real estate taxes, and traditional American values of saving, cost-watching, frugality, and "making-do with what worked before."

The idea of business domination of the local community has been attacked by political scientists and sociologists who maintain that a wide range of groups determine the course of political action in the community. In their view all local groups have a voice. Local, municipal, regional, and national political leaders are all important in shaping policy, but they are by no means the *only* important political voices. These observers would maintain that it is also possible for professionals, liberals, labor leaders, women's groups, college professors, and pressure groups of all kinds to enter the political scene—the choice is free to whoever chooses to enter. This view, best illustrated in the works of Wildavsky, holds that the balance of power in the community is basically a reflection of political interest, the willingness to acquire training for political action, and the personal effectiveness necessary for political success.

Until the late sixties, a major issue of this particular clash between the old and the new has been the school budget. To the educationally minded upper-white-collar and commuting professional classes, good schools have become essential to their way of life. For them, foreign-language studies, musical programs, college-preparatory courses, string quartets, and outside speakers have become indispensable elements of modern upper-middle-class education. The rub is that all these things cost money. For the original (old-line Republican) residents of American communities and their local business spokesmen, any increase in school services and programs violates the decency of past practice and the sanctity of the tax rate, not to mention traditional small-business anality. For the small shopkeeper—pressed by costs on all sides, threatened by large retail outlets, and dependent on a clientele of commuters—"holding the line" against modern profligacy usually has been a losing battle.

In any town, village, suburb, or city the balance of strength varies between the traditional and the new. In some communities such as Great Neck, and in many university towns, the new commuting professionals dominate; the old forces have been defeated. In other communities they have not yet succeeded or they have failed. From this point of view a town such as Springdale was relatively primitive when we studied it. There the same aspirations of the professionals were present; but because of their small numbers and their lack of self-confidence, they had not succeeded in dominating the town's institutions. Still, a few professionals had been able to dominate the cultural, though not the organizational, life of the town. But this was almost twenty years ago. Since 1954, when we completed our field work in Springdale, new interstate highways have been built, IBM has constructed a major installation in a nearby town, Cornell University has greatly expanded, and the density of professionals has noticeably increased. Even Springdale, bordering on the upper New York State tier of Appalachian poverty, has been unable to maintain the hegemony of the older American values.

In the American South, where primitive patterns are endemic, the situation differs from Springdale only in that the representatives of the older order are willing to go to extremes to defend tradition. In Springdale it was not a crime, even in 1954, if a Democrat who was sympathetic to the Republicans occasionally won an election. Moreover, the town fathers would, if necessary, make concessions on school policies formulated by Democrats in Albany. In the rural South, dominated by redneck Democrats, the fight has been much more brutal. Step by step, every effort to tamper with tradition has been fought, even when the opinion of the entire nation and the power of the federal government have been aligned against that tradition. But Southern rural and small-town redneck traditions, as opposed to Springdale's Yankee Republican tradition, have been slower to feel the effects of modern industrialization and corporate penetration. The deep rural South is twenty years behind the southern tier of upstate New York; but it is clear that the South is changing in the same direction as Springdale, and there is no doubt that its tradition will not be able to hold out indefinitely. In the urban South, in industrialized rural areas, and in university towns this penetration has proceeded much as it has in the North. In the South, however, the rejection of tradition has found its vehicle in an emerging Republican party which, while conservative, rejects the older forms of redneck, cornball localism. Increasingly, the Southern Republican embraces much of the sophisticated life style of the new middle class without necessarily accepting its politics or racial attitudes.

In Springdale the John Birch Society has been prominent in attacking university-based forms of modernism and un-Americanism. In some instances the Birchers may have been supported by university professors, but their membership is largely dominated by small-town businessmen and middle- and lower-ranking officials of regional branches of conservative national concerns. In the South, by contrast, the new professional classes appear to be liberal, but the fear of being tarred with traditional insults has led them to avoid being charged with liberalism.

In the North, middle-class white suburbanites, many of whom fled the city to escape from the blacks, have discovered that blacks, for perhaps the same reason, want to join them in the suburbs. Where blacks have migrated to the suburbs, they have become a major political issue for whites. Even aside from the housing issue, blacks cannot be ignored. Most suburbanites work in the cities, and some work in occupational areas that are the object of black penetration. Others, as owners of urban property and as supervisors of blacks, experience the effects of black anger, riots, and demands. Almost all middle-class adults, regardless of where they work, react against what they regard as the blacks' lack of law, order, safety, and decorum. They are offended by the "arrogance" of black demands and the unwillingness of blacks to suffer as they feel they and their parents did in the process of mobility. What is more, educational, social, and political programs designed to correct the injustices of past discrimination, segregation, and exploitation all cost money. In some cases the bussing of blacks into white areas has been rejected even when the plan entailed no extra cost. Ultimately the money is understood to come from the taxes of the affluent white middle and upper classes. At this point, white middle-class liberalism becomes expensive and produces the most dangerous form of racism, a racism which is not expressed by conscious racial attitude but by budgetary and fiscal selfishness and conservatism which prevent manifest solutions to racial problems.

In any event, the critical element in suburban culture is the same: the percentage of the new middle class that is the spearhead for a new tradition. The existence of this class only reflects the structure of business in towns where industries are highly bureaucratized and no longer locally owned, or where the service professionals have become numerically important. As the percentage of professionals and middle-class or upper-white-collar workers increases, their influence in the community is greater. To the extent that they can make their presence felt, they are the destroyers of local political traditions.

THE NEW MIDDLE CLASSES AND URBAN REFORM POLITICS

In the Northern and to a lesser extent in the Southern urban centers, the same middle-class trend has produced a new phenomenon in the politics of large cities. In the past, urban political machines, especially Democratic ones, were organized to coopt ethnic groups and the working class into the party apparatus. Mayor Curley (portrayed accurately in Edwin O'Connor's *The Last Hurrah*), Boss Hague, and Carmine De Sapio, not to mention a host of other figures, have been symbols of those ethnic and working-class groups which might otherwise have felt excluded from the American tradition. In this special sense, the older urban Democratic party has been a socializing agency. Urban Democratic party patronage was in effect a pre-bureaucratic welfare scheme for the un-Americanized urban mass which benefited from the corruption of the Democratic party. The ethnics and lower classes would have had no other source of social service, except for weak self-help organizations. The Democratic party, in addition to its business of politics, was a welfare institution, and made its claim to power primarily on the basis of these functions. To ethnic groups and the lower classes, this meant jobs, food baskets, and a small share of the graft. The successful ethnic politician served as a model of hope for all his "cousins" and served to validate the system of equality and opportunity in which the ethnic groups wished to believe. Everyone could point to an ethnic "cousin" in Congress or on the city council and, at least vicariously, feel that he had "made it" in America. This older system of politics was oriented to whites, even though they were Irish, Southern European, Slav, or Jewish. Negroes were excluded from prestigeous public positions.*

Acceptance of the ethnic immigrants by white Protestants did not come easily, because the ethnic style was hostile to indigenous white American Protestantism. Language, food habits, and, above all, religion, separated the immigrant from the native community. Yet the older Protestant elite could not fully express its resentment for the simple reason that the immigrant was doing the basic work necessary for the industrialization of the United States. Capital development in the mines, factories, transport, and agriculture depended on the hard-working, aspiring, uneducated, and illiterate immigrant who felt he could sacrifice himself for the sake of a future in which his children would reap the benefits. The Protestant businessman needed the immigrant, no matter how hostile and discordant his values. Thus it was on a very practical business basis that the Protestant elites came to terms with the ethnic groups, and the Democratic party in the North was the vehicle for this accommodation.

This ethnic history is now almost ancient. After World War II, descendants of white immigrants, in large measure because of the G.I. Bill and subsequent educational opportunities, were selectively admitted into the American affluence. Ethnics whose parents came from

* Compared with the ghettoization of the European immigrant, the black ghetto was the perfect example of segregation. Throughout the political history of the immigrants' incorporation into American society, the Negro remained unrecognized and invisible. It was difficult enough for America, a Protestant, anti-Catholic, anti-semitic country, to recognize the European immigrants. Acceptance of the blacks as descendants of the slaves has been even more difficult.

Vitebsk, Bohemia, Armenia, and Sicily now live in the suburbs. The *new* urban lower classes are less clearly composed of the older ethnic groups. Negroes, Puerto Ricans, Latin Americans, and the unsuccessful rearguard of Slavs, Poles, Jews, Italians, and so on, make up the polyglot of urban lower-class society. The traditional system for political (but not social) integration of immigrant groups no longer works either in the suburbs or in the cities because the integrity of the older ethnic ghettos was destroyed as the second and third generations became economically and geographically dispersed, differentiated, and stratified. While municipal tickets must still, by the older convention, contain an ethnic mix, they must also now make some appeal to the new middle class. For example, in New York City a professor of psychology whose name happened to be Timothy Costello, combining the Italian and Irish, was included on the ticket. Municipal and suburban politics have adapted to the new composition of the middle class.

When the members of the new middle class elect to live in urban areas, they live in pockets of affluence surrounded by disorganized lower-class urban slums and black ghettos. In their communal life they have divorced their private and political lives from their work establishment, as well as from the traditional political machine.

These same forces are at work in the suburbs, where they are more obvious and visible. The separation of work and communal life is central to the very definition of the suburb. Ethnic ghettoization in the suburbs has given way to ghettoization based on class, occupation, and status categories. Urban Democrats can easily become Republicans when making the short move from the city to the suburb. The new suburbanites have become interested in the political issues surrounding suburban life, especially the schools and public services, so that the politics of the suburban middle class are also separated from its formal work life, though related to the education, skills, and training that qualify the members of this class for their occupational standing.

One problem for the new middle class has been that of finding a political identity for itself. Having separated itself from the traditional ethnic political machinery, and regarding itself as educationally and culturally superior to both its ancestry and to the traditions of American Babbittry, there has been almost no place in American politics where it could attach itself. The older Democratic party stood for uncouth bossism in the cities, and the Republican party stood for conservative social and fiscal policies. Against this political corruption and nineteenth-century frugality, the new middle class created a place where it could express both fiscal liberalism and an educated self-image.*

In short, a major innovation in American politics since World War II has been the growth of the liberal, educated, professional, cultivated, professorial, white-collar political constituency, often characterized by vocalness and high-minded morality. It was almost inevitable that at a national level Adlai Stevenson should become the political hero of this group, for he represented the idea that education, professionalism, and culture do not disqualify one for political participation. When Arthur Schlesinger, Jr., and other intellectuals first attached themselves to Stevenson in 1952, there was even an air of Rooseveltian "class" and cultivation that suggested the earlier New Deal Brain Trust. John F. Kennedy, John V. Lindsay, Robert Kennedy, and Eugene McCarthy played the same role vis-à-vis the liberal, educated middle classes, which in all too rapid succession shifted their loyalties from Stevenson to Kennedy, then back to Stevenson and then to Lindsay-Kennedy, then to Eugene McCarthy and partly back to Robert Kennedy after he entered the presidential race.

The legitimation of the college-educated middle class and intellectuals in American politics would require a special study, which we do not propose to undertake here. But any such study would have as its central character Robert M. Hutchins, former president of the University of Chicago, who, during the thirties, instituted the University of Chicago Round Table. In Chicago at that time educators and intellectuals carved out a slice of American public life for themselves. The last chapter of this special study would also deal with Hutchins and his Center for the Study of Democratic Institutions, which represents in the age of high philanthropy the same thing the Round Table represented during the depression. Out of this history came an

* C. Wright Mills, in the last chapter of *White Collar,* was uncertain as to the political center of gravity of the new middle class. We think the middle class has an essentially schizophrenic character. A liberal fiscal interest in community culture competes with both a fear of blacks and the idea that the hard-earned money of the middle class will be spent on them.

identity focus for the political leanings of the urban and suburban middle class.

These political leanings were institutionalized in a middle-class movement in the cities, which has been called "reform politics." This version of reform politics is substantially different from the older reform movements of the nineteenth and early twentieth centuries, which concentrated on political honesty, Protestant purity, and, especially, *a low real estate tax.* Contemporary reform politics in the cities has the advantage of being uprighteous, public spirited, concerned with the general welfare, and on the side of the angels. This constellation of attractions allows the educated sons and daughters of immigrants (some of whom had been radicals in the thirties) and elements in the older Protestant classes to participate actively in politics in competition with the established ethnic lower-class machine. In dozens of cities the reform banner has meant the purification of politics for the cultivated, politically minded middle class.

Whenever the new leaders, parading under the banner of reform, win out, they find themselves in an ambiguous position: they must carry out the reform against the old established interests. Usually the success of the reformers in promoting alternatives to the old machines has resulted in the cooptation of reform leaders into the established political structures, in the same way that Adlai Stevenson was coopted at the national level by Lyndon Johnson. In the end, many of the reform-minded middle class thought Stevenson sold out or was duped on the Cuban invasion and the Vietnam issues. Even after his death, posthumous letters were adduced to show that Stevenson had privately maintained his integrity, despite his compromised public positions. Stevenson was especially important as a symbol of integrity and character for liberals after the assassination of John F. Kennedy and before Robert Kennedy emerged in sharp profile. When Robert Kennedy decided to become the leader of the liberal-intellectual reformers, it was much easier for the new middle class to forget Stevenson (whose liberal star had begun to wane before his death). When McCarthy challenged Robert Kennedy, he was able to do it because of his ability to claim the moral superiority of his position on Vietnam. It would appear that the reform and silk-stocking movements in the cities and the suburbs provide a new avenue of political mobility for those who cannot or do not wish to compete on the basis of corrupt, ethnic, machine politics. The new educated political aspirants would in addition be excluded from ethnic politics because they are overqualified in education, culture, and "intellectuality." The new reform (but not radical) movements are a response by the politically minded middle class to their exclusion from politics on the older machine terms.

In the process of continuous cooptation of reform politicians into the conventional political system, reform rarely wins. From the point of view of the rank and file of ideologically committed liberals, the cooptation of leaders is treasonous; thus the disenchantment with Adlai Stevenson, with John F. Kennedy before his death, and with all reformers after they have been in office for awhile. Even Eugene McCarthy lost supporters for his new politics when he played traditional Senate politics after losing his bid for the presidential nomination. For the committed, activist liberal, there is a passion to political interest which makes it difficult to accept even necessary compromise. Politics is no game; it is a genuine and meaningful way of expressing ideals and attitudes which are denied in all other areas of his public and private life.

Within the last five years a new middle-class reform style has also made itself felt. This is the style of the college radicals, liberals, and left activists who had been looking for a political base. Not all have joined extremist splinter parties, and not all have dropped out of politics. Given issues on which a radical perspective seems relevant, such as Vietnam, the military-industrial complex, poverty, or the reform of the Democratic party, such groups may find, or may have already found, meaningful opportunities in local clubs of the Democratic party. Given their passion, their high degree of political experience at a relatively young age, and their singlemindedness, they constitute a major problem to the older leaders of the party establishment.

THE RELATION OF NEW MIDDLE-CLASS POLITICS TO THE CORPORATION

For the professionals and the higher white-collar echelons in management and executive positions, work in the bureaucratic institutions does not provide opportunities for self-determination, altruism, and high-mindedness. The bureaucratic and professional work situation usually involves either a toeing of the organization's authoritarian marks, which place a premium on compliance, or it involves a careful concern for one's occupational self-interest at the expense of one's ideals. Most bureaucratic and professional work requires narrow horizons and does not permit the intrusion of personal ideologies and ideals. Because this limited and restrictive quality of bureaucratic work conflicts with the education and cultural interests of college-educated bureaucrats, they are forced to seek outlets for their interests, talents, and ideals in spheres other than their place of work. Politics is one of a number of areas that fill this cultural gap. The interest in politics, then, represents some search for ideals and for meaningful activity which is otherwise denied.

For the organizational bureaucrat, local politics is especially attractive. As an employee in an organization with a national or international jurisdiction, his work life does not overlap with the life he leads in his residential community. If he lives in a large urban center, he can become anonymous in the urban mass. If he lives in the suburbs, the organization does not care too much what the commuter does in his private life or in local politics so long as his activities are not linked to the corporation.

The case is quite different where the political focus of the firm coincides with the employee's home life. In a smaller town which contains the headquarters of a nationwide corporation, the politically minded member of the middle class is forced to be much more circumspect. He cannot escape identification with the firm because of the size and character of the community; the firm is always a part of both his public and private life in a way that it is not for a suburban-dwelling employee of the urban-based corporation. The individual is forced to participate as a representative of the firm, or he doesn't participate at all. In Rochester, New York—admittedly an extreme case because it is dominated by only three firms—one experiences the quality of the company town. Employees cannot participate in politics as representatives of the firm, nor can they escape from local ideologies and political pressure, but take the company line whenever the immediate interests of the company are at stake. When the nationally based corporation is located in a small or middle-sized city, the employee has little chance to exploit the advantages of urban anonymity. William H. Whyte, in his books *The Organization Man* and *Is Anybody Listening?*, tells us that the corporation does not grant very much freedom, and when it does grant any, it tends to be in those areas that do not matter to the company.

The situation of the corporate employee, whether in the city, the suburb, or the company town, is quite different from that of his counterpart, the university professor. The very fact of being dominated by a university rather than a corporation makes the university town a special case. Professors have a tradition of opposition to university administrations which at times allows them to participate in college and civic affairs regardless of the "company line." In addition, the rise of radical student politics has often forced mild-mannered professors to respond to student pressures and adopt a militant stance in opposition to university administrations and local communities.

In urban and suburban areas in which a single firm does not dominate, a certain amount of political freedom is available to anyone who wishes to take it, so long as he does not publicly offend corporation policy. The greater the number of corporations in a given community, the greater the freedom. In Rochester, because three corporations coordinate their policies at the highest level, there is little independent political life for their employees. For this reason Rochester has, until recently, seemed to be a more peaceable, unified, harmonious, and organized community than were the earlier company towns. Only black minorities and "ungrateful" workers could upset this equilibrium. Outside agitators, trade union organizers, university professors, and students were a source of danger. When Saul Alinsky was called to Rochester in the mid-sixties to help organize the black community, the increased activism that followed resulted in relatively minor demonstrations and race riots.

Where a single corporation does not dominate, and where there are a number of forces trying to influence politics, the older, pre-bureaucratic, industrial paternalism does not work. The inability of any single or coordinated group of corporations to dominate the community allows for a political pluralism at all government levels. So many forces and counterforces are present that no one group succeeds in dominating the others.

POLITICS IN UNIVERSITY COMMUNITIES

The situation in the university town has been studied extensively because it is so accessible to university professors. As a result, since World War II, professors of political science have emphasized the voluntaristic character of American communities and have neglected to emphasize such structural factors as the composition of the labor force. We believe that structural analyses would indicate major differences in findings. A New England university town is a case in point.

The university, located in a rural town, expanded between 1944 and 1960 from less than two thousand to fifteen thousand students. In 1948 it was converted from an agricultural college to a university. The heritage of eastern Connecticut, the locus of this town, was poverty ridden, ethnic, and nonindustrial. After World War II the university became the major employer and dominant industry in the town. Even before its expansion in the fifties, this university, in a manner not dissimilar to that of the dominant industry in a company town, was the major political power in the community. The highest officials of the university exercised the political power: the president and the provost presided over local political affairs and were able to extend their influence into state and national politics. Whenever the community was split on a decisive issue, the provost was called upon to act as an "impartial" moderator for the town meeting. Over the years the university succeeded in maintaining local prohibition and its own police jurisdiction over its campus, in preventing industry from entering the town, and in influencing zoning policies favorable to the university and its personnel. Though this dominance was not total, it was effective in all crucial instances, and naturally generated resentment among the townspeople.

The demographic composition of this community changed with the expansion of the university. As the university increased almost tenfold in size, and a large number of commuters moved in to enjoy the cultural benefits of a university town, the typical school battle was fought and won. New schools were built, tax rates went up, and local shops prospered. Industry is still excluded, and the university, as a collectivity, has its way on those issues which are central to it. One new feature, not found in most other new middle-class suburbs or in this town before World War II, has been the entrance of professors—particularly professors of political science—into party politics both as "local citizens" and as experts. Political science professors claimed special expertise in local and state politics and intergovernmental relations. Within the Democratic party, a high-spending reform faction (the "university crowd") occasionally breaks ranks with local taxpayers. This reform faction has influenced the selection of the town supervisor, though it has not been able to change any of the traditional political arrangements in the community. Despite the fact that professors are playing at local politics, the system continues as before. As the tradition of community studies indicates, major decisions in the society are not being made at the local level.

The university town described above is without an industrial base. Because it is isolated, it probably provides the ideal setting for the entry into politics of liberal professors who do not wish to accept the pre–World War II professorial role as classroom lecturer, researcher, and writer of textbooks. This same phenomenon has occurred in most of the university towns and cities studied by the pluralist theorists, though they have not made this interpretation of the communities they studied.

The newer politics of the university professor in our example go far beyond party politics or local and state government. Professorial radicalism and libertarianism have permeated the cultural milieu of the university. These new political and cultural styles have been imported somewhat belatedly from national student movements, particularly from Berkeley and Columbia. These cultural importations, however, are sufficiently sensational in eastern Connecticut to rock the Yankee and ethnic conservatives. The new movements have included sexual freedom, conspicuous homosexuality, public pornography, drugs, communes, mod and hip dress styles, and studied dirtyness in speech and personal appearance. In politics this style has included opposition to the Vietnam War, university-sponsored war research, university cooperation with draft agencies, ROTC, and Dow Chemical recruiters. At the local level, students and professors violently opposed the presence of state police on the university campus. Needless to say, these activities have polarized the faculty, the local community, and the entire state. By and large they have strengthened the hands of those opposed to the new forms of cultural and political revolution.

Studies of university communities over the past twenty years have neglected another major aspect of middle-class politics. The social, cultural, political, and intellectual movements that have overwhelmed the university campus and community are nationwide and international in scope, just as are the structural changes that have affected the composition of classes in all communities. In confining their studies to the university town, the pluralist theorists have missed its relations to the outside society.

The professor as technician has been interested in much more than the local community. He has been a consultant to national and state government agencies and bureaucracies, to national and international business firms, to nonprofit organizations and foundations, political parties and pressure groups. In fact, the new programmatic professor has been responsive to opportunities for earning more money by accepting grants and consultantships. In most instances, professors have identified with the roles provided by their second jobs. Conservative professors have tended to consult for business, industry, and Republican government. Liberals have consulted for government, trade unions, philanthropic foundations, or have tended to keep their consulting secret.

During the Kennedy administration, liberal professors became more self-confident and articulate because so many of them were selected for prestigious or well-paying governmental consultantships. President Kennedy affirmed the cultured, professorial style. Lyndon Johnson offended the academic community because of his Southwestern populist, political-boss style, and because he quickly began to purge Kennedy's academic advisers. Moreover, as the Vietnam War became an issue, students and faculty began teach-ins and, initially, peaceful protests. As the war escalated under Johnson and Nixon, the protests became more strident and appeared to generate the welter of movements that now dominate the universities. Liberal professors, among whom are now included former student protestors, now help to determine the political atmosphere of the university community even in the reaction they produce. President Nixon, in staffing his administration, may have sensed intuitively that this was a problem. He recruited a minimal number of professors, and most of them were relatively conservative. Moreover, he has not been able to retain the loyalty of those whom he has appointed. In this new way, national politics and national institutions have helped shape the climate of local politics.

The employment of professors as consultants for business and government has not interfered with their image of themselves as being free, independent, objective searchers for the truth, endowed with the right to struggle with the university and the university community for freedom from pressure and harassment, especially political harassment. Their idea of their pure motives allows them to advocate any political cause while being exempt from criticism—since that would be an infringement on their academic freedom. The professorial self-image also includes notions of cultural superiority over pluralistic businessmen and the great unwashed.

By his emphasis on professional independence, the university professor thus achieves the equivalent of what the city dweller gains through the anonymity of the metropolitan area, and what the suburbanite achieves by living away from his work. The great majority of professors, however, are still politically inactive.

10. *Philanthropy and the service economy*

THE RELATIONSHIP BETWEEN PRIVATE AND PUBLIC PHILANTHROPY

The American economy has created armies of clerks, teachers, welfare workers, administrators, experts, managers, and supervisors, and has thereby multiplied the size of the employable population. These secondary, tertiary, and more "advanced" occupations have usually been considered intrinsic to the rise of the service economy. The federal battalions of clerks, bureaucrats, and soldiers provide an additional source of job opportunities, some of which are created in order to administer the creation of new opportunities and a new economic distribution.

The expansion and growth of private philanthropy is an additional facet of the service state insofar as philanthropic redistribution achieves the same economic ends as job expansion in industry and government. In effect, philanthropy is an additional mechanism by which the problem of overproduction finds a resolution counter to the Marxian prediction.*

* The following discussion does not deny that philanthropic activities may be inspired by the highest ideals of Judeo-Christian charity, by ideas of stewardship, or by the need to find meaningful uses for surplus time and money. Nor does it imply that all philanthropy is indirectly subsidized by the inheritance and income tax laws, or by efforts of wealthy families to retain control of their holdings despite inheritance tax laws. We are dealing here not with the motives for philanthropy but rather with its consequences for the society as a whole.

Modern philanthropy produces nothing but services, including information, and it is these services that are its major contribution. Theoretically, the market for services, in contrast to other forms of economic goods, is limited only by man's imagination. For example, some advocates of psychiatry suggest that every member of the population should have psychiatric treatment; if this became a reality, it would constitute the maximum marketability of one kind of service. Extend this to include dozens of other forms of health, recreational, educational, and cultural services, each specialized and differentiated for lower, middle, and upper classes, and the prospects of economic development through the expansion of services seem unlimited. Thus there is little danger of overproduction of services: whatever dangers may occur, philanthropy facilitates the use of services by providing them for nothing, or so far below cost that they may properly be called philanthropy. Theoretically, in a philanthropic service economy the problem of overproduction can occur only if the service agencies are unimaginative in their discovery of needs. The expansion of services is limited only by the capacity of public and private economy to meet the costs for providing these services and by the capacity of the economy to expand its primary productive functions so as to free resources and manpower for such services. We will leave it to the economists and other ideologists to argue what the optimum limits of services might be, though the limits to expansion would be defined by either the lack of resources or the lack of appreciation of the benefits to be derived from the services. It is as much a social and political issue as an economic one.

Both the government and private sectors share in meeting the costs of philanthropy. Although the dollar volume of government investment in philanthropy is incomparably greater than private philanthropic investment, the administrative structure in both sectors bears only a slight relation to funds. For example, even though the government carries a disproportionately heavy share of the total cost of philanthropic services, the number of units distributing these vast amounts of money is small in comparison with the number of private philanthropic units. Of private nonprofit *foundations* alone, there are thousands, while welfare, religious, educational, charitable, and philanthropic organizations are so numerous as to defy tabulation. On a dollar-for-dollar basis, it would appear that the government distributes its philanthropy much more efficiently than the private sector: one committee in Washington can decide in one afternoon to give a physics department in a university $1 million, and spend little time making the decision (though it takes many more people and much more time for the physics department to spend the million, the more so as the proportion spent on services is greater than equipment costs). The proportion of the budget devoted to administrative costs reflects the difference between large-scale "budget-intensive" expenditures as compared with labor-intensive philanthropic investment. As the size of the grant increases, the time invested in making the decision decreases. To the extent that the government operates as a large-scale producer of philanthropic dollars, the difference between government and private philanthropy can be likened to the distinctions between industrial and pre-industrial economies.

Private philanthropy is essentially pre-industrial; it is better understood on the model of the craft system, where the product is made to order for a specific client. For example, it is difficult to imagine the mass production of standard units of psychiatric family counseling services for a mass consumption market such as the one that exists for shoes or ready-made clothing. The psychiatric counselor is essentially like the tailor or shoemaker of an earlier era who measured each client individually and tailored his product to meet the client's individual needs. Under the craft system, the customer, like our hypothetical patient, had to come to the shop not only to have his measurements taken but for a fitting or two as well. Generally speaking, private philanthropic welfare expenditures take the form of servicing the client; the government, as a general but not a universal practice, prefers bulk purchasing of standardized units of service. Depending on the state of the arts and sciences, it purchases its services from handicraftsmen and smaller suppliers of services, who are quite often subcontractors. In short, the government uses a putting-out system.

In emphasizing volume and mass production, government philanthropy tries to follow an industrial model. What is being mass produced is not, of course, a product, but the low-cost distribution of large sums of money; it is mass purchasing of individualized services rather than mass purchasing of a standardized product. Just as industry has moved in the direction of capital-intensive investments (automation) and away from labor-intensive production techniques, so the industrialization of philanthropy is measured by the ratio of administrative salaries to the total cost of services: the small staff which produces the distribution of vast sums of money corresponds to the automated factory. In this sense government philanthropy is technologically superior to much of private philanthropy which remains in the labor-intensive handicraft stage.

Obviously, this model cannot be applied rigidly to mark the differences between public and private philanthropy. Several private philanthropic organizations have achieved a high measure of industrialization —for example, some of the very large private foundations such as Ford and Rockefeller. Contrariwise, some government agencies (such as a Veterans' hospital) go so far as to dispense the service, instead of purchasing it from others (as in federal support for child welfare services). This simply indicates that neither private nor public philanthropy has a monopoly on modern philanthropic technology, but that (1) the government is in a better position to purchase this technology because its capacity to use it depends on heavy capital resources, and (2) where direct creation of craftlike services are the essence of the philanthropic activity, the private sector with its pre-industrial technology is far superior in its ability to provide unique services.

As the size and scope of government philanthropy increase, the services themselves are standardized and rationalized. Standard forms, procedures, programs, machine teaching, standard curricula, larger classes, standardized diagnoses, computerized systems management, and cost-benefit schemes—all work in the direction of the "objectivity" required by large-scale bureaucratized management. In psychiatry, the most individualized craftlike service based on a one-to-one relationship gives way to group therapy, lobotomy, chemical treatment, and "mental health" classes. Even the forms of rapport, spontaneity, warmth, and involvement are standardized through the systematic training of professional service workers, custodians, and parental surrogates and models. But even as these new devices are instituted, the objectivity, impersonality, and mass production produce resentment: the client, the individual, is lost in the shuffle. The response to demands for recognition of the individual can be met on a professionalized mass basis by incorporating him into the therapeutic process. Sensitivity training, T-Groups, group dynamics, psychodrama, achievement motivation programs—all are designed to produce warmth, spontaneity, individual recognition, and self-motivation within the framework of a large-scale production of services. All of these methods have in common the attempt to reduce the cost per case by large-scale treatment, in other words to expose more and more clients to social service agencies.

In addition to seeing industrial and pre-industrial forms as a means of dividing government and private philanthropy, it is also useful to look at the dynamics between them over a period of time. In the short run it is always difficult for the government to spend money on projects that do not have a socially useful appearance. Tax dollars are supposed to be reasonably rational, to provide services which the community accepts as being needed, and to have some relationship to the community's resources. Given the laissez-faire tradition of modern society, it has been hard to justify philanthropic services as producing economic returns. Ideologists for governmental philanthropy justify expenditures on the basis of necessity, rationality, and usefulness. They know that the public is more likely to resist changes in services than changes in products or technology, because changes in services are more likely to upset settled, hallowed patterns of thinking.

In the long run quite different processes operate: the public can accustom itself to changes in the definition of social needs, the acceptability of previously radical forms of governmental expenditures, and new ratios between expenditures and resources. This is particularly true when the cost is born by economic efficiency and innovation, and thus is never felt as a pinch in the taxpayer's pocketbook. At this point private philanthropy begins to play a major role. Because private philanthropy has little public accountability, it can indulge itself in the never-ending activity of creating new needs for services, embellishing and elaborating old needs, and exposing new groups to old as well as new needs. As a result of these efforts, many new needs are accepted as legitimate by the public.

Once such legitimacy is achieved, servicing the need may eventually be too costly for private philanthropy alone. Government agencies must assume a role in servicing, or government must offer subsidies from tax-based funds. In this way the range of public welfare, health, educational, and cultural programs and in the long run the size of governmental budgets are increased. Once the government steps in and takes over any area of need, private philanthropic organizations are free to engage in exploration and creation of new needs. This cycle repeats itself over and over again. In the division of labor, private philanthropy is historically a research and development agency, and its general movement is always in the direction of further innovation at the expense of ongoing services. In this sense private philanthropy is a significant economic institution in that it provides a perpetual mechanism of expansion. This is true despite the fact that its advanced forms are bureaucratic in character and managed by government agencies.

The Ford Foundation is particularly "modern" in emphasizing its research and development role. As a matter of policy, it specializes in "seed" programs, new experimental efforts which it finances on a "test" basis. Once the program is "successful," it is usually turned over to a government agency. The Ford Foundation has started community action programs, urban renewal and land development and housing programs, school decentralization and urban education programs, and manpower training and development programs. In this way it has developed a major portion of the innovative domestic policies in America. It has acted similarly in relation to American international policies.

In noneconomic or community terms, philanthropy has the capacity to create, to destroy, or to make obsolescent older ways of dealing with an area of need, and to create new methods, organizations, and markets for newly defined needs. Philanthropy thus provides a form of creative destructiveness in the services, exactly parallel to that of the entrepreneur as described by Joseph Schumpeter.

The heroic role of the fund-raiser must be seen in the light of the analysis offered above. These entrepreneurs who create new causes and then go out and collect the money to support them are capitalism's current equivalent of the risk-taking entrepreneur of an earlier era. The philanthropic entrepreneur performs the function of stimulating the flow of currency from primary production, personal hoarding, or consumption into socialized, collective services. The stimulation of the consumption of social services, however, supports the market economy to the extent that that income made available to the government would not have had as strong a multiplier effect.

PHILANTHROPY AS A SYSTEM OF COOPTATION

Traditionalists in the political and business community have regarded government philanthropy as a waste, feeling that all adults should enter the labor market. The public support of nonproductive consumers and nonproductive agencies is for them wasteful and immoral. Opponents of waste have always failed to comprehend the higher economic and political dialectics of public and private philanthropy. Theories opposed to forms of collective waste show a lack of awareness of its social and economic advantages. Any success in eliminating waste would subvert all the social and political meaning of philanthropy.

The mechanism of the market *per se* tends to maintain the present process of income distribution. We can also regard it as axiomatic that those who have higher incomes tend in the long run to share in the power distribution of the society. Thus the process of income distribution tends to maintain any ongoing systems of power.

All features of the system of income distribution which accentuate the concentration of wealth also contain the potential for increasing the resentment and desperation of those who lose out. Those with the power and intelligence to think in terms of rational alternatives may either: (1) permit income inequities to produce so much dissatisfaction that force must be used to maintain order; or (2) successfully justify the ongoing distribution of income and wealth by means of myths, ideologies, and propaganda; or (3) redistribute income within or outside the framework of the market in order to mollify potential opposition and avoid a confrontation with those groups which are dissatisfied with a decreasing share of the total wealth. The ultimate rational choice is between using naked force and using psychic or economic devices to avoid the use of force. In Machiavelli's phrase, the opposition must be either annihilated or embraced.*

* The alternatives stated here imply a degree of rationality on the part of policy-makers which may not be historically justified. Considering the role of left-wing political action, democratic socialism, and trade unions in the history of the rise of the welfare state, the redistributions which have taken place appear to be much less a Machiavellian embrace than victories won by the opposition through political action which the rich and powerful have strongly opposed. The system seems to have a rationality not always possessed by its dominant actors.

Under the logic of philanthropic redistribution, blind market decisions are "corrected" by private or public philanthropic decisions. From the point of view of the history of Western political economy, the redistributions have been concessions to:

1. Individuals with little or no income. This has resulted in direct relief which in recent history has reached such proportions that we shall devote Chapter 12 to its evolution.
2. Individuals of higher social status whose economic position or whose authority is not commensurate with their social position in the community—intellectuals, scholars, professionals, and administrators, to whom we shall devote Chapter 11.
3. The spiritual expectations of the different groups that make up the community. These groups are important in such areas as religion, education, higher and mid-culture, leisure and sports, cults of violence and foundations for peace.

Those with little or no income have scarcely anything to lose and are willing to take desperate measures on slight provocation. Philanthropic investments in relief, even at low levels, are the cost for minimal commitment to the society and avoidance of violence. If such minimal relief is accepted, the poor will not become a problem. If, even after accepting the relief, they do become a problem, it is because outsiders tell them they are insufficiently rewarded. Other outsiders may also organize them and develop in them the capacity for organizing themselves.

All expanding societies are likely to produce expectations for reward that are higher than the rewards received. To attract desirable candidates for the organizations that govern the economy and society, large numbers of youth are induced to aspire to these positions. Fewer are selected to fill them. The difference in numbers provides the selector with freedom of choice and makes the position seem attractive to the aspirants, but it also guarantees a certain number of discontented, rejected aspirants who feel under-rewarded, betrayed, rejected, or inadequate. If the rejected blame the system rather than themselves, they can become discontented and a source of discontent for others. Each expanding system thus tends to generate its own disappointed office-seekers, its well-off, educated, political malcontents and revolutionaries.

In our society, with its immense bureaucratic and corporate growth demanding large numbers of educated personnel, the number of potential malcontents is larger than has been the case in any previous society. Here is a fertile breeding ground within the system for high-level opposition to the society. This discontent calls for a special kind of philanthropy aimed at intellectuals, scholars, professionals, and administrators, each of whom may have his own price for cooperation with the system. Philanthropy, to the extent that it coopts these groups, is an implicit transaction: toleration or support of the system in return for philanthropic support to intellectuals, scholars, professionals, and administrators. Under a fully developed system of philanthropy, the transaction is a continuous one (though scholars move from grant to grant and institution to institution) and is not terminated until the parties to the negotiation die. Here Robert M. Hutchins and his Center for the Study of Democratic Institutions is an excellent example, as are the Guggenheim, Rockefeller, Ford, and other "intellectually" oriented foundations. Philanthropy in this case provides its own higher dialectic: by its support of "intellectuals" it creates new groups of applicants for philanthropy and also provides the resources and institutions for absorbing potential leaders and subsidizing them within the confines of their own institutions.

Politically, then, philanthropic institutions are a mechanism for the manufacture and absorption of would-be elites. They are also a means of pensioning off members of the elite who are temporarily defeated. Thus defeated politicians, university presidents, and government administrators quite often are put to pasture in a foundation, where they help to define policy for the victors and for the society at large. Sometimes they re-emerge (as we shall see in Chapter 11) from such pastoral retirement and again become active leaders in government, universities, and other foundations.

It appears paradoxical that educational institutions, themselves philanthropic, should engage in the manufacture of would-be elites only to force philanthropic institutions to absorb the overproduction. This paradox is resolved if we recall the relationship between philanthropy and the problem of leadership in society. Without philanthropy it would be impossible to reward all who aspire to leadership positions at levels appropriate to their expectations. The universities' continuous manufacturing of would-be elites has the side effect of providing a surplus of aspirants for the preferred positions in the established economic and political institutions, a surplus without which these positions would lose their preferred quality. So long as there are more aspirants than openings, it is possible to find individuals who are motivated to perform within the established order. The overproduction of would-be elites has become a necessity, though some of them can never be absorbed in the central economic and political institutions other than those of philanthropy. For these reasons philanthropic institutions have become socially and politically indispensable.

More important, however, philanthropy apparently solves the crucial political problem of how to keep apart (a) the unorganized, minimally committed, resentful, potentially desperate groups who are not participants in the largess of the society, from the (b) higher-status, educated, but surplus leaders. The joining of these two groups, especially in times of crisis, often leads to further instability and outright revolution. In our time it appears that these two groups can be kept apart by a price differential—the difference between subsistence relief for the poor and the affluent relief guaranteed by public and private foundations to academicians, intellectuals, and professionals. The 20 per cent or, as some say, the 40 per cent of the people who subsist at substandard consumption levels remain an unorganized mass so long as their potential leaders are the beneficiaries of the higher and more affluent philanthropy. Occasionally philanthropy will try to organize social outcasts by using coopted intellectuals in programs that may cause local upheaval but prevent potentially greater disturbances.

Sometimes the coopted indigenous poor believe the propaganda they are fed by program directors, take their program seriously, and run away with it. They thus embarrass the foundation and the political groups which sometimes employ foundations, and alienate other groups who have political influence. The inability of foundations to control their clients and to anticipate responses to their own programs is their single most important inefficiency in the process of cooptation. When they fail, foundations hasten disaffection and violence rather than postponing them. Both public and private philanthropy now have enough self-conscious sophistication to calculate the extent of aid necessary to keep disaffected groups from joining on a mass scale for society-wide action; but they are incapable of judging when any group of leaders or followers will stay bought. In an affluent society, money is insufficient.

In an affluent society, income redistribution begins to take other forms than direct relief. The job market in the private economy, as well as public and semi-public philanthropic employment, can be regulated to produce income redistribution for social and cultural rather than economic goals. During the Great Depression the WPA had its artists, writers, and painters; now these cadres are more usually subsidized by the cultural foundations, indirectly at government expense. Scholars and intellectuals who are potential ideologists have been able to find both public and private sources of subsidization in most of recent history. While there may be differences over time in the levels of price supports for intellectuals, the existence of the subsidies serves to eliminate the intellectuals as potential leaders of the disaffected and the resentful in the mass.

As men do not live by bread alone, there is always some community demand for circuses. The high-consumption society has shown that it is possible to run more than one circus at a time: the masses have more than one opiate. It is to the "credit" of the free-market philanthropy that it permits the putting of any and all shows on the road. No act, no scene, no cause need go without financing but for a modicum of initiative in finding a source of funds. Where every cause can find a budget, it is difficult for an ideologue to remain disaffected or for resentments to accumulate.

But here too the dialectic is more complicated. Philanthropy deals even with those who have no cause or have not yet found one. It provides a great cafeteria of causes where one can choose a dessert according to the fancies of his taste. The myriad of philanthropic causes seems to leave no one, not even the cynics, untouched and unaffected, for the affluent society can afford to bribe the artists, scholars, and intellectuals into doing their own work, asking nothing in return except that they keep busy at it.

The philanthropic system becomes fully articulated at the point where each philanthropic official with a cause throws himself into the support of his *own* higher spiritual cause. Everyone is free to indulge his own intellectual, cultural, or psychological needs, investing as he chooses in the hobbies, sports, arts, religions, intellectual pursuits, and ideologies of the day, and while doing so contributing to the functioning of the economy by the contributions he makes to his cause. But even if one does not contribute money, one can make a still higher form of contribution by receiving philanthropy. As it permits him to follow his own higher pursuits, it dissuades him from other more destructive activities. Thus philanthropic activity supports the power and distributive arrangements of American society, and is functionally indispensable to the American way of life.

Of course, the system does not work perfectly. Some groups and individuals are not yet aware of the personal opportunities available in allowing themselves to be coopted. They may lack information or the linguistic and literary styles necessary to apply for and receive the benefits of philanthropy. Some middle-class youth, so long as they live off the philanthropy of their parents, have no need for the more systematic philanthropy of the government and the foundations. They can afford to remain free as long as they are young, have few personal commitments, and keep their fixed costs low.

Other groups may be too hostile to the society to demonstrate the attitudes necessary for successful cooptation. Some groups of black nationalists and ghetto youth who fall in this category are coopted in spite of their alienation. Others, for ideological or political reasons, resist the whole system of cooptation because they are aware of its implications. Sometimes an individual, while aware of the implications, thinks he can beat the system by accepting its benefits without repaying the expected political commitments and loyalties. He either remains free or discovers after the fact that he has already been coopted.

11. *The intellectual and public policy*

Federal government and private philanthropic expenditures for higher education increased in astronomical proportions between 1940 and 1968. These "investments" in education have resulted in a new set of institutions geared to examining, influencing, and creating government and social policy, both at home and abroad. Today, as never before, intellectuals and professional technicians are producing a stream of monographs, reports, books, studies, papers, treatises, and compendiums in far greater quantities than man has ever known. The fact of this stupendous production of written material, which no one man is capable of digesting, is worth examining. Who produces all these documents? Why do they produce them, and where in society are the producers located? We know that in the past intellectuals were socially rooted either in the middle and upper classes or in the practicing professions such as law, journalism, or the clergy, and only rarely in the pre-modern university academy. Now the university appears to be the major employer of intellectuals and the fountainhead of a literary explosion.

The expansion of the universities since the beginning of World War II and the great increase in the number of college graduates and Ph.D.'s have produced a corps of technicians, aides, speechwriters, symbol manufacturers, ghost writers, investigators, and policy proposers who are now employed by practical men in all institutions. These people, called intellectuals in the sense that they deal with symbols and ideas, have become professionalized in exactly the same sense as the engineer. Unlike the engineer, however, these professional intellectuals are free from much of the routine grind of daily work: they carry light teaching loads and enjoy government and foundation grants and subsidies for their research.

The professor's project budget is the initial economic base that supports his independence within the university. The project budget sustains both the existence of graduate students and the fiscal solvency of the university, which takes a percentage "overhead" out of every project budget. The major feature of project money, whether its source is government or business, is that it is given on a contractual basis, a different contract for each project, so that the investigator's independence rests upon his capacity to secure a succession of contracts. For this reason the direction of research follows changes in budgetary, political, and industrial policy. Thus, for instance, in the social sciences we have had periods of heavy expenditure and intense concentration on military sociology, Kremlinology, the sociology of international propaganda, the sociology of housing, gerontology, mental health, poverty, narcotics addiction, delinquency, crime, violence, land reform in underdeveloped countries, demography, population problems, military elites in new nations, Vietnam, core-city problems, pollution, ecology, and law enforcement. Interest in each of these areas has reflected a major concentration of interest by a government agency or a philanthropic organization. At any given time several of these areas of research have been available to academic and university constituents whose intellectual focus is responsive to these outside opportunities. The ability to anticipate these budgetary inducements, as well as knowing how and to whom one applies for a grant, is a genuine talent among professionalized intellectuals. Within the university and in research organizations, one's status depends partly on the size of his grant, its duration, the number of research assistants employed, and the value of the equipment to be purchased.

A full-scale analysis of the intellectual's new codes and conventions would be interesting but would understate his influence in the formation of public policy. To understand the wider significance of the intellectual, one must understand his relevance to the theory of public opinion and leadership in a democracy. Up to now, two general theories of public opinion have been used to legitimize the democratic process.

1. The first holds that public policy is created by pressure groups. The pressure group puts its argument in terms of general societal advantages that will accrue if policies are adopted which coincide with its vested interests. In a society with many pressure groups, policy is formed by compromises between interest groups. The need to compromise necessarily limits the demands of competing groups. In this theoretical framework, the role of the intellectual is to represent and express the claims of competing groups. Intellectuals become the symbol manipulators (the public relations men, propagandists, and ideologists) for all interest groups, and often do so as technicians. As spokesmen for their own field, or as employed consultants, their intellectual position is that of proponent for the audience for whom they provide values, goals, strategies, and ideologies. Since academic intellectuals face all audiences, they manufacture and contribute to all ideologies. In addition, they have, of course, their own academic ideology which glorifies "for its own sake" the pursuit of knowledge, science, the university, and the value of intellectual life.
2. In the second theory, which is based on the romanticism of Jean Jacques Rousseau, public policy is derived from a consensus based on the general will. It is presumed that at any given time in society there is a general will which a government takes into account in arriving at its policies. Class and other interests are subordinate to the general will, and, moreover, the general will is independent of class interests. The classic problem for this theory is to concretize the concept of general will: Who is to give expression to the general will? All too frequently this problem is answered by the man on the white horse who considers himself to be above petty class interests and hence claims directly to express and symbolize the soul of the nation by some intuitive process. The result is not policy based upon consensus but a

consensus based on some degree of submission to leadership. Charles deGaulle had been the most recent exponent of this position.

In modern society it has sometimes been argued that public opinion polls act as an expression of the general will, even though all sophisticated analyses of such polls seem to indicate the contrary. It is generally known that people respond to public issues directly in terms of class interests and life styles. "Public opinion" as measured by the poll is presumed to be the measured product of the operation of opinion-manufacturing social forces, organizations, and institutions, and is continuously changing in response to events and manipulation.

In the theory of the general will, intellectuals are regarded as above class interests and serve the function of expressing the general will. Needless to say, it is difficult to find intellectual classes which do not have interests of their own, though many claim this function.

The rise of the giant universities since World War II and the great increase in the number of intellectuals which the economy is now capable of supporting have produced a new set of claimants to the function of providing the "disinterested" definition of public policy. Under the claims of the professional and academic intellectuals, knowledge itself is presumed to provide a disinterested (in the sense of articulating a general will) basis for the formation of public policy. In the academic community this claim to disinterestedness is asserted by the left, the right, and the middle.

The claim to disinterestedness has found a powerful ally in the modern philanthropic foundation, which, simply because its source of funds is not derived directly from economic activity but rather is based on *rentier* income derived from capital holdings and stock investments, can claim a disinterested approach to public issues and public policy. Since the advent of the heavily endowed foundation, public issues ranging from war and peace to poverty and the performing arts have been defined from the apparently disinterested perspective of philanthropic selflessness.

The most recent claimants to this function of disinterested advocacy have been the radical youth and professional prophets who use Hegelian justifications to support their position. While they recognize that they represent a minority of the population, their views are based upon the belief that only they possess innocent, free, and uncorrupted values in the society. The validity of their actions is justified on the ground that they embody the future evolution of their society, that they are right because the future will prove them right. Since they represent, and in fact are, the future, the establishment is obligated to accept their views regardless of the means by which they present them. Public opinion and the reality of the future, not the present, validate their actions.

THE NEW OPINION-FORMING AGENCIES

From the early years of the Carnegie Foundation in the twenties to the Ford Foundation in the fifties, American philanthropy has supported a wide variety of projects. The foundations have stimulated the reformulation of higher and lower educational policy for the society at large and for professional educational movements. From the Flexner report on medical education in the early years of this century to Charles Silberman's report on secondary education in the seventies, almost all areas of professional and educational policy and practice have been appraised by foundation-supported projects. In their other enterprises the foundations have attempted to define world population policies (Milbank and Ford), regional and area development policies (Carnegie and Ford), foreign policy (Rockefeller and Brookings), cultural and artistic policy (Mellon, Ford, and Rockefeller), leisure-time policy (Twentieth Century and Rockefeller), urban race and poverty policy (Rosenwald, Ford, and Twentieth Century), and so on. The foundations have shaped and financed a large part of the cultural "explosion" in America (Rockefeller Fund Report on the Performing Arts) and have been responsible for major innovations in the medical, physical, biological, and social sciences. The work of the Ford Foundation alone has set in motion the present emphasis on gerontology, urban policy, delinquency, poverty, fertility planning, population control, and urban black education.

In terms of international relations, foundation "area programs" have produced a large crop of indigenous and American specialists in the major developed and underdeveloped regions of the world. The careers of experts on Russia, Latin America, Africa, the Middle East, and China have been financed according to the needs of American foreign policy and the aspirations of the foundations. Between the efforts of the International Institute for Education, the Social Science Research Council, the American Council of Learned Societies, the Ford Foundation, the Wenner-Gren Foundation, and so on, no area of the world has been left untouched. "Policies" have been formulated for specific countries (Nigeria, Ghana, Vietnam, Egypt, and so on), and these policies have been implemented by direct financing, indirect aid, research programs, training programs, and by employing anyone who can help in the realization of stated policy. The foundations have thus stated goals for America and the world and have attempted to achieve them. If we add these activities to their experimental "seed" programs, we can see how great the foundations' influence on social policy can be.

Compared with other organizations engaged in the manufacturing of opinion, the economic resources of the foundations are great. When they wish to do so, they invest their money in any area they regard as "fruitful." They understand that their "investments" may produce important ideological and tangible returns. A half-million- or million-dollar investment in a position paper, a panel report, a "study," or a "special report" may have the importance of a policy paper from a major, and certainly a minor, government. The investment not only supports the intellectuals who do the work but may result in a marketable idea. Like the capitalist entrepreneurs of an earlier time, the foundations are willing to risk their capital on venturesome projects, even if the results cannot be foreseen. Reports, studies, and monographs resulting from these investments may focus public opinion on a given issue and suggest guidelines for action. Edited, censored, and purified for public consumption, the final report is only a lure to an undetermined constituency which, depending on other factors, may or may not respond. But the point is that the very *process* of developing such studies and reports in itself creates opinions, issues, and policy positions.

Mechanisms such as the conference, the panel, the joint steering committee, the president's commission, the advisory board, and the joint commission are used to assemble viewpoints and crystallize policies. These mechanisms usually involve consultation with leaders of those organizations concerned with given policy areas. Thus the work of a panel study group like the Rockefeller Fund Report on the Performing Arts incorporated almost all major artistic and organizational leaders in the arts, who after two or three years of discussion reached a working consensus among themselves. The panel report is based on a prior policy agreement developed by these leaders, but only after intricate negotiations and complex compromises. After the negotiations and compromises, the unanimity of the report or policy statement gives their statement a high degree of authority in all relevant areas of the field in question. Such public agreement among "experts" and leaders breeds confidence in the minds of the lay public. Thus the panel and conference procedures become in themselves a means of defining issues and manufacturing consensus.

When the foundation report is released, cooperating publishers, critics, columnists, press officers of the institutions whose leaders are panel members, and members of ad hoc citizens' committees are briefed to issue prepared statements publicizing and supporting the report. Subsidized copies of the report are distributed to all interested and important figures in public and private life. Conferences are planned to discuss the report's implications. Follow-up articles in magazines, newspapers, and journals extend the range of coverage and the depth of exposure. Radio and television interviews with key participants are programmed to coincide with the rest of the publicity barrage. If these means of dramatizing the issue are successful, a television documentary is apt to follow close behind. Thus, within a period of two years, all these processes are capable of creating a salient public issue and defining public opinion on it. A major part of what we consider to be public opinion is a result of a continuous process by which foundations, government agencies, and universities define issues for the society at large.*

The relationship of the academic community to the foundations is of special interest. The academic community is involved primarily in presenting technical background information and editorial skills to the

* At the governmental level, commissions such as the President's Commission on Violence, the President's Panel on the Crisis of the Universities, and the Kent State investigations are recent examples of a process which in the governmental sphere is extremely old.

foundations. Presidents and deans of universities operate, in addition, as public figures who help to organize support and lend authority and respectability to the final report. The university president or the dean is usually a person who no longer engages in intellectual work, though he is likely to have achieved his position on the basis of intellectual accomplishments. In this sense he stands as an administrative symbol of scholarship. His identification with the report and his sponsorship of it acts as an intellectual imprimatur.

What is revolutionary about this university function is that the whole process of granting the imprimatur is carried on by individuals and institutions which appear to have hardly any vested interest in the policy issue itself. Conventional interest-group theory does not account for such a phenomenon.

The foundations have now entered areas which used to be the preserve of special-interest groups and the government. In other areas, such as overseas development or the subsidization of the arts, they have simply filled a vacuum. When the foundations enter a given area, they do so with great resources, with great numbers of coopted technical personnel, and with a reserve of talent which is precisely the same talent necessary for policy formation and the administration of programs. An investment or a crash program in a given area (Vietnamese hill tribes, for example) requires (a) individuals who are free to leave their jobs for long periods of time with little loss to their parent organization (b) administrators who can carry out an organized distribution of funds, (c) consultations with innumerable government agencies and officials whose administrative jurisdictions touch on the area, (d) substantive specialists of all kinds from the professorial ranks, and (e) the joint cooperation of a group of universities whose resources will be pooled to cover the total range of technical needs. Large- and small-scale operations thus reach into a variety of organizations, agencies, and institutions in the search for personnel. Any foundation is a clearinghouse for talent. Professional organizations and various government agencies maintain standardized directories of personnel and their skills, listed according to categories relevant to social and political policy. It is thus a relatively easy matter to find a group of specialists on almost any subject.

It follows that these pools of talent become available to the government and the universities as well as to the foundations. At the highest levels, government as a matter of course employs its Rusks, Bundys, Gardners, Weisners, Hellers, Heards, DuBridges, and Milton Eisenhowers, all of whom are university and foundation officials who have distinguished themselves as consultants over the course of a lifetime. In the same way, university professors and deans and college presidents operate as consultants, though in their case they either do so while still employed by the university or take a leave of absence to serve in areas relevant to their academic or administrative skills. The same process occurs in reverse, where government and military officials, after having achieved prestige, resign or retire from their main careers to go to the foundations and the academy (Stassen, Dwight Eisenhower, Gardner, Bundy). At almost all levels there is a three-way traffic in personnel among government, universities, and foundations.

INTERLOCKING DIRECTORS IN POLICY-MAKING

In an earlier age it was the businessman who shuttled between his corporation and government; but from the New Deal to the Nixon administration the businessman was not a major source of technical aid to government. Instead the professor, the college president, and the foundation official assumed this role, a fact which irritated many businessmen. During the New Deal, the Brain Trusters (Tom Corcoran, Raymond Moley, Benjamin Cohen, Laughlin Currie) and social workers and planners (Harry Hopkins, Frances Perkins, Rexford G. Tugwell) who "never met a payroll" were the object of scorn by businessmen who felt themselves to be the sole possessors of practical knowledge. During the ensuing thirty years, businessmen grumbled and complained about their loss of this function. Today, however, they would never employ the argument of impracticality against a Kissinger, though they might against a Schlesinger. The role of the intellectuals in World War II must have played an important and convincing part in this acceptance. Perhaps it was the professorial developers of the A-bomb and H-bomb, working in their makeshift labs under Stagg Field at the University of Chicago, who demonstrated for all time that in things that count the academician could be "practical."

There is no doubt that General Leslie Groves and Wild Bill Donovan were enormously impressed by the work of the physicists and the intelligence specialists in the Office of Strategic Services. Even Herbert Marcuse was then acceptable in the OSS. Ph.D.'s, if not refugees themselves, displayed a flair for learning foreign languages and knew what to do when dropped behind enemy lines. Besides, government discovered that intellectuals liked their work and, if given sway within their specialties, worked well and patriotically.

During and after World War II the scope and complexity of government operations increased geometrically as America found itself the dominant industrial and world power. Only the universities could create and train the specialists which the government needed. Government and foundations subsidized the programs necessary to train the specialists who, once they were trained, were hired by the government and foundations from the universities they had subsidized. After twenty years of intensive investment and several generations of eager candidates who responded to the clear and present danger, the requisite pools of talent have been produced.

The term *pool* implies a certain amount of interchangeability and, what is more important, a social matrix of interpersonal commitments and involvements. The specialists, technicians, professional intellectuals, administrators, and professors form a "community" above and beyond specific institutions, universities, and agencies.

As a result of this development of paralleled careers, middle- and top-level officials in government, foundations, and universities have come to know each other on personal, professional, and official levels over the period of their careers. Thus the penetration of inter-institutional cliques, as we have already described it, occurs at the simplest interpersonal level. Each individual operator, whatever his current institutional base, has a personal constituency in those other areas which include his students, professors, colleagues, subordinates, or superordinates. On an informal basis each can call upon his friendly "contact" for information, advice, and informal private opinions, and each can use the other as a source of support and personnel. In this way, without undue effort and with a minimal anxiety arising from the normal uncertainties of bureaucratic warfare, worldwide projects that involve a variety of institutions can be organized with the appearance of a high degree of efficiency.

At a public level this integration and efficiency are achieved through institutions that are now the showcases of inter-institutional coordination. They are called the "review panel," the "steering committee," the "advisory board," and other rubrics used by hundreds of government agencies and philanthropic foundations. Their chief feature is that they are composed of "outside" experts, "outside" meaning that the participants arc selected from agencies other than the one doing the selecting: a government "panel" is composed of experts from the universities and foundations or from other government departments, and a foundation "panel" is composed of experts selected from anywhere except the foundation in question. What is common to all panels is that their members know each other from other contexts and from a complex structure of other interpersonal commitments. In vulgar language, the panel members are attuned to the dictum, "I'll scratch your back if you scratch mine." This dictum is never openly expressed. The etiquette of bureaucracy demands that all participants accept the pretense of objective, value-free, affectively neutral group decision-making, in which consensus is reached by a language of subliminal gestures. The total relationships of the participants to the unspoken agreement come into play.

The panel has the quality of the older businessman's club, where it was understood that deals could be made in a private sanctuary. But the bureaucrat, being a public official whose acts go "on the record," does not always have the luxury of a private arena. The harassed, publicly scrutinized professional bureaucrat creates the equivalent of a club by *sub rosa* forms of communication. He acts in public but is not seen by the public which is witness to the act. In this sense the linguistic euphemisms of bureaucracy are functional.

The members of these panels, advisory boards, and steering committees are primarily concerned with distributing federal and foundation money on a scale that is impressive even to the businessman who is accustomed to dealing in large sums. As they decide on requests for grants, research projects, grants-in-aid, and subsidies to universities and corporations, and in the process evaluate the personnel, these consultants make policies which result in the allocation of huge amounts to those who can be expected to use the funds in ways consistent with policy.

A concrete example may be helpful to the reader who is unaware of this process. One influential member of a government review panel—a professor whom we shall call Smith—visited Washington three or four times a year throughout the sixties as a consultant, for which he earned $100 a day. His role was analogous to the dollar-a-year man of an earlier period. Smith is an expert who knows everyone in his field; as an adviser he decided on the policies of agencies which distributed millions of dollars in subcontracted funds. Because he was a star figure in his field, he sat on a large number of government review panels and remained a member of at least two foundation steering committees in his area of specialization. When Smith made a decision on one committee, it was necessarily with reference to what he had seen, heard, and done on other committees. This is natural enough, even though inconsistent with the theory of role segregation as propounded by theorists of administration. In a very simple and straightforward way, Smith coordinated the funding policies of a variety of institutions.

Smith also created, in the process of his everyday work, a staggering network of interpersonal commitments by the simple process of allocating funds to individuals and institutions whom he knew, trusted, liked, and respected. In the private, as opposed to the public, world, this is known as "empire building." When a star figure in one of these inter-institutional networks has access to millions of dollars which he can direct to his own institution, his stature, prestige, and power within his own institution know no limits.

With the advent of the Nixon administration, Smith lost his influence with the political masters of the bureaucracies he served. Today he remains influential only with the foundations. Moreover, he has lost much of his influence within the academic world. A new set of consultants has come to the foreground, and the flow of funds has been "democratized." Nixon has had good reason to distrust academics and the bureaucratic agencies that employ them. When possible he has hired businessmen, especially from the Midwest. Given the differential in salaries and the indispensability of businessmen to their businesses, the comparable salaries have attracted inferior consultants and civil servants.

In some instances inter-institutional stars combine their academic role with political contacts at the highest levels of government. Thus, for example, some cabinet members become university presidents, and vice versa. When this happens, as is the case for a school in the far Northwest, to mention only one, the program of an entire university may be based on the inter-institutional skills of one man. In the case in question, the power of this single administrator is overwhelmingly felt in every nook and cranny of university life. This former cabinet officer was able to tap his former government contacts for scholarships, fellowships, building funds, research contracts, and salary subsidies. He was thus able to take a second-rate institution and, at least in budgetary terms, convert it into a first-rate school almost overnight. Such a career pattern is not at all unique, and in part accounts for the large number of former government officials who are now deans and college presidents. The process is analogous to the employment of former generals and admirals by defense-oriented industries.

A change in administration may affect a university negatively or positively. Thus a university which has received millions of dollars for buildings, staffs, fellowships, and operating costs can lose all of these with a shift in the federal budget or the loss of influence of a major consultant. Such universities are apt to scratch for enough funds for staff and to heat the building generously donated to them by the government. The most recent dramatic case is the demise of many language and area studies programs at universities. American foreign studies programs require linguists, anthropologists, and presumed experts in such fields as Kremlinology, Sinology, and Southeast Asia. The Nixon administration has cut these programs back drastically, and labor surpluses have emerged. Universities with programs in such areas have tried to influence public policy to maintain them.

Such examples abound, and wherever they exist they represent a major change in the structure of the university, one result of which has been a new type of conflict on campus.

In most of the larger schools, and in many of the smaller ones whose existence depends on the new sources of funds, there is sometimes a conflict between scholars who are not oriented to project research or outside funds, and other scholars who are. Scholars not oriented to projects feel devalued by what they regard as money wasted on piddling research which is rarely completed and not significant anyway. Others resent the fact that the curricula, staff, and character of the university are determined by the availability of funds to persons with "proper" contacts. This is a battle, sometimes silent, occasionally open, always brooding beneath the surface in almost every major university. In part it is a struggle between the older generation, which regards itself as intellectually principled, and the middle generation, which their elders regard as having "sold out." At another level it is a battle between "idealistic" students and their professors. Or, apart from status categories, the issue may be joined as one of integrity versus corruption and intellectual degeneracy. As a result, government and the foundations determine not only the character of the special funds in the university but also their relative importance in the total mix—thus the whole academic tone of the university.

THE FUNCTIONS OF THE UNIVERSITY

Before World War II the university was virtually alone in the field of organized intellectual production; after World War II a number of new institutions were created to carry on similar activities. The range, scope, and sponsorship of these institutions are extremely broad and diverse. For our purposes it is necessary to suggest only a few examples. Advanced study centers (known in the trade as think tanks) free scholars from university duties for the purpose of intellectual interchange and completion of work in progress. This institution is favored by the foundations. It preserves the quality of the community of scholars, though it detaches professors from students, who previously were thought to be part of the university. More to our point are the creations of the armed services, the State Department, and the CIA, which during the early phases of the Cold War established and subsidized various "nonprofit," "disinterested," "scholarly" institutions designed to formulate and evaluate public policy. The public knows these subsidiaries as the RAND Corporation, the Operations Research Office, the Special Operations Research Office, the Systems Development Corporation, the Institute of Defense Analysis, and several "Centers of International Studies," the one located at MIT being the best known. The idea behind such organizations was to broaden the base of intellectual involvement in public policy formation, discussion, ideas, and collation of information without establishing explicit government agencies. For a number of reasons, this solution has not been entirely satisfactory.

If the consulting institution depends exclusively on contracts with one major government department, it is too easily designated as a front organization for that department—for example, the RAND Corporation as a front for the Air Force, or the National Student Association as a front for the CIA. In order for a front organization to be valuable it must not appear to be a front, so that in this respect the universities and the foundations serve the purpose much better than an obvious front like RAND. For this reason the work of the Operations Research Office or the RAND Corporation loses a measure of credibility for disinterested research, especially among the academicians: everyone knows their one source of funds. So long as Project Camelot* was thought to be a sociological enterprise and not generally known to be sponsored by the Department of Defense, there seemed to be no problems. As soon as Defense Department sponsorship was publicly revealed, credibility was totally destroyed, if not for all social scientists certainly for intellectuals in the underdeveloped world. By contrast, Michigan State University's wholesale collaboration with the CIA and the Defense Department in Vietnam was not only a viable front for more than five years, but even after its exposure by *Ramparts* magazine it could maintain an element of academic credibility by the fact that for a while the public refused to believe that Michigan State was totally corrupted. The university can always exploit an element of ethical ambiguity, and in this respect has advantages as a front organization not enjoyed by more transparent fronts like the RAND Corporation. One major disadvantage of the university as a front is that it is especially vulnerable to demonstrations, riots, occupations, and fires provoked by radicals and peacemongers.

Even more important than these special consequences of the cooperation among universities, the government, and foundations is the independence and freedom which the government gains from such arrangements. Any government agency is known in advance to have a

* Project Camelot was a Department of Defense worldwide study of sources of internal rebellion, which enlisted the services of social and political scientists from many countries.

vested interest. All of its work will be judged accordingly and will be regarded as propaganda by anyone who wishes to discredit results. The CIA realized this and accordingly used the technique of fronts on a worldwide scale. Its policy was successful for a remarkably long time, and was vitiated only after glaring public exposure. For this reason a private foundation or a university is much better equipped to carry out government policy than a government agency. This is especially true in the area of international relations and intelligence-gathering, where the audience for the intellectual product is the outside world and where the government is much more apt to be suspect even among friendly allies. Thus the Ford Foundation, the Rockefeller Foundation, the Carnegie Foundation, and university-based Centers for International Studies have been able to do much more than the government could if it were to enter similar activities directly. Moreover, when the government intervenes in such areas and its intervention is exposed, as was the Department of Defense's Project Camelot, sponsored through the American University in Washington, D.C., the fiasco has worldwide repercussions; a fiasco involving a private foundation or a university can be buried. While the university is a better cover for underground work than an institute or even a foundation, its historical tradition of righteousness makes it particularly vulnerable to exposures of its operating and financial structure.* If it is discovered to be financed by the Department of Defense or the CIA, it is likely to lose its sole source of legitimacy: its reputation for disinterested, independent, and high-minded activity.

In some cases, to be sure, overt government sponsorship can exist without destroying the credibility of the program. These exceptional cases are likely to be in the areas of education, the international exchange of persons, cultural programs, and, to a lesser extent, international propaganda. In instances such as the International Institute of Education or Radio Free Europe (which is supported by the CIA), federal funds are administered by presumed private corporations which cover their "kept" status by making appeals to the public for funds. This approach appears to work best in the area of education, where it can always be rationalized that in spite of a vested government inter-

* The exposures themselves are regarded as outside the boundaries of respectable academic research and hence as unethical.

est, education in and of itself is good and is therefore beyond contamination. Hence there is less need to fumigate funds by a system of front organizations in the area of education.

The clarity of political purpose implied in this discussion does not always hold. That is, in both foreign and domestic policy the last twenty years have been a period of experimentation and ambiguity, so that there are cases where jurisdictional lines between government, the foundations, and the universities have not been easily defined. Under such conditions, responsibilities may be tossed back and forth during times when it is not yet clear who can best handle a given area. For example, the Ford Foundation, perhaps because it entered the field of large-scale philanthropy relatively late and thus was forced to find "new" jurisdictions for itself, took pride in establishing seed programs and "demonstration projects."* It hoped by these means to demonstrate their potential to a government which has not yet entered these areas. When one of these programs is successful—as, for example, population control, urban youth problems, or gerontology—it invites local, state, or federal governments to create similar programs. Having defined an area, the foundation may phase itself out of that area and pass it on to another agency.

As an illustration of the process in reverse, the federal government may appear to take over a field which it later abdicates to private foundations after it lends an initial impetus. This seemed to be the case in the performing arts, where the Hecksher Report was originally financed by the federal government but was not used as a basis for attempting to coordinate the performing arts. This failure of government initiative led the Rockefeller Foundation to establish its own panel on the performing arts, through which, in effect, a program for the performing arts in America was established. Later, President Johnson, with his National Endowment for the Arts, attempted to recover this jurisdiction, but the foundation was reluctant to return it to the federal government. Only after much persistence by the National Endowment did the Rockefeller Foundation "surrender" the arts.

* Its most successful seed programs have been *seed* programs—the development and dissemination of new hybrid corn and rice have helped to alleviate the pressure on the food supply. The Ford Foundation has been less successful in disseminating birth-control information and devices, most effective in the physical sciences, and, like everyone else, weakest in the social sciences.

The surrender was temporary. President Johnson appointed as director of the National Endowment Robert Whitehead, whose major background was in private theatrical production. After a troubled tenure of office, President Nixon replaced Whitehead with Nancy Hanks, who had administered the Rockefeller Report on the Performing Arts.

Clearly, much of the initiative in these matters is provided by the executive departments of the federal government or by the foundations, rather than by those who live or work in the areas affected. This is natural enough, for these are the agencies that provide the funds. Nonetheless, the universities are a major beneficiary of these processes because the personnel for most projects are trained in and recruited from them. Irrespective of who sponsors the program, the source of personnel is the same, so that, by and large, change of sponsorship only results in different application blanks, work sites, and paymasters, as far as the university is concerned.

Foundation and government executives do not always agree on who should predominate in certain areas. At times, different agencies compete and may even drive one another out of a given jurisdiction. At times, joint steering committees composed of members of various agencies and their higher-level executives agree to divide jurisdictions and coordinate activities. Depending on circumstances, resources may be pooled for the purpose of integrating all work in a given field; this seems to be the case in the field of population control. Anti-trust laws do not apply in such coordination, though impulses toward regulatory legislation vis-à-vis the foundations have begun to appear under the instigation of Congressman Wright Patman of Texas, who rightly or wrongly appears to fear their growing economic and political power. Patman is most concerned, however, with the use of foundations as a tax dodge and as a base for stock market manipulations.

Apart from the grounds on which Patman's fears rest, the foundations occupy a powerful position in relation to the universities. By threatening to withdraw support, they can pressure individuals and universities to cooperate in programs they consider vital. While any university can refuse to cooperate, it does so at the risk of being left holding a bag of heavy costs left over from older programs, and no new sources of support. If the university commitment to nonteaching functions is deep (in some cases as high as 80 or 90 per cent of the operating budget), it is difficult to back out. Doing so would mean the collapse of an entire institution and with that the economic basis of the life styles of most of its members. In this way the foundations (as well as the government) introduce order and stability into the world of ideas and the academic marketplace.

This is not to say that the universities produce no new ideas. It only means that they are directed toward areas where new ideas are to be found. Foundation executives, university presidents, and professors do not consider themselves as mere appendages of the executive and legislative branches of government. Many of them are better paid than their counterparts in government, in positions which they themselves may once have held. They tend to feel that they are more efficient and better qualified than their government counterparts. Moreover, operating out of the foundation or university, they feel a freedom to be more creative, less constricted, and better able to construct new and imaginative policy proposals. As a result, it is probably true that they can lead rather than follow government policy in many areas. In the world of ideas they can act as a "research and development" branch of the government. Bureau officials within the government understand the constraints of their own positions. Such constraints do not operate with equal efficiency in the private sphere, so that private operators become responsible for creating government policy without the need to acknowledge conventional interest groups or the legislative branch of government. Thus the foundations are in the special position of being able to act more directly than the administrative and executive branches of government.

From the government's standpoint, when the foundations and the administration reach a policy consensus, they have at their disposal a massive apparatus for educating the public to the agreed-upon policy lines. The process of arriving at "long-run" policy positions has not been accounted for in conventional interest-group analysis.

Behind the government position paper, policy report, guideline, statement, and so forth, stand a number of academic consultants. Usually they are linked together by a foundation report which in the first instance provided a basis for their recruitment. The very creation of the policy report contains within it a supporting constituency for the policy, since its makers gain an interest in supporting their own product. The academic community that researches and writes the report also becomes a supporting constituency. But much more than this is involved. Researching a report and writing it involve a massive mobilization of personnel and talent. Experts in all relevant fields and activities are consulted. Hundreds of key people are interviewed. The process of mobilizing support and expertise for each stage in the making of the report ultimately involves broad segments of key opinion and institutional leadership of the society. The report, though ultimately written by a professional writer, is much more than a report. It is also, if successful, an *institution* which coordinates opinion.

Occasionally some celebrities and technical consultants rebel at the direction they are asked to take, at the agenda, and even in the selection of participants to the conference. When this happens the participants will refuse to be coordinated, and will argue with each other in public and with the conference organizers. Perhaps the best examples of this are the White House Conferences (on Youth, Crime, the Family, Children, Juvenile Delinquency, the Negro, and so on) and presidential commissions (on Government Reorganization, Urban Affairs). These conferences and commissions are composed of lay leaders who, after deliberation in Washington, report their results to the President and thus focus attention on "new" issues originally "seen" and "defined" by the agency organizers of the conference or commission. Those in the agency who make the agenda and organize the conference play a key role. Massive discussions are held in advance in committee and plenary sessions. Testimony is taken and reported on TV, radio, or in the press. Arguments take place. Conclusions are reached. Formulations are made. Resolutions are voted upon. Final reports are submitted. Monographs, papers, and summary conclusions and recommendations are distributed to the public, specialized journals, and the mass media. The public is given sufficient time and opportunity to contemplate all of these procedures and all of this material. Professional associations may engage in deep debate over aspects of the policy proposals. When the final policy is announced from the White House, the movement to support it is well on its way if it does not already exist. Some observers have ridiculed the conference and commission method as a boondoggle or a fireman's holiday and have failed to see its usefulness in shaping public opinion.

THE ROLE OF THE PUBLIC IN PUBLIC OPINION

To return to the question of where the "general will" originates: it becomes increasingly clear that in contemporary society the general will emerges from the opinions and policies created, coordinated, and crystallized by foundations, universities, and the government. It is also clear that the opinions and policies created by these groups become part of the general will only insofar as these groups can successfully define issues for the public and convince politically decisive groups that the policies they advocate should be adopted. The government-foundation axis (which is differently constituted, depending on time and the issue) competes with other interest groups who often use more conventional methods of propaganda. What emerges from this competition is of course not the general will at all, but merely public opinion or policy as formulated by those who express it.

Much of what we have described concerning the cooptation of academicians as technicians and as public-opinion crystallizers has been part of a secure tradition in American life at least since World War II. Exposés of secret CIA support and similar embarrassments during the sixties only dramatized what was already known, in most instances, by academicians, foundation executives, and government officials, though probably no one realized the full extent of such cooptation.

The blasé attitude toward such cooptation was not even moved by publicizing the names of CIA recipients of funds in the *New York Times* before the appearance of a longer article in *Ramparts* magazine. *Ramparts* simply focused the issue and added moral indignation to it by linking the cooptation of the universities to the Vietnam War. The full course of the exposure did, however, add new dimensions to public knowledge of the cooptation of totally new segments of American institutions into the combined public-opinion apparatus. Thus the public discovered that nonacademic intellectuals, critics, avant-garde writers, editors, and leaders of the intellectual establishment were used as fronts and, in the more extreme cases, as articulators of administration policy. While detailed cost figures are not available, it seems they were bought at even lower prices than academicians. For airline fares and expenses-paid attendance at vacationlike international and national conferences, they would not only lend their names but would do genuine intellectual work (in the form of writing) for CIA-subsidized journals and magazines which they could call their own. To be sure, in some cases their own hatred of communism and their own radical past made them especially willing to cooperate. But nonideological businessmen in the same position would have asked for "cash and let the credit go."

The cooptation of large numbers of college students and youth organizations is more understandable, despite the tendency of youth toward radical attitudes. College students who were coopted frequently did not have the experience to realize or the ideological training to resist what they were asked to do.

Labor leaders, socialists, and Christian radicals were willing to accept any support necessary to sustain their higher causes. Commercial book publishers and the university presses were willing to accept funds for less noble purposes, and in doing so disseminated justification of policies over wider and wider areas.

In all of these respects, however, the CIA was doing in one area exactly what the foundations, the government agencies, and the universities had been doing in other areas since World War II. The fact that the CIA and the Department of Defense have received most of the publicity in the case of Project Camelot has only deflected attention from the full range and intensity of the total process. But the continued exposure of university front organizations, especially by radical youth organizations, has served to destroy their effectiveness. This has produced a crisis in the entire machinery of university involvement in technical consulting and public-opinion formation, a crisis reinforced by the cost cutting of the Nixon administration, and by the tendency of some radical youth to bomb or burn computer centers provided the universities by the federal government.

The effect of such exposures has also been to deepen the disenchantment of youth and to provide grist for the propaganda mills of radical students. Students have attacked their own university's connection to the Defense Department through military contracts; programs of the Institute of Defense Analysis and the CIA; ROTC; and recruiting by specific industries which are considered part of the military-industrial complex. Exposures and confrontations have partially destroyed the credibility of universities, have become the basis of new forms of thought-control originating from the left, and have forced universities to divest themselves of some programs and modify others. From the standpoint of government, student radicals have endangered previously successful programs and threatened "law and order." Government intervention increasingly becomes nonfiscal; not only the police but also the withdrawal of funds where violence occurs are a major danger to those universities that have relied heavily on government financing. By and large, however, the foundations, being private philanthropic organizations, have not been bothered except for a few nonprofit corporations that have been exposed as fronts. New institutional forms have not yet been created to overcome the difficulties, though it appears that further exposures will make it necessary to develop alternative machinery.

If this whole foundation-government-university network can be seen as a public-opinion machine, then it is little different from the total agitprop mechanism as defined by Lenin and Trotsky and implemented by Stalin to manufacture public opinion in the Soviet Union. In this respect the major similarity between the United States and Russia is that public opinion and public policy are manufactured from the top with the aid of communications and technical specialists, university professors, and staff institutes. The major differences in the agitprop apparatus of these two countries are:

1. In Soviet society there are few open and public institutions which are permitted to express opposition.
2. There is as yet no free press in Russia which, regardless of its own vested interests, is able to kick over the traces from time to time and make exposures as did *Ramparts* or the *New York Times*.
3. American students and intellectuals who are not coopted can continue to expose and demonstrate against the system without immediate fear of direct reprisal or sanctions, provided they do not provoke the police to a direct attack.
4. Agencies which can independently act as pressure groups on the central government are not allowed to exist in the Soviet Union. Pressures by various bureaucratic interest groups do exist, but these are exerted *in camera,* except in the case of a few literary intellectuals.
5. Since it is apparent that many Russian citizens are aware of the official nature of the machinery of propaganda and public-opinion-making, they are unwilling to accept official definitions at face value.

In fact, Russian citizens are more likely to become specialists in interpreting the motives, sources, reasons, and weaknesses that evoke public statements. In short, Kremlinology is not a monopoly of American university Russian specialists and correspondents: the ordinary Russian is apt to play the same game. In America the equivalent agitprop apparatus has evolved without a theory or the appearance of a central design. It grew like Topsy. American citizens are thus more poorly equipped to evaluate the official nature of public statements, information, press releases, "lines," and so forth, for they are only dimly aware of the mechanisms by which these are produced. Nonetheless, news-management failures and selective misinformation produce disillusionment for those who once believed, and the same skeptical attitudes and cynicism have emerged. Radical college youth have seized upon the exposures of universities as a basis for demonstrating and picketing against university administrations, projects, and institutes. Regardless of their motives and methods, the students have served to focus public attention on the extent of cooptation of the university and its professors.

There are limits to what can be done with propaganda and managed news. It is extremely difficult by the manipulation of symbols to convince a group which has clear-cut, simple, and direct economic interests to surrender those interests for the sake of ideological, patriotic, or distant psychic benefits. Rather, the interest groups in question learn the language and rhetoric of official prose and learn to mask their own interests in these terms. Thus the entire society begins to talk in bureaucratic and official language, often parodying it, so that the consensus, when it appears to be achieved, is the consensus of linguistic styles.

12. *The philanthropic cooptation of the lower classes*

The foundations, government agencies, and the universities have become major factors in the attempt to influence public opinion. In the process, foundation and government officials and university professors have been major recipients of the new public and private philanthropies. Part of their role has been to devise plans for the philanthropic cooptation of the poor. Such plans are not only aimed at solving the problems of the poor but are also designed to help the poor accept the system, or in other words to prevent violence and urban riots, and to maintain law and order.

As we have already suggested, the established structure of society cannot be secure if there is organized mass disaffection at the bottom. A major problem for any society is maintaining either the positive or passive support of the lower classes, who by virtue of their class position do not benefit substantially from income and wealth distribution. What mechanisms can be used to achieve this support? To what extent are these mechanisms similar to those used to secure the assent and cooperation of the middle classes?

CHANGES IN THE CONCEPTION OF THE POOR

Welfare in America up to the New Deal is a history of private philanthropic institutions. The Protestant ethic and its descendant, laissez-faire capitalism, suggested that the poor had earned their just rewards; the economic system rewarded individuals according to their economic contribution. Thus if the poor suffered, it was because they were either morally or economically inferior, the underlying assumption being that any man with enterprise, energy, and a willingness to defer gratifications for the purpose of investment could succeed. In American economic development, large expenditures for welfare and charity would have been a drain on savings used for reinvestment.

When charity was unavoidable, it was accompanied by a hazing of the indigent and powerless client. He was forced in innumerable ways to admit his dependency and to submit to conscious and unconscious attitudes of sufferance, tolerance, and condescension from those who distributed the charity. The poor paid for this charity by acknowledging the moral superiority of their betters. The "means test" and similar legislation placed the poor beyond the pale of respectable society and denied them the minimal pleasures of life. To receive charity it was necessary to show one's betters that one was suffering. The poor affirmed upper-class moral superiority by denying themselves the pleasures of drink or sex, pleasures which the Protestant upper classes in fact denied themselves. This aspect of the Protestant tradition has been fully described by George Bernard Shaw in *Major Barbara,* and by George Orwell in *Down and Out in Paris and London,* in which Orwell describes his poignant encounter with the moral virtuosos of the Salvation Army. Orwell draws the complete picture by indicating that this punishment was inflicted on all those who enjoyed life.

The New Deal signaled at a national level, *but not at a local level,* the beginning of a change in attitudes toward the poor. In the thirties, society began to recognize that poverty was a human problem with human costs. People began to see that personal economic failure could be the result of a failure in the operation of the economic system. No doubt the high visibility of poverty and unemployment helped to create this redefinition of social attitudes, but it was also true that the intellectuals and social workers of that and earlier eras played the role of educator to the public. People such as Jacob Riis, Jane Addams, and, later, under Roosevelt's administration, Harry Hopkins and Frances Perkins, contributed substantially to this revolution in thought by following careers of selfless help to others. The origins of this social welfare movement are located in England, where the selflessness of the work of such individuals as Booth, the Webbs, and the Fabians represents one of the highest flowerings of Western industrial society—which in its laissez-faire period has not been known for its humanity.

During the thirties it became relatively easy to adopt humanitarian attitudes because of the number of the unemployed. Mass unemployment made it difficult to equate being poor with moral failure. Older arguments seemed unsuitable to explain the new poor of the thirties, who were precisely those working-class and lower-middle-class individuals who strove hardest to maintain middle-class respectability and had lost their jobs through no fault of their own. New social policies were instituted and embodied in social security and social welfare legislation. These became a basis for retaining the new attitude toward public responsibility for the "lower classes," even in the prosperity that followed World War II. In the postwar period almost all sectors of society were prepared to accept or unable to resist these attitudes.

The attitudes of the thirties and their continuation into the present do not explain the current interest in poverty. If they did, the work of Leon Keyserling, who was a major prophet of the thirties, would not have gone unheard. He fought unsuccessfully and for the most part singlehandedly, keeping aloft in the affluent society an interest in the economics and humanitarianism of New Deal welfare capitalism. Factors other than ideology were at work in generating the new interest in poverty.

THE ROLE OF INTELLECTUALS AND ACTIVISTS

In part, the reopening of the poverty question can be traced to John Kenneth Galbraith's widely read study *The Affluent Society,* which pointed out the unresolved problems that existed in a self-satisfied and self-congratulatory society that prided itself on its tinsel and, in John Keats's terms, its "winged chariots." But by itself Galbraith's reopening of the issue was not enough. Michael Harrington's book *The Other America* helped to make poverty a public issue. A crucial event in this literary-intellectual history was Dwight Macdonald's *New Yorker* review of a whole series of books, including, in addition to those mentioned, books by Gabriel Kolko, Robert Lampman, and Gunnar Myrdal, which not only pointed out inequities in income distribution but showed that these inequities were increasing rather than diminishing.

Macdonald's review happened to reach John Kennedy, who at the time was campaigning for the presidency in the West Virginia primary election. Kennedy appropriated the poverty issue and in a series of campaign speeches linked it to the idealism of the thirties and the challenge of the future. When elected, Kennedy redeemed his campaign pledges by creating the President's Committee on Juvenile Delinquency, the Area Redevelopment Administration, and the Appalachian Development Program. In total these programs, both in reality and in projection, involved less than $1 billion and could justly be called tokenism. But apart from their inadequacies they became the basis for a government version of a new philanthropy aimed at the lower classes.

The implication that the poverty program is no more than a product of the ideological and intellectual efforts of scholars and moralists is certainly an overstatement of the case. Much earlier, in 1954, and independently of government, the school desegregation decisions (which were the result of the activities of blacks themselves) helped to mobilize black civil rights activities. It is difficult to overestimate the psychological effect of the civil rights movement on the Negro community, for it showed the Negro that changes in the system were possible. One major consequence of the *Brown vs. Maryland* Supreme Court desegregation decision was the spontaneous and unplanned anti-segregationist activity of youths and students in the South. The ability of the youth, and what is more, black youth, to find a means of expressing their idealism and taking direct action spread like wildfire throughout the nation and touched the white liberal youth of the North. As a result, "youth" as a category became motivated and activated for the first time since the thirties, an activation that remains disturbing and incomprehensible to the older generation, whether they were radicals, liberals, or conservatives in their own youth. Apparently the older generation would have preferred to regard the issue of discrimination against the Southern Negro as resolved, reflecting their personal accommodation and adaptation to a system with which many had maintained a measure of tension.

Black and white Northern liberal youth demonstrations in the South rapidly caused leaders of black communities to move to the front as quickly as they could to prove they were leaders. In placing themselves at the head of these new movements, black leaders adopted a tone of Christian righteousness, humility, moral superiority (Martin Luther King, Jr.), or radical passivism (Bayard Rustin). These ideologies overturned the older ideologies of the NAACP and temporarily overshadowed those of the consumption-minded black bourgeoisie. By 1960 this change in ideological tone had become so great that black leaders could no longer live in an upper-class cocoon within a segregated community. By 1960 all Negro leaders were forced to compete with the newer rhetoric of civil rights and the emerging rhetorics of black nationalism and militancy.

In the meantime, the belief within the black community that change in the abysmal conditions of segregation, poverty, and exploitation was possible stimulated large numbers of black youth, black ghetto dwellers, and Southern masses to reject the conditions under which they lived. The opening of these new possibilities led to direct and immediate demands, frequently utopian, which went far beyond anything the dominant white community and its leadership were prepared to grant. The excess of demands over response was illustrated very early by President Eisenhower's unwillingness to press the school desegregation issue to the limit. The subsequent history of the black revolution has shown that strong new demands have been resisted even after urban riots and threats of violence. Both delay and underfinancing have been characteristic of government response. Many blacks and some of their leaders, especially the more militant ones, soon began to feel that American society owed them immediate reparation for three hundred years of deprivation. They seemed not prepared to accept less. The reasoning of these groups focused on the parallel of the federal government in its response toward veterans after World Wars I and II: the logic was that disproportionate exploitation and deprivation deserved extraordinary compensation. These demands by blacks have been denied on the grounds that they are unreasonable, and that blacks, like other groups, should pull themselves upward gradually in the American tradition of "just rewards for proved usefulness." They are expected to demonstrate their right to receive rewards by hard work, morality, and self-discipline. The tradition of rewards appropriate to effort could only develop in a society where hard work and self-discipline have "paid off." Slavery, discrimination, exploitation, ghettoization, and segregation isolated the lower-class black from this tradition, denied him the opportunities to live within it, and justified inefficiency and lack of "motivation" and inner discipline. Under a system of slavery or equivalent discrimination, industry and efficiency would only result in the expropriation of the products of hard work. All work that produced more than minimal levels of return increased the profit to the slave owner and resulted in minimal gains to the slaves. The impairments produced by slavery and discrimination are not easily overcome. It is difficult for blacks reared in a tradition that devalues skills to acquire new work habits when adjusting to the white man's economic system.

The civil rights movement showed blacks that they could publicly vocalize their demands, and this fact altered the quality of their demands in a fundamental way. They could now address themselves directly to the white community and its leadership. They had learned to voice indignation, to state positively their demands, and to threaten violence to achieve them. The blacks created new myths by rewriting history and by creating a new black history which anchored their claims in the distant past.

Black acceptance of this new history, and the denial of their demands, led to an intolerance of the white man's delay and neglect of their problems. Black aggression, previously turned upon the self or upon other blacks in self-destruction and intracaste hostility, could now be turned outward upon the society at large. Thus the black power movement and urban race riots threaten white society. Liberals in particular now experience guilt, and older ethnics, along with Southern rednecks and the white politicians who live off prejudice, have become increasingly resentful. Backlash psychology is the major response to the civil rights revolution.

Perhaps liberals, more than any other group, were susceptible to black claims which were stated in terms the liberals believed in and could recognize. But when John F. Kennedy and Lyndon B. Johnson responded to the new humanitarian definition of the situation, they were only partly responding to their own liberal sentiments. Below the sentimental level, they also were responding to the clear and present political and social danger thrown forward by the open expression of black aggression. Neither Kennedy nor Johnson were purely ideological and idealistic in their policies.

FEDERAL POLICY TOWARD THE POOR

When John F. Kennedy took office he established the President's Committee on Juvenile Delinquency, designed as a major device to treat the issue of lower-class, slum (i.e., black ghetto) youth problems. For purposes of historical accuracy, it is useful to note that the foundations, particularly the Ford Foundation, were unusually prescient in having already designed programs to overcome problems of delinquency and poverty. Among these were Mobilization for Youth in New York City (then at the outset of its development) and the New Haven Community Development Program, Inc. Both already existed as functioning examples and became, as intended by the seed-program theory of the Ford Foundation, the models for the President's Committee. The foundation programs were small-scale test markets for the much larger federal programs. Compared with what happened later, both of these pre-existing programs have been conspicuously successful. In part this is because they operated with fewer of the political pressures of government programs and with more freedom from public scrutiny.

The Ford Foundation, through such consultants as Richard Cloward and Lloyd Ohlin, apparently adopted the approach of Saul Alinsky toward poverty and delinquency. Alinsky of Chicago during the thirties developed the approach of activating the indigenous poor to solve their own problems. The Ford Foundation built this approach into Mobilization for Youth and the New Haven Community Development Program. Alinsky, on his own, has continued to activate the poor, not only in Chicago but wherever his growing organization (the Industrial Areas Foundation) has been invited to help in the organization and activation of the black poor. Most recently his sponsors have been newly militant church groups in urban centers.

Robert F. Kennedy, as head of the President's Committee on Juvenile Delinquency, was given the task of redeeming his brother's campaign pledge to do something for the youth and the poor. But Robert Kennedy developed a special philosophy which went far beyond the immediate definition of what was required. His approach, following the Ford Foundation and Alinsky, was to coopt grass-roots participants from among local leaders. The leaders would help define the programs and would be used to alleviate the internal stresses and tensions in the community. In theory, only those who suffered from the problems would have a voice in their resolution. This meant bypassing: (1) local and state governments; (2) almost all established welfare and social service agencies; and, most crucial, (3) the established political machines of the Democratic party.

The bypassing of all vested interest groups meant in effect that Robert Kennedy was creating a new urban grass-roots political machine that potentially would have been the successor to the older urban ethnic politics of patronage. It would appear that the Kennedys, who earlier in Massachusetts had learned to circumvent traditional vested political interests, were now applying that formula experimentally on a national scale. By dealing directly with ethnic leaders, Robert Kennedy was establishing institutions that would be responsible to himself personally and independent of all other forms of control. A major novelty in this enterprise was that the entire operation, in contrast to the older system of municipally based ethnic patronage, was to be financed by federal funds. In an implicit and unheralded way this policy presaged a major revolution in American politics: no less than a recognition that older forms of municipal bossism would be destroyed, that the older ethnic politics would become obsolete, and, finally, that all welfare patronage would come under the aegis of a federal dispensation. Robert Kennedy's imagination went far beyond the system's capacity of acceptance.

According to Robert Kennedy's plans, local grass-roots leadership for new anti-poverty programs would include some indigenous politicians, heads of vested social service agencies, some leaders of municipal governments and their relevant departments, a selection of receptive local businessmen, clergymen, and congressmen. Two hundred of them were incorporated into local planning committees. In the original formulation, the only group conspicuously not represented was the poor. Not until much later, when the President's Committee on Juvenile Delinquency was replaced by the Office of Economic Opportunity, did the poor come to be recognized as a potential pool of talent for community action programs.

In the sixteen original communities where local community action programs were set up by Robert Kennedy, no poor were represented; all other groups, including Republicans, were. Republicans could be included because the local boards were ostensibly nonpolitical, high-minded, socially conscious, and not connected to the operations of traditional politics. The cooptation of Republicans lent credibility and legitimacy to the entire "nonpolitical" nature of Kennedy's new type of nonpartisan political machine.

Within the sixteen communities originally selected for participation in the program, local politics took on a new complexity. Since Kennedy had coopted most relevant local groups as participants in the governing boards, his program brought together a number of divergent interests. What happened in the sixteen cities in question was a struggle for local control of the program and its funds. The issue at stake was whether established organizations and the mayor's office would receive federal funds or whether new organizations would be created to receive them. The latter alternative would upset the established structure of community power. At the same time, power struggles began to occur between the various local leadership groups to gain control over the governing boards and the communities themselves.

In half of the cities selected for the new delinquency programs, the new organizations proposed by Kennedy were stillbirths: local leaders and municipal administrations could not resolve conflicts among themselves over the distribution of authority, funds, and patronage. Where established municipal administrations prevailed, no change could take place, and Kennedy was not able to reconstitute municipal politics.

Mobilization for Youth, the only one of Robert Kennedy's programs to enjoy even partial success, had the advantage of having been started earlier with Ford Foundation funds. When the President's Committee on Juvenile Delinquency was established, its support of MFY was added to that of the Ford Foundation. Even with the advantage of double sponsorship and a head start, MFY ran into a number of difficulties:

1. Staff consultants and social workers at MFY took the ideology of community activation seriously. They began to rouse the poor over issues of rent, housing, and education. By doing so they irritated municipal and neighborhood welfare, educational, and real estate orga-

nizations, which resented interference in their affairs by troublemaking amateurs. Moreover, established municipal interests in these fields and established party politicians saw these new activist social work programs interfering in affairs which they had successfully pre-empted as their own.

2. President Kennedy did not or was unable to devote himself to the problem of securing new funds to maintain and expand the program. Congressional resistance, lack of public emphasis on the problem, and intraparty bickering at the municipal level restricted large-scale spending.

3. From the point of view of the program sponsors, including the Ford Foundation, the problems that emerged were problems that plagued almost all other urban poverty programs. Even though the program was based on the Ford Foundation concept of managed innovation and change, many of its activist staff were more activist than top Foundation executives. Some of the Foundation grantees, like Mobilization for Youth, oversubscribed to Foundation philosophy, having believed in aspects of the philosophy before joining the community action programs. Mobilization for Youth was extremely effective in activating parents and youth, whether delinquent or not, on New York City's lower east side. Part of this effectiveness was based on the fact that youth and adults were paid fees and wages to act as militant activists. Some were hired by the hour for specific "demonstrations" and others by the year as consultants. The youthful demonstrators enjoyed their tasks since they found them more pleasureable than traditional forms of leisure and delinquency. Indigenous adult consultants took their own militant roles seriously since these new roles often coincided with their own legitimate aspirations. But with the aid of Foundation grants and the Foundation itself, they enjoyed a new respectability and power which grass-roots social action could never provide. It is not surprising, as we have indicated, that some consultants and youth made demands that were embarrassing to those in the program who were capable of being embarrassed. They attacked the New York Board of Education, the Welfare Department, the New York State Employment Service, the police, the courts, and the mayor of the city. Ultimately, the mayor retaliated by investigating the organization. Evidences of

theft, lechery, drunkenness, budgetary mismanagement, commingling of funds, and sheer incompetence and nonperformance of contracted obligations were alleged. No criminal charges were pressed, but a few officials resigned under pressure, budgets were reduced, and Mobilization for Youth lost its militancy and most of its financing.

In this instance the Ford Foundation was saved by its seed-money philosophy from its own inability to control its staff and its clients. Indigenous consultants who became convinced either of their own omnipotence or their "mission" because of their affiliation with an all-powerful Foundation, became a source of embarrassment to the Foundation. The seed-money philosophy allowed the Foundation to disassociate itself from Mobilization for Youth. New York City municipal government and various federal agencies were left to clean up a mess begun by the Ford Foundation. These government agencies harvested the crop seeded by the Foundation.

The death of President Kennedy cast the entire youth and poverty programs in a new light. Robert Kennedy, as head of the President's Committee, became a lame duck and stayed in the Johnson administration no longer than was respectable. Sargent Shriver, who remained to accept the position as head of the Office of Economic Opportunity (OEO), which was Lyndon Johnson's vehicle for coping with the poverty issue, appeared to want this job enough to adopt the program philosophy of the new President.

The new administration's plan was (1) to pour greater amounts of money into OEO than had previously been dreamed would be politically possible, and (2) administratively to reorganize the entire enterprise so that it would be carried out by established welfare agencies and party organizations controlled by loyal party members. By these measures the apparatus set up by Robert Kennedy was either circumvented entirely or put under the control of municipalities.

THE STRUGGLE TO REPRESENT THE POOR

The greater funds under Johnson, coupled with the freedom offered to local political machines and established welfare agencies, generated an enormous interest in OEO and all other poverty and youth projects. Because OEO offered a clear and visible funding opportunity for anyone wishing to come forward, many new agencies and organizations began to "relate" themselves to the new program, which until that time was generally regarded as too small to bother with.

1. City mayors looked to the new programs and budgets as a means of financing existing services through the federal rather than local budgets, and expanding existing programs at no added cost. The possibility of federal subsidies for municipal welfare programs looked like a partial resolution of local tax problems.

2. Social workers, charitable religious groups, private welfare agencies, community councils, and especially the research branches of all such groups saw in the new funds an opportunity to expand welfare programs under their aegis. They entered the contest for their fair share of the new funds with an ideology based on superior technical knowledge and a professionally established means for communicating with the poor. In these terms they claimed to be the most qualified recipients of the new funds.

3. The established community elites, many of whom did not live in the communities they represented, and especially those who had been coopted to the President's Committee, felt they were the legitimate heirs to the expanded budgets because by their own definitions they *were* the poor. For them, operating as ghetto leaders and feeling responsible for their constituencies, the federal funds offered a chance to solve local community and patronage problems.

4. The universities suddenly discovered there was a great deal they could do for the poor and stepped up their research efforts accordingly. Private, quasi-university research organizations suddenly realized that the poor could use their services. Many were organized for this purpose.

In short, all of these groups thought the poor could most properly come under their jurisdiction. For the first time in American history, being poor could become an economic asset for those who were not poor.

Soon a new body of "experts" came into being. After a short period of retooling, social workers, psychologists, psychiatrists, sociologists, urban anthropologists, ecologists, community health specialists, lawyers, accountants, and administrators were ready to make a special occupational claim based on their presumed expertise in dealing with the poor. Poverty became the basis for the creation of a new class of professionals which were "getting rich off poverty."

As well as creating a new professional "field," the new programs, which ostensibly were designed to solve the problems of the poor, inevitably attracted a large number of people who had an ideological and political interest in the deprived lower classes. Socialists, radicals, civil rights types, black nationalists, and older political activists from the thirties saw in the new programs and poverty organizations a way of influencing social policy in the direction of their own ideologies. In some instances these types were social workers who were employed in the programs and tried to influence policy from within. In other cases professional political activists such as Saul Alinsky set themselves up as pressure groups to point out the flaws, weaknesses, and fraudulence of the entire program. They preferred a structural resolution of the poverty problem.

As head of the Office of Economic Opportunity, Sargent Shriver attempted to adjudicate the various claims for funds and the staggering political pressures from above and below, particularly in Congress, city hall, and the executive branch of government. Shriver took the law literally by insisting that the poor be defined in terms of income, and, as a vital concession, that the poor actually be represented on the boards of community action agencies. In New York, for example, a City Council Against Poverty was set up. This council was to have a membership of approximately one hundred and would "be composed roughly as follows: 32 poor persons chosen by neighborhood groups in sixteen poverty areas in the city, fifteen officials of the city government, fourteen representatives of voluntary and social welfare agencies, eleven representatives of eleven major neighborhood groups in the city and various representatives of civil rights groups, religious, business, labor and ethnic groups." Inclusion of the poor threw all groups which claimed to represent the poor into confusion, since their legitimation now depended on proving that they actually knew some poor. A scramble ensued to find some real poor persons to be on the boards.

In one case a recent migrant to a major Eastern city became a representative of the poor in an otherwise undistinguished community action organization. He was elected to its governing board, resigned after an attempt to take it over, but as a representative of the poor became one of the top municipal officials in the municipal agency which controlled self-governing community action agencies. For him the American dream came true. It was discovered later that his rags included a degree from a Southern university.

Most of the local and genuinely poor were unaware of the larger issues and political struggles going on, simply because poverty usually results in a restricted and confined life. But social workers, with their techniques of "reaching out," were at times able to find some poor who could serve the purpose of representing other poor on the boards. This novel theory of economic democracy, designed to supply one-third of the membership of the boards, was not always easy to apply.

In New York and Philadelphia, where elections were held for the poor to enable them to elect their own representatives, no more than 5 per cent voted. Finding a mechanism that would allow the poor to elect themselves was not the only problem. Finding the poor was the major problem, a problem that could be solved only with considerable effort.

Usually the representatives of the poor on the boards and commissions were paid salaries of $75 to $100 a week. If they were *bona fide* poor, this meant they were no longer poor but now occupied a new kind of white-collar position. If they were merely "poor," they now had a stake in complying with the demands of the paid officials in the poverty program who presumably were their subordinates. The officials used the best techniques of education and indoctrination to insure that the poor understood the programs that were being designed for them. If the poor did not understand, or refused to understand, they were fired and separated from their paid positions in the poverty program. They could then revert to the status of clients in the programs they had helped to design for themselves. In a few cases the poor gained control of the new programs and caused untold problems for their sponsors. The incorporation of the poor into the decision-making process was fraught with difficulties.

THE NEW SERVICE BUREAUCRACIES

The procedure by which the poor were incorporated was accompanied by an increase in the number of new programs—the Job Corps, the

Manpower Development and Training Act, Head Start, Upward Bound, the Neighborhood Youth Corps, and remedial educational and therapeutic programs in an unimaginable variety. Many of these programs were designed as mass-production enterprises. Because it was necessary to "involve" the community, programs that had a dramatic and visible quality were enacted first; hence the proliferation of novel-sounding program names. For the same reason, many of the programs involved parades, arts and crafts, and especially dramatics and music activities, all of which have the quality of stimulating and demonstrating movement and action. While the activist, dramatic, and externalizing quality of these programs did not solve the poverty problem, nevertheless, coming as they did in the summer of 1965, they were probably successful in forestalling or at least mitigating dozens of riots that might otherwise have occurred during that summer.

Not all of the poverty effort, of course, was directed at forestalling riots. There were also long-term programs such as job training. In the job-training program the trainee was originally paid $1.35 an hour, a rate of pay which he could get without undergoing any training if he worked on the open unskilled market. Even if the individual finished his training, he still faced a market for jobs that required no training or for jobs that do not exist either because the skills involved are in contracting industries or because the jobs in question are unionized by Jim Crow industries and unions. Thus this program contained within it the danger that the trainee would discover that his training was useless, the chance that high dropout rates would jeopardize the program itself, and the danger that the trainee would riot and strike out against both inhuman treatment and fraudulent promises. Worsened frustration seemed to be built into these youth programs.

Apart from the black youth, most poverty programs today provide opportunities at a clerical, social work, white-collar, and professional level to groups that have been created in response to the existence of these opportunities. Blacks and whites in this category find themselves earning good incomes but able to do little about the problems they are supposed to help resolve. In some instances they feel they were employed only to enjoy the perquisites of the office and must alleviate this guilt by threatening violence and riots. In this way they can convince themselves that they are still activists and militants. They have become a new black and white bourgeoisie without a manifest function —but at the same time the major beneficiaries of the poverty funds.

This new black and white welfare bourgeoisie maintains a relationship with the rest of society that differs from that of the old black bourgeoisie described by E. Franklin Frazier. Instead of playing the role of aristocrat, this new bourgeoisie plays the game of agitator, revolutionary statesman, and bureaucrat. Organizational procedures, memoranda, forms in triplicate, dittos and duplicating equipment, office furniture, intercom systems, bullhorns, applications for grants, and continuous meetings, demonstrations, and trips are the substance of their way of life. In their world the whole external shell of revolutionary planning and conspiracy and foundation and government bureaucracy is re-enacted by individuals who, because of past exclusion, have no knowledge of the substance behind these forms. Their attachment to form rather than substance parallels the process of emulation described by Frazier in his description of the life styles of the older black bourgeoisie. Thus the new revolutionary welfare bourgeoisie acts out a form whose original forms they have never seen. The result is a visible inefficiency, mismanagement, lack of bureaucratic skill, incompetence, and insufficiency of training in the new bureaucracies. From time to time all this is revealed in the eruption of local and national scandals, such as in the HARYOU program of New York, where the most elementary bookkeeping and accounting procedures were deficient and hundreds of thousands of dollars were misplaced.

Coupled with this fetishistic reliance on bureaucratic form, the poverty programs have shown a thorough appreciation of the value of public relations and the concept of the image. In the face of their lack of security in their newly won positions and their lack of traditional legitimation, a substantial part of the activities of the new poverty bourgeoisie was oriented toward creating a positive image, with the result that most programs were geared to providing public relations for real and potential constituencies.

The civil rights and nationalist ideologies of the blacks provide a particularly convenient position from which to reply to critics of the poverty program, for regardless of the basis of the criticism, all critics can be labeled as racists, exploiters, and representatives of the hostile, repressive establishment. Criticism from idealists who demand that a program reach out and do something for the actual poor is labeled as immature. Such critics, it is claimed, have authority problems and do not understand the realities of the world—especially if they will not allow themselves to be coopted into the official programs as respectable revolutionaries and bureaucrats. Thus the programs are inviolate against any angle of liberal criticism.

We have talked as if the poverty programs have produced almost no results. While this may be true as far as the poor are concerned, there have been a number of other unintended results that are highly significant.

1. It has produced a new class, a poverty bourgeoisie, which though small in number is based on opportunities which previously did not exist. Thus the poverty programs distribute opportunities, though not necessarily to the poor.

2. Many professionals and ideologists who used to work in civil rights and protest movements have been coopted as officials in poverty programs. The poverty bureaucracy has become a career line for youthful ideologists and protestors who face turning points in their careers. Their concern with bureaucratic survival often mutes their passion for protest and converts them into officials.

3. Most important, this new class has a vested interest in legal representation of the poor. The category of the poor is thus a new legal entity in American society. To the extent that it exists, it further violates past fictions in democratic theory which hold that social, racial, and economic inequalities will not be recognized by the law. The suggestion here of a new form of segregation is reminiscent of the feudal estate.

CASTE AND CLASS IN THE COOPTATION OF THE POOR

The consequences mentioned above are irrelevant to the solution of the problems of the lower class. Yet all of the poverty programs have stimulated hopes on the part of those actual poor, particularly in the black lower class, who are sufficiently trained in recognizing middle-class fraud. The day of reckoning is postponed until the poverty programs are connected to institutional solutions which can produce tangible results; but even when such programs are so connected, the achievement of tangible results is usually so slow that it fails to pacify the poor. Thus riots and violence will continue to be a major, irrepressible part of the urban scene.

While the discovery that their aroused hopes may not be fulfilled has led to greater disenchantment and more violence among the poor, there are nevertheless a number of mechanisms by which this effect can be temporarily forestalled.

1. First of all, the poverty programs are continuously coopting the poor's leadership by absorbing activist leaders into official positions. This is the same process that historically has been used to coopt leaders of other ethnic groups in the United States. It robs the civil rights and community action movements of some of their potential for direct action. In the long run, however, this process is not likely to work, since new activist leaders will replace those who have been coopted.

2. American military commitments have provided a substitute set of opportunities for the poor who voluntarily or involuntarily become soldiers. The drafting of each black by the armed services helps to reduce the unemployment rate of black youth. But, again, this only forestalls and exacerbates the problem, because the returned veteran finds it all the more difficult to revert to his old status. He has become accustomed to a soldier's income and the right to kill.

3. The effect of large promises and minimal offerings stimulates demands for real and substantial programs and convinces the poor that they have a chance to get results on the basis of their emerging organizational strength. Continuous pressures from below may force government leaders and politicians to convert fake programs into real ones whether they originally intended to or not.

The creation of new social and economic expectations creates a dilemma. If, after hopes for opportunity and equality are raised, these hopes are either crushed or remain unfulfilled, idealistic philanthropists and opportunistic politicians help to create a mass disillusionment and a backlash that could result in the polarization of the entire society.

President Nixon, in the early period of his administration, was caught in this dilemma. Aware of the danger of race riots, of his lack of black political support, and perhaps even of the possibility of a greater backlash, he was also aware of the needs of his middle- and upper-class constituencies for "budgetary" responsibility (fiscal racism), their fears and anxieties caused by race riots and lack of law and order at a time when the war in Vietnam was still unresolved. He tried to ride both horns of the dilemma by encouraging token black capitalism, by recruiting a few civil rights leaders and liberal urbanists, and by firing them as soon as they demanded effective action. So far he has done much less than either Kennedy or Johnson in initiating or maintaining anti-poverty programs. His only positive solutions have been to increase the budget for law enforcement agencies and to threaten their use.

The great danger in American society vis-à-vis the lower class would be a complete reversal in policy by a federal administration representing the old middle-class ideology of "make the poor suffer." With such a policy reversal the administration might simply drop poverty programs altogether. This is not an impossibility, especially since the waste, confusion, and mismanagement that are characteristic of present programs have already begun to offend middle-class tidiness, anality, and respect for property values as embodied in a psychology of low taxes. This morality is very much alive among the newly prosperous ethnic working and lower middle classes, among residents of small towns in all parts of the country, and among all those retired people who are struggling against inflation; any proposals to reverse liberal policies toward the poor are thus politically appealing. Those who wished to reverse this economic policy could also claim that they were forestalling backlash and vigilante repression. Finally, the dilemma is exacerbated by the fact that any elimination of promised opportunities is in itself sufficient to cause riots.

Racial violence in the form of urban riots, looting, quasi-organized black nationalist vigilantism, and the individual and nonpoliticized violence of black rage has already begun to work in this direction. As such actions and events have proliferated, they have begun to produce a kind of backlash, white racism, and white nativism more virulent than any known in this century. The cry for law and order, the issue of crime in the streets (though crime is a genuine problem) are, in large part, an expression of this backlash psychology. A majority of American voters in the 1968 elections voted for a presidential candidate who used one or another of these slogans as part of his appeal. In the final analysis, it appears that race was not the decisive factor in the election: a generalized, diffused dissatisfaction with the Johnson administration was. But the specter of a racist, backlash psychology remains; the possibility that further racial violence will provoke overreaction among lower-middle-class, working-class, and middle-class whites into an American form of fascism cannot be dismissed. The possibility of such violence remains great because white political leaders and their constituencies appear unwilling to initiate programs that, though expensive, will promise more than the tokenism of the past.

Another threat to the development of effective programs is posed by some new leaders of the poor, the bureaucratic professionals, paraprofessionals, and bureaucratic revolutionaries who feel they have a vested interest in controlling and managing the poor. If, as is now occurring, they develop a feeling of special privilege, they will regard themselves as exempt from the ordinary criteria of administrative and budgetary accountability. Criticism of mismanagement can then be deemed as racist, irresponsibly radical, or rightist conservative and representative of the established powers. This would link their vested interests to existing programs and proposals regardless of their effectiveness. The possibility of achieving different anti-poverty and welfare programs that do not require their special services is limited, if not precluded.

For example, programs involving broad fiscal policy, economic planning, real urban renewal as opposed to black removal, industrial expansion, making the ghettos livable by the use of paint and polish, or any policy that attempted to get to the root of the problem and that would achieve the same results as social service projects would be opposed as an infringement on the bureaucrats' privileged access to the budget. More effective programs, not yet fully explored, have been opposed by leaders of the poor who are more concerned with protecting their own jobs than with the substance of those programs. The poverty bureaucracy now established may well become a means by which racial inequalities are legalized. Thus trainees and enrollees in racially unbalanced poverty and welfare programs all too often regard their program, their job, or their stipend as a right which is always inadequate and on the verge of being withdrawn by white racist politicians. Job training consists of large doses of race ideology, committee work, planning, and the acquisition of no skills. It qualifies the trainee only to make further threats and demands for poverty funds with which to sustain his sense of threatened and injured manhood.

Some leaders of the poor will become professional and social celebrities and will find themselves socially acceptable to and lionized by white society—especially the radical chic—precisely in proportion to their having a constituency that is socially unacceptable. In this sense the social cooptation of leaders would serve to maintain on a larger and more complicated scale the subordination of lower-class groups.

White political leaders and foundation officers, especially those of old Protestant upper-class backgrounds, appear within the past several years to have adopted this strategy. Black leaders have been given control of ghettos and ghetto schools, and poverty, social work, and educational positions. Token aid for housing has also been made available, and loans to black businesses, all of the small variety, are means, hopefully, of avoiding riots. Black power thus comes to terms with white power. Black power, operationally, means power over the black ghetto by black bureaucrats and black ideologues. This includes the power to exploit, threaten, and repress other blacks and other minority groups in the ghetto. White officials, teachers, and businessmen, among others, are to be replaced by native rulers. The native rulers, if they become committed to their own careers, will, hopefully, guarantee the peace. And surrendering political jurisdiction over the ghettos to blacks is a substitute for vast expenditures in housing, education, job training, and social services which would be necessary to solve the objective problems of the black poor. Black power appears to be a means of avoiding such expenditures. The trouble is that black power cannot attain these purposes. It cannot guarantee law and order because bureaucratic and nationalistic militants have trained themselves to threaten violence. Sometimes they are believed by their constituents; sometimes they are carried away by their own rhetoric, hence violence is always possible.

The chief danger of present poverty, civil rights, and black nationalist programs is that they rest upon the magnification of race separatism, race loyalties, and race differences. Let us imagine that the poverty and civil rights programs of the past ten years were continued and were successful, and that the poor entered into the economic system at levels commensurate with expanding economic functions and their numbers. It would still require at least several generations before blacks could in substantial numbers move out of service, unskilled, and blue-collar occupations. They would, because of their late entry into modern industrial society, remain a substantial plurality of the blue-collar and lower middle classes. As a result, race and economic issues would continue to be chained together, and those who are opposed to the economic interests of these classes would still be tempted to introduce the race issue. Thus the purely economic interests of the working classes would be more difficult to express because of the confusion of race and economic issues.

To prevent this confusion, leaders of both the black and white lower and lower middle classes would have to suppress race issues and attempt to find common economic and social grounds for their demand for full participation in the society. This solution appears to have been adopted by the United Auto Workers in Detroit, where blacks participate in their union primarily as union members, and in civil rights and race organizations as blacks. Such a response is possible only when blacks have full social and economic acceptance by their union and by management.

This acceptance can only operate effectively when blacks have been employed for sufficient lengths of time to achieve equality in seniority and thus are not laid off before whites. Equality of opportunity must coincide with equal training opportunities so that blacks have equal seniority with whites at all skill and occupational levels. Finally, there must be no premium on being black or white.

Such a solution involves enormously difficult problems for those committed to racially unbalanced poverty programs. All of the pressures for maintaining and establishing poverty and specialized welfare programs are based on racial and civil rights injustices which maximize racial identity and separateness as the basis for their jurisdictions. Most programs that are not oriented to fundamental economic solutions maximize these racial differences.

Purely economic solutions, not based on racial identity, would deprive race leaders and indirect colonial rulers of their jobs, perquisites, and functions. In a number of instances, attempts to institute such programs have resulted in mass demonstrations by the poor—demonstrations led by threatened leaders.

Insofar as racial leaders have allowed themselves to be engaged primarily in civil rights, nationalist, and racially based poverty programs, they may be unable to make the switch from racial to occupational and economic grounds. If the switch cannot be made, their programs and ideologies may become devices for continuing the separation and segregation of the races.

In most present poverty programs and ideologies there is the inherent danger of creating a separate world of the poor which will be circumscribed by program boundaries and a separate leadership corps. With the bureaucrats and indigenous political elites having a vested interest in a quasi-legally defined "culture of poverty," the basis exists for a permanently subsidized, socially segregated lower class and a permanent corps of colonial officials. This is the new lower-class philanthropy.

If present trends continue, a new caste system may replace the present *de facto* second-class citizenship. The new *de jure* second-class citizenship would be based on the operation of federal programs and budgets supported by law. The system would be administered by indigenous leaders and their white bureaucratic masters and counterparts who would manage the new colonial administrators, and the net result would be a new caste position for the American black which surpasses the old primitive Southern caste system in its capacity to cope with modern organized society. Modern bureaucracy could create a more efficient caste system. The low-budget policy of the Nixon administration has appeared to cut off this possibility.

13. Rejection of the new society by radical youth

As fewer and fewer primary producers are necessary to maintain American industrial productivity, the lower and impoverished classes find it more and more difficult to enter the productive sector of society. Instead they come to depend on the federal budget as a major source of support. In structural terms, an increasingly large percentage of American middle-class youth find themselves in the same immediate economic position as the poor. There is little or no demand for them on the primary labor market, and the age at which they enter the labor market has become higher and higher. Many youth now remain in college until past their mid-twenties, and more and more of them attend college through the age of twenty-one or twenty-two. Middle-class youth differ from the lower-class poor not in terms of their relationship to the market but rather in terms of the level at which they are supported by the philanthropic systems. They also differ in terms of the financial reserves available to them (their parents' assets) and their long-range prospects. Radical youth movements in America are best understood by understanding the major elements in the contemporary American revolution.

THE SOURCES OF STUDENT RADICALISM

Student radicals have been estimated to be about 2 per cent of the total college population. At first they were concentrated in the better-known upper-middle-class universities and colleges; now they are becoming diffused through all colleges and comprise a larger percentage of the total student body. In a confrontation with the police or college administration, they may also draw to their support various hippie or other disaffiliated students as well as those who may resent the stupidity of the police and administrators who deal with radical students. It is by now obvious that the number of disaffiliated students far exceeds the number of radical students, and that the vast majority of students in all universities are mainly concerned with completing their education, getting a degree, and entering the adult occupational world. Nevertheless, the "critical mass" (the number of student activists necessary to close or destroy a university) may be relatively small, perhaps from 35 to 150 students. Given an issue and the unintended cooperation of the police and the college administration, they can gain the support of up to five hundred or a thousand students. Since it takes the initiative of only a few to seize and occupy buildings, to provoke violence, and to destroy property, this small number may be sufficient. Their provocations are important, for the students are collectively our own children and the property to be destroyed is collectively of value to the whole society. Even in the eyes of the establishment, education involves not only job training for individuals but the perpetuation of the cultural traditions of the civilization.

The small number of radicals does not permit us to treat them as mere "deviants" or as individual psychological misfits. These youth are the result of the whole operation of American society which has helped to produce the youth revolution. Most of the young radical students have come from the upper middle class, primarily the new middle class. Their parents are prosperous professionals, administrators, and bureaucrats. Most of the parents have succeeded in the new middle class as a result of the middle-class revolution in the post-World War II era: they are college graduates and, in comparison with the American past, are relatively educated, cultured, and liberal. They have been tolerant, permissive, and warm supporters of the children's educational and cultural aspirations. If anything, they have been so interested in their children's aspirations and achievements that they have "invaded the privacy" of their children. In other words, they have attempted so much to influence their children in positive directions that children with inclinations toward self-defined, positive achievement have had to resist the pressures made by parents in their own behalf. In short, parents, by overidentifying with their children, have robbed them of their independence, especially of the means by which adolescent youth discovers itself and its own identity. This has been called personality absorption.

In their own youth the parents had different problems. As children of immigrants or as small-town farm boys and girls, they could rebel against the "ignorance," lack of culture, lack of sophistication, political innocence, and "un-Americanism" of their parents. Their own revolution against their parents and society forced them into the mainstream of American society.

Unlike their parents, contemporary middle-class youth are already there. They have a surfeit of culture, sophistication, and middle-class respectability. They have no experience of the depression or deprivation which spurred their parents to seek a college education and accept the enjoyment of middle-class prosperity in the post-Keynesian bureaucratic society. As a result, the youth take prosperity and affluence for granted: while enjoying it and at times seeking to discover the feeling of poverty, they also complain of the shallowness of middle-class life. Their parents, regardless of their present liberalism or past radicalism, feel that their own prosperity is a personal accomplishment. In enjoying the fruits of their economic and social achievements, they unwittingly force their children to enter the ratrace. From kindergarten through high school, and in many cases through college, youth feel they are the victims of their parents' aspirations. They feel they have been manipulated and exploited to achieve goals which will embellish their parents' self-image as accomplished, cultured, educated, and important people. The children not only resent this but are likely to see their parents as frauds. To them the parents' self-image is more an image than a reality.

Because their parents have an immigrant, small-town, or rural lower-middle-class background, and because their parents have only imperfectly absorbed the culture, sophistication, and life styles which they cling to for themselves and demand of their children, the children feel all too often that they are being exploited and manipulated for ends that are insecure at best. They feel that the permissiveness of their parents is not genuine but only a compromise between insecurely held values and a desire for "mere" success. When the parents are "swingers" or "beautiful people," the children are asked to absorb role models and cultural styles that are so ephemeral as to be little more than sophisticated nothingness. The children become beautiful people and resent and attack either their parents or the educational institutions that would make substantive demands on them.

They also see contradictions between their parents' work and their parents' values. Their parents' managerial, bureaucratic, or professional occupations make them appear to the youth to be mere clerks, technicians, paper-shufflers, and functionaries in large-scale organizations and businesses that pander to lower values and goals than the ones which their parents taught them to value. The youth regard their own goals and values as superior, so that their image of their parents as relatively warm, permissive, but manipulative and exploitative hypocrites is confirmed.

FORMS OF YOUTH REBELLION

The youth respond in many ways. Some freak out. To do so is to give up the ratrace for the pursuit of personal values, music, dancing, bizarre dress, and sexual styles which emphasize immediate gratification and are noncompetitive, nondisciplined, and anti-ratrace. To the extent that this style has an ideological base, it emphasizes love, communitarianism, personal pleasure, and hostility to the impersonal, bureaucratic, and disciplined. It values passivity, subjectivity, innerness, the sensual and nonrational experiences of mood, color, touch, and beat, and a mixture of all these in kaleidoscopic effects that defy linear exposition. It draws on versions of Zen Buddhism, Indian mysticism, witchcraft, American Indian peyote culture, primitive tribalism, and anabaptist communitarianism. This freaked-out generation sustains itself with pot, LSD, amphetamines, and other drugs which symbolize both its rejection of the square world and its identification with a youth culture that is presumably nonexploitative, nonmaterialistic, anti-rational, communitarian, and idealistic. This entire culture is, of course, sustained by commercial adult institutions and mass media, the DJ, the music packager, adult prophets of perpetual youth, and (with respect to drugs) the pharmaceutical companies and the Mafia.

Most radical youth reject the overall approach of the freaked-out generation, the hippie, the crazy, or the yippie, though they sometimes pursue some of the activities of that group. These include pot but not addictive drugs; folk music but less rock; the sloppiness of Che or Fidel dress styles but not the ultra-mod; sexual freedom but not a sole preoccupation with it. They reject freaked-out culture mainly because that culture permits the establishment to continue in existence. Pure hippies, in their eyes, cop out from the revolutionary struggle to transform the world, while pure crazies merely mock politics and middle-class culture.

The political stance of radical youth cannot be understood solely in terms of reactions to the family, problems with parents, or distorted psychological reactions to personal conflicts. Apart from personal and psychological factors, American society has supplied the basis for their reaction. In the late fifties and early sixties the children born after World War II were in their late teens and began to enter college. In college they sought new avenues to express an idealism which may well have been instilled by the liberalism of their parents but which was denied by their images of those same parents' philistinism, hypocrisy, manipulation, and psychological exploitation. Their idealism sought an anchorage in *ideas* that could express both their discontent and their desire for new goals for action. A reservoir of ideas was conveniently made available to these youth by an older generation of radicals. The older radicals, the critics of Western society during the thirties and late forties, had evolved a critical, leftist image of American society which supplied the youth with the ideas they needed to objectify their idealism and contempt.

THE NEW AND THE OLD LEFT

The older critical generation included sociologists, social theorists, philosophers, economists, and free-lance writers—Norman O. Brown, Paul Jacobs, Norman Mailer, Marshall McLuhan, John Kenneth Galbraith, David Riesman, Daniel Bell, Lewis Feuer, and Hal Draper are leading examples. These authors, some radical and some liberal, presented images of American society which, together or separately, were not necessarily consistent, politically radical, nor related to the uses which youth made of them. But they did supply the raw materials out of which youth could work out its own often inconsistent and ever-changing programs. This is not to say that these thinkers alone supplied the framework out of which the ideologies of youth emerged. Rather, these men were the outstanding representatives of several past generations of critics of Western society going back to the predecessors of Marx, Weber, Veblen, and Freud. Thus if one wished to assign responsibility to the suppliers of the radical ideas, it would have to be distributed among the entire left-of-center intellectual tradition and the teachers and writers who disseminated that tradition. Also responsible would be the center and right-of-center individuals and institutions that evoked the criticisms in the first place.

This overall criticism of American society includes the notion that it is dominated by bureaucratic or power elites which manipulate or control the rest of society for economic and political ends. The middle classes are turned into conformists, bureaucratic hacks, and one-dimensional men. The people are brainwashed by mass media which both render them passive and subject them to a tasteless, mindless mass culture. Life is experienced vicariously, and the true sources of man's creativity, emotionality, and sexuality are denied. Instead, a sterile rationality alienates man from his emotional, sexual, spontaneous, genuine self and identity. The society rewards passivity and conformity by making consumer goods easily accessible, by allowing permissiveness in personal consumption, and by permitting self-indulgence so long as no one upsets the political applecart. In the meantime this same society neglects the poor, the black, the mentally ill, the grape-pickers, the aged, the Indian, the ill, and the Vietnamese peasant. Necessary social expenditures and values are sacrificed to individual hedonism and profits. Everything is geared toward exploitative corporate profits, largely at the expense of the underdeveloped areas of the world and under a neo-colonial policy that practices outright intervention and repression when the rights of American business are interfered with. The universities, the foundations, and the government are agencies by which the industrial-military complex and a power elite govern America and corrupt all that they touch. All of the white-collar world, including the students, are the objects of manipulation and brainwashing which, if they accede, makes them dehumanized, automatons, and careerist functionaries. The major themes of this ideology could be extended indefinitely, and, as taken over by youth, have been so extended.

YOUTH DEMANDS

Radical youth movements are much more complicated than freak-out styles. While the radicals base themselves on the same ideological themes, they have attached themselves to a succession of heroes such as Mao, Castro, Che, Regis Debray, Frantz Fanon, R. D. Laing, Daniel Cohn-Bendit, Eldridge Cleaver, Huey Newton, and Malcolm X. In addition, the objectives of particular youth movements, demonstrations, sit-ins, confrontations, and busts have been limited and specific. As they have evolved, student youth movements have touched a bewildering variety of issues in odd combinations which reflect both past demonstrations and a congery of unrelated and often opposed political ideologies. The epidemiological character of these movements, their uneven rates of borrowing from each other, and the effect on them of the success or failure of past demonstrations have resulted in an almost incomprehensible pattern of the political activities of radical youth. As a result, it is impossible to summarize all the demands of the student movement. In one university the demands may include forty-six items, in another five. During any one sit-in, demands may shift, escalate, or be dropped with changes in the situation or with changes in the leadership of *ad hoc* groups. During a given period a great number of demands in different universities will focus on one issue, such as draft evasion, while at another time each campus may emphasize issues peculiar to its local situation.

Over time the demands have included free speech, free sex, no university cooperation with draft boards, no recruitment by Dow Chemical or the CIA, abolition of the ROTC, and no university defense work. They have included anti-draft demonstrations, the burning of draft cards, demands for the unilateral pull-out of troops from Vietnam, and provision of sanctuaries for draft evaders.

In the university the demands have included rights to a voice in the hiring, firing, and promotion of professors, rights to determine curricula, rights of control over mixed dormitories, protection of the rights of pregnant professors, and seats (up to a majority) on all university committees and senates. Both black and white students have demanded open enrollments, the admission of Negroes on a quota basis, segregated and unsegregated housing, black and "third-world" institutes, and the employment of black and third-world professors. They have protested on issues of university expansion into ghetto areas at the expense of ghetto housing, and they have demanded university-subsidized ghetto housing for the poor. They have struck for peoples' playgrounds and against the enclosure of the college commons. At times they have struck against excessive or increasing fees, against cafeteria food, and against class schedules. They have demanded exemptions from examinations and the abolition of grades; liberation from required courses and from subject matter which, by its nature, requires discipline and protracted study, especially mathematics, the sciences, and languages; resignations of professors, deans, presidents, and trustees whose ideologies are not acceptable. They have demanded that others of the university staff be fired because they are repressive and have denied academic freedom to students and student groups. They have struck over the right to be immune from raids by the police, especially "pot" raids, but also from arrests over panty raids. Frequently they have struck in order to achieve immunity from crimes committed during protests designed to achieve other ends.

Off the campus, students who were not necessarily radical helped to make Eugene McCarthy a serious candidate for President and helped to drive President Johnson from the Democratic primary. By other means they helped to elect Governor Reagan and President Nixon, and they may be in the process of unwittingly electing rightists, conservatives, reactionaries, and racists whenever they affect the election process by provoking white conservative backlash. Some radical groups intentionally provoke backlash actions by the establishment in order to accelerate polarization and ultimately to bring on the revolution.

If we scrutinize the full panoply of these demands, we can classify them into three major types. The first deal with Vietnam. This includes draft resistance, demonstrations against the war, the ROTC, military research, and cooperation between the university and the draft board, and support for Eugene McCarthy. These demands reflect the students' special class interests in that they hope to avoid fighting in a war which they consider senseless, at a time when they feel they should be doing other things.

The second set of demands is geared toward control over the university, its staff, curriculum, rules and procedures, housing policies, and admission policies. Radical students regard the universities as theirs or as jointly owned by themselves and their teachers.

The third set of demands concerns the universities' policies toward housing, planning, and the poor. While these issues have stimulated a number of dramatic demonstrations at Harvard, Columbia, the University of Pennsylvania, and elsewhere, they have not taken hold as issues with great dramatic appeal.

Seen in a broader social perspective, the student demands are not as unreasonable as members of the older generation may think. Certainly demands relating to the war reflect a personal interest in the political process, rather than "pure ideologies." The demands for student participation in the university administration reflect a profound disenchantment with both the university and the students' own role in it. In some cases universities are large and dehumanized, and when professors and administrators neglect students in favor of consulting work, research, and expansion per se, student demands appear to be appropriate. But the same demands are made in large and small universities, in research and teacher-oriented universities, in "liberal" and reactionary universities, and in professional schools as well as graduate schools. In fact, the greatest dissatisfaction and the greatest demands appear more often in liberal universities than in conservative or reactionary ones. It appears that liberalness and permissiveness are often interpreted—not always incorrectly—as signs of weakness or indecision on the part of faculty and administration within the university. With few exceptions, the students have focused their demands on issues of the larger society as they touch upon the university. Thus students, with the exception only of the McCarthy campaign, the Weatherman bombings, and the 1970 election campaigns, seem to want to make the revolution on the campus: almost without exception they have reached for issues which do not interfere with their presence on the campus or the completion of their degrees.

In comparing their stated aims with their accomplishments, it is clear that students have not been unsuccessful in their campus-based revolution. They have forced universities to include students on faculty committees, senates, and boards of trustees. They have achieved coed dormitories and the elimination of parietal rules. They have forced universities to sever their connections with military research and, in some cases, to sever or limit their connections to the Defense Department. They have ended university ROTC programs and have forced universities to cease cooperation with draft boards. At least temporarily they have stopped university "invasion" of ghetto territory, and they have increased black enrollments in some major universities. By their support of McCarthy and their direct attacks on President Johnson, they contributed to Johnson's decision not to seek the presidency. With the help of Mayor Daley, the Chicago police, and the TV news reporters, they contributed substantially to the victory of President Nixon.

The demands and successes of the student movement do not exhaust the full range of ideological objectives that radical youth espouse. According to their ideology, the university and the student movement are a vehicle for social and revolutionary "change." For the radical youth, the idea of "restructuring" the university is simply preliminary to creating a base for radicalizing the entire society. The ultimate demand of radical youth movements is for a total political and economic revolution in American society—the end of the military-industrial complex, the exposing and replacing of the power elites, and the end of imperialism, neo-colonialism, and racism. According to this ideology, the university is the central institution by which the American establishment operates. It not only trains new cadres of technicians for the corporations and colonial administrations, but becomes the research and development branch of capitalist, military, and imperialist establishments. Some groups would destroy the universities as a means of destroying the establishment, arguing that *no* universities would be better than the present ones, which serve only to perpetuate the establishment. Other groups would merely gain control of the universities in order to make them serve their own political ends rather than those of the establishment. The most extreme radical students, some of whom are foreign students, reject the whole idea of focusing upon the university as a key object of attack. For them the objective of the youth movement is to create an alliance between the world's students and intellectuals, blacks in Africa and America, the oppressed working class, and the underdeveloped nations, especially—but not only—Maoist China. Their objective in forming this alliance is to pull down or destroy the whole establishment.

Thus the idea of changing the university is only the first step. As a consequence the welter of specific student demands, often contradictory and confusing, can never be met because many of them are demands which no university can meet. Other specific demands can be met in terms of their manifest content, but radical students have operated on the premise that the granting of particular demands will be followed by new demands that are more extreme. Each student success leads to an escalation of demands. Sometimes demands can be met by coopting students to student-faculty committees which are made part of the administrative apparatus. In this way some students become a part of the establishment by protesting against it. They, like older intellectuals, are to a point cooptable.

REVOLUTIONARY MEANS AND THEIR IMPLICIT PSYCHOLOGICAL VALUES

Up to now we have talked mainly about the ends of the radical student movement. Apart from its ultimate, underlying revolutionary objective, its means are much more important than its ends.

In their righteousness, youth feel entitled to picket, demonstrate, sit-in, occupy buildings, and prevent, if possible, the operation of the university. Professors and students have been threatened, beaten, and at times terrorized. Presidents and deans, as well as professors, have been escorted from classes and offices. Files have been looted for evidence of university cooperation with the industrial-military complex and the police. Papers have been burned, including draft registration data and scholarly manuscripts. Mail has been opened and destroyed. Buildings have been bombed and burned, furniture destroyed, and walls defaced. All this is done in the name of freedom.

In defense of free speech and free education, universities have been closed and classes prevented from meeting. Lecturers have been harassed on the grounds that they were fascist and anti-democratic. The rights to education of the vast majority of students have been denied and deferred on the justification that all change is introduced by a radical, revolutionary elite minority. Change, it is argued, is not possible without busting a few heads. In these times of violent and not-so-violent upheaval, the university ceases to function as an educational institution—though radical youth would argue that the experience of "revolution" is an education in itself. The excitement, the feelings of communal brotherhood, the endless meetings, the debates, charges and counter-charges, the folk singing, the exhilaration of mob action, provide a sense of euphoria, ecstasy, and "sterile excitation," as the sociologist Georg Simmel put it, that becomes a value in itself. The feelings of communal brotherhood and the euphoric loss of conventional senses and of limits of self (the sense of being a stranger to oneself) are major by-products of all revolutions and pseudo-revolutions which, once experienced, are an incentive to continue the revolution indefinitely in its most intensive and violent stages. A student revolution helps to overcome the sense of isolation, alienation, and impersonality that youth sometimes experience simply because, as youth, they have not yet made commitments either to work or to others. Commitments mean that personal activities are, at least in part, routinized and rationalized, that is, reduced to methodical and organized procedures.

For adults the necessity of doing one thing in a systematic, methodical way over long periods of time runs counter to the need for immediate and total involvement which revolution, violence, and mob action evoke. Of course, some adults, faculty members, and even university administrators can experience the same sense of enthusiasm, euphoria, and involvement as well as commitment to temporary crises situations—those who are perpetual youths, those who regress to their youth, or those who wish to escape from routine and the boredom of their own careers and work. The campus crisis, both in preparation and in operation, so well described in the case of Harvard by Steven Kelman in *Push Comes to Shove,* allows one to suspend one's normal sense of reality and to experience new and different emotions and moods at relatively intense levels.

Unfortunately, during campus crises the normal work of a university, such as teaching, research, and administration, must be dropped. From the standpoint of what is *usually* considered education, a campus crisis results in the wasting of a year or at least a term. In China, where youth revolts have been part of the cultural revolution, the education and training of the entire youth population appears to have been delayed for at least five years in a society that desperately needs technicians, teachers, administrators, and scientists in order to carry out its own stated objectives.

American society has been more fortunate than China. Its youth revolts have occurred in American colleges and universities and, in most cases, have been of short duration. Moreover, they usually have been confined to the liberal arts and social science faculties, which produce no well-defined product. Science and engineering colleges have suffered little from the campus revolts. Since a major function of the American university in recent years has been to take youth and professors off the primary labor market, campus revolts and crises do not interfere with the productive sectors of society. The relative isolation of American universities, in contrast to the cultural revolution in China, has so far prevented the youth revolution from having a major impact on the rest of society.

From the standpoint of individual colleges, their students, and their staffs, however, college crises have often been disruptive. Besides the loss of scholarly and educational productivity, individual faculty members have frequently resigned from a crisis-bound university, and applications for admission have declined. Thus a first-rate college, after a prolonged student revolt, can in a short time become a second-rate college. Other colleges may profit from hiring its professors who resigned. The supreme irony of events occurs when professors resign from one university (such as Berkeley) because of student revolts and join another faculty (such as Harvard) only to find that the student revolt has followed them.

One question still unanswered is whether youth can destroy not just one university but the entire university system. If the university were to become politicized, polarized, and the center of continuous conflict not only between radical students and faculty or administration but also among the faculty and between various radical and nonradical factions, it is possible that no conventional educational functions could survive in the university. Instead it would become a center for ideological and political experimentation and conflict. If this should become the standard—and it is a definite possibility—then the problem of conventional education will become intensified. Since the educational functions of universities are important to an industrial society, these functions will have to be met elsewhere.

YOUTH IDEOLOGIES: RIGHTEOUSNESS

To argue, as we have, that youth's feeling of righteousness is the cause of extremist and violent student tactics overstates the case. An explicit motive for such tactics is also to be found in the political strategy of radical youth groups. Violence as a tactic has two separate advantages. First, it can aim at provoking a response, especially police intervention. Once this is done it aims at provoking police brutality, counterviolence, and excessiveness. After these two stages are accomplished, the student or faculty radical can call foul play, denounce the administration, condemn the police, and rally the noncommitted students to the cause of the revolution. By this process noncommitted students are, they hope, politicized and radicalized, or at least converted into potential radicals or revolutionaries who will participate in future actions. Thus even when radical students are defeated on a specific issue or in a specific crisis, they count the crisis as a victory if they can cite large increases in the number of participants in the student revolt. Since the overall goal of the student revolt is not the specific crisis but the radicalization of the entire society, the gain in actual or potential adherents to the cause is more important than small victories or defeats. The present is only preparation and recruitment through crisis, and confrontation is a major goal. Only the last victory, the last great battle, counts.

Conversely, radical students are often disappointed when the police are not called or when issues are settled without violence or crisis, even if in that situation the students have won their specific demands.

ACTIVISM

While righteousness is one of the major contributions of youth to a radical ideology, it is not their only contribution. Another of their contributions is activism. Activism has many dimensions, but it can best be described by what it is not. Radical youth have been critical of the older generation of leftists and radicals, especially of the noncommunist left, who appear to them to spend their time in endless argument and debate. Young radicals have argued that the polemics of the old left and its concern with statements of aims and methods are major preoccupations which prevent it from actively engaging in organizational work, demonstrations, strikes, and crises. Thus the old left was never able to create a revolutionary situation.

Young radicals, responding to arguments for and against the "end of ideology," began to argue for and participate in immediate direct action. It did not matter whether goals were clear, aims agreed upon, or an imagined blueprint for the new society worked out. Youth argued that the goals, aims, and outcome of revolution are never more than an emerging possibility. They are shaped spontaneously by the process of revolution itself and cannot be predicted. Therefore, radicals can ignore long-term goals, ideologies, and blueprints and proceed to the immediate task of creating the revolutionary situation. What matters is not thought and planning but radical sincerity and a willingness to commit oneself to short-range actions that are morally unimpeachable and radical in spirit.

Activism as a pure value is only one approach. Another is the destruction of all corruption for its own sake. Since society is repressive, corrupt, and undemocratic, it is only necessary to destroy and not worry about what comes after the revolution. Once all forms of repression have been destroyed, the leaders of the new society will be able to restructure society so that true freedom can be realized. This argument frees the revolutionaries from accountability for their immediate actions and allows them to engage in revolutionary action self-righteously.

The activist ideology has a long and disreputable old-world ancestry. The anarchist Nechaev glorified nihilist violence. Bakunin, also an anarchist, placed special value on individual acts of violence. Lenin, though seen by some biographers as a disciple of Nechaev, denounced the senseless, unorganized violence of the Narodniki and the anarchists, as Marx had earlier denounced Bakunin. Conventional Marxism, and especially Leninism, emphasized discipline, organization, control, and the professionalization and bureaucratization of violence and action. Lenin and Marx laid great emphasis on the ideological control of violent action.

Georges Sorel, the French social philosopher, on the other hand, rejected sterile rationality in making a revolution and emphasized the need for the mytho-poetic, the irrational, and the emotional element in revolution. If scientific grounds were to be the basis of revolution, Sorel felt that the revolution would surely fail, for trade unions, business, and government would be able to solve the technical problems of capitalism by the equivalents of a welfare state. If a true revolution was to be achieved, it had to be achieved on emotional and irrational grounds. Only in that way would it be possible to secure a society rich in emotional, nonrational ends. Violent action would not only polarize the classes, it would also add the myths of violence and heroism and thereby attract the masses by overcoming the greyness, drabness, and alienation of a sterile and rational existence.

Sorel's argument was picked up by Mussolini who, on this basis, converted socialism to fascism which was to be heroic, athletic, dangerous, masculine, and Roman. Fascism would give the masses deeper, richer, and higher values to aspire to, and would again overcome the sterility and rationality of bourgeois existence. Mussolini's argument was in turn picked up by the National Socialists, particularly Alfred Rosenberg, who, in combining it with racist theories advanced by Comte de Gobineau, De Bonald, Houston Stewart Chamberlain, and Nietzschean ideals, created a myth of the Nordic superman. He was to be active, nonneurotic, anti-intellectual, uncomplicated, strong, heroic, and athletic. He achieved his strength through his job, valued his honor, and was not afraid of blood or bloodshed. The Nazis were activists unabashed by legalisms, principles, ideologies, or programs. They engaged in direct and immediate action. Because they saw it as decadent, they hated Jewish and bourgeois intellectualism, neuroticism, and introspection. The Nazis possessed the absolute truth and felt that they had the *right* to impose it upon a majority—and, if necessary, to destroy the majority.

This is not to say that contemporary radical youth directly emulate Nazis and fascists, or that they are aware of the anarchist origins of their thought. On the contrary, most would deny all such connections.

It is only an emotional affinity to activism and direct, immediate, and violent action that characterizes radical youth and a vast variety of anarchist, fascist, Nazi, and communist revolutionary movements.

In all of these movements there is a basic romanticism, a worship of the direct, the real, and the intense emotional experience. The subjective, the self-questioning, and self-doubt are alienating from reality and immediate experience. Separation from others, or the lack of a sense of community, are indicators of this social alienation, whose causes are capitalism, the establishment, the system, bourgeois society, commercial culture, careerism, and professionalism. Overcoming the causes of alienation through revolution, confrontation, and crisis becomes a way by which youth feel that a revolutionary can achieve an intense, exciting, and nonalienated existence. At the same time the dialectic guarantees that after the revolution alienation will be permanently abolished. André Malraux, in *Man's Fate,* Dostoevsky, in *The Possessed,* and Albert Camus, in *The Stranger,* document this phenomenology at perhaps its fullest and most dramatic level; and Max Weber, in *Politics as a Vocation,* presents it in terms of social science.

While it is more an emotional affinity than a direct intellectual borrowing that results in a connection between the "ideology" of radical youth and their forms of activism, for the ideology itself there is a direct theoretical basis in the works of Herbert Marcuse and Norman O. Brown. Marcuse draws his emphasis on alienation from Marx, especially the early Marx, who saw modern industrial society splitting men from each other and separating the life functions into distinct and separate spheres. The emotional, the expressive, the creative, and the physical were separated from the rational, the intellectual, and the artistic. One of these elements was so separated from all the others that by itself it became the basis of Marcuse's one-dimensional man—a monstrosity who developed one faculty at the expense of all others. But in addition to all of this, modern capitalism made sterile rationality its guiding principle. The rationality of the marketplace has prevailed over the direct, human, social relationships of barter and the small self-sufficient community. Modern capitalist society has created the most advanced forms of alienation, which can only be destroyed by ending the system of private property. The solution to this state of affairs is scientific socialism, which would end property and therefore the state, end repression and alienation. Men could then finally return to their full and original social nature.

Marcuse and Brown justify their rejection of modern industrial society on Freudian grounds. They argue that Freud demonstrates the importance of the emotional, the irrational, the sensual, and the sexual as the roots of personality. These are the sources of the energy of man, his creativity, his art and poetry, his myth-making, and his experience of himself as a warm, emotional, human being. The primary sexual energy, eros, the libido, the pleasure principle, and the id are repressed in the process of early socialization. Once this energy is repressed, it transforms itself into myth, poetry, the arts, and other forms of cultural creativity. It expresses itself in human play, games, ceremony, and ritual. It enriches the emotional and sensual life of the individual because, even though disguised, it is present, and, as transformed, is available to the social, cultural, and artistic life of the individual and society.

So far Freud, Marcuse, and Brown agree; but at one point Marcuse and Brown depart from Freud. They argue that industrial society is so rational, repressive, impersonal, and manipulative that individuals are unable to reach down to the sources of their creativity. They not only are repressed by the system, but they unwittingly repress themselves. Since psychic energy is not permitted gradual and continual release, repression enters and becomes a source of alienation, or the eruption of overrepressed energy becomes a source of psychic breakdown. Only by manipulation through the mass media are individuals permitted the privilege of emotional identification. But such identification is spurious. These individuals identify with premanufactured cardboard gods, pseudo-heroes, and television- and cinema-induced violence, pornography, and heroics, which, in their very artificiality, fail to provide the necessary release. They fail because they reduce individuals to passive spectators of life and culture consumers rather than allowing them to become creative producers. All the individual can do is assert himself by engaging in a self-directed activism which can destroy the capacity of the system to manipulate.

YOUTH AND BUREAUCRACY

These arguments, and especially the activist solution, are attractive to youth. In the extended adolescence of contemporary American society, youth are free from the commitments of adulthood. They have a great deal of time to ruminate over their ideals, their goals, and their occupational destinies. If they are middle and upper middle class, their affluence, culture, and education have exposed them to the highest values in Western society. Their image of their parents and of the occupational world they will one day be forced to enter leads them to expect rationalistic, sterile frustration. This anticipated frustration is a major source of their sense of alienation. But their frustration is intensified by subjectivism and the normal ruminations and self-preoccupations of youth. In turn, their subjectivism is intensified and extended by the length of time they remain youth. The desire to escape the sense of self and of alienation leads them to value activism, and the activism is directed against the system that is oppressive to them. Those theorists who can give positive theoretical and intellectual expression to the emotional longings of youth can provide their world with meaning no matter how limited or incorrect the theories may be.

The longing for a rich, involving, nonintrospective, nonrational, and emotional experience is the same for both the radical student and the freaked-out hippie. Both seek to escape the dull, neurotic, routinized present. Both seek rich, intensive, exciting experience. Both seek danger, either the danger in drugs or the danger in violence and confrontation. Both emphasize communitarian values: one group, the brotherhood of violence and the political commune, and the other, the brotherhood of the sexual or loving commune. But the hippie retreats into the passivity induced by drugs and the drug-induced, enlarged subjective experience. The political radical gets his kicks from the excitation of violence, conspiracy, and mob action. Because the psychological values sought in both movements are so close, the two movements are competitive. They draw from the same age groups, the same sense of alienation and disaffiliation, and the same rejection of the square world. But one movement leads to retreat from the world and the other to violent confrontation with it.

Yippies and crazies get the best of both worlds by burlesquing and provoking the square, and sometimes the radical, world. Individual hippies and yippies will join in the demonstration and confrontation, at times burlesquing it and at other times entering into the spirit of it. In the latter case, they will loot, burn, destroy, and provoke, despite their ideology of love. Individuals in all three camps will switch back and forth between camps, trying out first one approach then another, returning finally to the original camp that in the meantime has changed its line.

The emphasis on activism takes other forms as well. Activism, the rejection of apathy and of being manipulated by others, especially the "system," the "power elite," and the "establishment," means in an affirmative sense an emphasis on participation and on democracy. "Participatory democracy" thus becomes a major form of activism, aimed at transforming the bureaucratic system in the here and now. It has led to the formation of youth-directed poverty programs, reading programs, community action programs for student power, and student participation in curricula, personnel, and grievance committees, and in student-faculty senates.

In all of these activities a select group of college youth and young independent radicals are given an unusual opportunity to experience the operation of large-scale institutions, to participate in the decision-making process, to wield power, to negotiate, and to learn how to manipulate symbols, agenda, and people. Youth, through these "revolutionary" activities, have reversed a century-old trend in which the wielding of power was reserved for elders. In the eighteenth and early nineteenth centuries a youth could only hope to become a prime minister. In the twentieth century he negotiates with university presidents, heads of states, and officials in the mass media. He achieves this prominence by mastering techniques of organization, agitation, and public relations. He uses these techniques in a setting where, because of the de-emphasis of formal bureaucratic, political machinery (which is deemed undemocratic), he can become the leader of a revolutionary movement. The emphasis upon, and the mastery of, techniques of leadership and the use of power is truly awesome because of the absence of limitations upon its exercise. Youth learns to use bureaucratic power without experiencing its customary restraints.

But once the youth becomes a successful leader and participates in governing both revolutionary movements and universities, he can be coopted into the organizational machinery of the bureaucratic university establishment. He learns to enjoy student-faculty lunches and meetings. He also learns to appreciate the importance of his position and the seriousness of the deliberations. At one point he begins to enjoy the prerogatives of power and his prestige as a leader. Frequently he is denounced by his revolutionary peers for hogging the limelight, selling out, or creating a cult of personality. A college youth who is organizationally successful in revolutionary campus politics is likely to become a college president, a dean, or, at least, a best-selling journalist. If not that, at any rate he is likely to become a celebrity and a public lecturer, as long as he keeps the spotlight upon himself.

Because a bureaucratic society needs individuals who can understand and manipulate power, revolutionary training is perhaps the best training a youth can get for a career in the establishment. Historically, youthful radicals, both in the success and failure of their revolutions, have become the political and bureaucratic leaders of the establishments in their adult years. Youthful rebelliousness and revolutionary training lead to a competence in the techniques of political usurpation.

THE FUTURE OF THE UNIVERSITY

At the time of this writing, it is difficult to assess the full implications of the radical youth movement. We have indicated that some youths will gain invaluable training which will qualify them for important positions in the establishment, university, business, and government. By the simple process of shifting their political commitments as they grow older and acquire an economic stake in the society, they can come to terms with the establishment. Their specialized background, training, and preoccupation with power should make them far more effective and perhaps more ruthless and authoritarian bureaucrats and leaders than the older generation of bureaucrats, many of whom were softer-hearted members of the old left.

Certainly many of the universities that have been experiencing prolonged youth revolution have been permanently damaged. The youth revolution may well continue because the conditions that produce it are structural, that is, related to the class position of middle-class youth in a bureaucratic world. If it does continue, it will penetrate more and more schools. Until now, prolonged campus crises have led to a migration of faculty from campus to campus. In the future, migrant faculty will be more and more likely to find revolutions migrating with them.

In some cases radical students leave the universities they have made second-rate because they have become dull, and at times they follow the professors they have driven out only to make new revolutions for them.

As long as the student revolution affected only a small minority of universities, its major effect was to ruin some universities and enrich others. But when student rebellions affect a majority of campuses, the effects are more profound. In addition to reducing the labor force, the universities provide technological, ideological, and personnel support for the New Society. If the universities become radicalized, politicized, and polarized, all of these functions, as well as genuine intellectual functions, may well be driven from them.

As an initial step, faculty members who, because of their technical functions, can secure employment in business, government, or foundations may discover that these institutions provide more freedom for them to work in peace than do the universities. In the meantime, these professorial émigrés will be replaced by young ideologues who, having graduated from the radical youth movement, look to a university career as involving minimum contact with the establishment. Some, at least in the first years of their professorships, will use their positions to activate, politicize, and radicalize their students; in doing so they will deepen and broaden the student revolt. Others, because of their organizational skills and preoccupations, will become deans, department chairmen, and university politicians. Conflicts between aging but "youthful" ideologues and ex-radical administrators will be part of the university scene for years to come, and will be concentrated in the social sciences and the humanities. The science departments will be freer from such conflicts, but conflicts between the science departments and other departments will increase. The two cultures will separate even more.

Meanwhile, government agencies, the Defense Department, foundations, and businessmen, under the pressure of student protest and because of the increasing "unreliability" of the universities, will be forced to create or expand their own research departments, special institutes, and foundations to do the kinds of work that universities formerly did for them. Universities may increasingly become teaching institutions by default, even if little teaching is done there.

Business firms will have to face the problem that many graduates of universities (especially the brightest ones) will not be interested in business careers. Others will come to business with a hostility to bureaucracy, organizational discipline, and the subservience implied in the bureaucratic organization of business. In the short run, business firms are likely to make concessions to extremely talented university graduates in the hope that these concessions will lead to full cooptation. But if the student revolution continues, businessmen may find that university graduates are primarily interested and trained in ideological and revolutionary methods. If this should be the case, businessmen in the giant bureaucracies may be driven to undertake the education of high school graduates themselves. Technical institutes and training programs already in existence will be expanded, and new ones will be created to guarantee personnel that have both the technical and administrative background and the organizational loyalties desired by industry.

The industrial giants have the resources and the personnel to create such training institutes. If they should create them, outside support for the universities would decline, and the universities would be abandoned to the ideologues.

THE FUTURE OF THE YOUTH MOVEMENT

At an entirely different level, one can imagine a youth movement that extends far beyond the universities. Radical, anti-war youth movements already have appeared in the army. Anti-war newspapers, demonstrations, protests, and lawsuits challenge the legitimacy and authority of the Vietnam War and the military command structure. In politics the new reform movements based upon Eugene McCarthy's presidential movement and upon postgraduates from the New Left and SDS have attempted and in some cases succeeded in taking over segments in the Democratic party. Again, while such movements may radicalize the party, they also cool off the radicals. As a result, some accommodation may be possible. At the same time, segments of student radical movements are attempting to migrate from the university into factories, unions, and race movements, in order to create a united radical front. In these areas they clash with the desire of both the blacks and factory workers for more consumer goods, higher wages, and greater benefits from a capitalistic society. They also face the intense hostility of workers and lower-middle groups who identify strongly with the achievements they believe they have made in American society.

At another level, postgraduate student radicals in such fields as teaching, social work, architecture, medicine, psychology, psychiatry, and so forth, have organized to threaten the "establishments" in their own fields. They have demanded reform and the restructuring of their profession and its practices. In each field being "radicalized," the demand for change conflicts with expectations for professional success. To the extent that the profession is controlled by an establishment that strongly identifies with its field, the demand for reform and change by talented but radicalized professionals may simply become a means for increasing the asking price in the process of cooptation. Individuals who do not wish to sacrifice their careers for revolutionary change can become "reformers" and liberals within the establishment. They can be accepted while allowing the establishment to continue.

But as the youth revolution continues, it will cease to be a youth movement. In the early 1960's the age of thirty seemed to be a dividing line which cut off youth from the establishment. But already a large number of young radicals are, by their own former definitions, no longer youths. Many have entered or have had to enter the labor force and become part of the establishment, even when their doing so has gone against their grain. As the youth movement continues, as "old youth" is replaced by "young youth," and as more of the old retire or die, then youth of all ages and shapes will have inherited the world. The battle will then be not only between young youth and old youth but between those who are now radical and those who are not. Nonradicals will be joined by those who graduated from a radical youth when they took over the perspectives of middle age or adulthood. Thus the conflict of the generations will be superseded by a conflict over the acceptance or rejection of the bureaucratic society, and over the degree of change necessary. It will be a conflict in which all ages, regardless of their youth, can engage.

14. Post-war efforts to lead the world

In its simplest terms, America's world power dominance since World War II is based on the ability to deliver fire power (from troops and materials to atomic and hydrogen bombs) as well as military, technical, and economic assistance to almost any area in the world. This concentration of power and capacity to deliver the goods are simply a by-product of the industrial, scientific, and technological might of a country with great human and technological resources. As a consequence this means that influence, responsibility, and leadership, whether exercised or not, have been forced upon the United States. In contrast to the post-World War II period, America up through the 1930s was unwilling to enter the European-dominated world scene, willing only to intervene in Asia and Latin America. Now American power and policy operates on a worldwide scale, leaving no areas untouched.

Immediately after World War II, with the Potsdam Conference and Churchill's Fulton, Missouri speech, where the phrase, "The Iron Curtain," was first used, America became the leader of the West. A number of historic factors provided the basis for this leadership:

1. American entry into World War II turned the tide from defeat to victory. American intervention, moreover, demonstrated to Americans that it could no longer, as it had attempted to after World War I, turn its back upon European or world politics.
2. At the end of World War II the United States, and only the United States, had the bomb.
3. Only the United States had the resources to prop up the economies and armies of the Western European countries. It did so through the Marshall Plan, UNRRA, CARE, NATO, and other forms of military aid. In doing this it made some of its former enemies prosperous allies. All of its allies were dependent on American aid and were forced to accept American foreign policy, even if at great cost to their national pride.
4. The American Navy by a show of force in Greece in 1946 successfully intimidated Russia. Shortly afterwards the American Air Force did the same thing by successfully overcoming the first Berlin blockade. Since then the "show of force," no matter how ineffective, has remained a decisive aspect of American foreign policy—as the Cuban, the Vietnam and Mideast crises demonstrate.

American leadership in the immediate post-World War II period was focused and defined initially by its direct opposition to Russia, and later by opposition to China. Regardless of any prior reservations, this international role was accepted by American presidents of both parties even though not all members of their respective parties have agreed to it. The former world leaders, Britain and France, and in short order West Germany, served initially in the role of advisors and mediators. In part they were a claque for American policy in order to make American world leadership appear to have wide support. As long as America's allies were economically and militarily weak they had no choice but to act in this manner, and, so long as American aid was an indispensable part of the economic and military recovery of Europe, resentments against American leadership were muted. But once American aid had done its work and European recovery and prosperity became facts, resentments based on the loss of glory and autonomy began to emerge. The Labor Party in Britain at an early date exhibited resentments against American domination of British foreign policy, and Adenaur, leading a Germany that had been vanquished, was always ambivalent about the power and resources of the United States. Later, England's resentments were expressed by Conservatives who looked to the continent for solutions and by leftists and radicals who opposed what they regarded as a British sell-out to the Pentagon and to John Foster Dulles. In Germany it was expressed by efforts to develop an autonomous foreign policy. DeGaulle's attempts to isolate American influence from the continent were perhaps the most extreme of these resentments which were, in part, intensified by his personal resentments over Churchill's and Roosevelt's neglect of him when he was head of a friendly state in exile. Since then, one of the goals of French foreign policy has been to insist on its independence from the United States, while hoping to benefit from its economic and military policies.

In the quest for a new autonomy, these countries have begun to assert themselves. Thus, while America has at times unwillingly been forced to accept the responsibilities inherent in its power, the countries over which it has most direct power are uneasy about acknowledging and accepting it.

Further complicating matters, American leaders (especially John Foster Dulles) have been reluctant to acknowledge that the source of their power is only economic and military. As George Kennan stated, and Senator Fulbright restated, the American tradition converts issues of political and economic power into moral ones.

From the early history of America, attitudes of moral superiority have been central in its foreign policy and in its view of non-Americans. George Washington saw European society as dominated by intrigue, deceit, tyranny, and immoral expansionism. James Monroe hoped to protect Latin America from the undemocratic expansion of the European powers. But American manifest destiny was used to justify our own expansive aims. We opened our doors to the oppressed, the tyrannized, the poor from Europe (but not from Asia) and congratulated ourselves for it while these groups provided the source of cheap labor power which, however, had to be controlled and kept in place. We avoided international commitments and responsibilities because this involved association with the tyrannical and degenerate powers of Europe in unholy causes, but we sent the

Marines to Latin America, North Africa, and China when vital interests were involved.

When Woodrow Wilson temporarily reversed American policies of nonintervention, he did so in the spirit of idealism, moral righteousness, and the acceptance of a new manifest destiny. When in the twenties America rejected the policy of direct and continuous intervention, it did so in the spirit of righteous superiority over corrupt and unredeemable foreigners.

The United States's entry into World War II followed by the apparently permanent reversal of noninterventionist policy in the postwar period were carried out in the name of moral righteousness. This attitude permits the United States to try to dominate the international and domestic policies of its allies and dependents and be silent in its support of dictators. In this, U.S. foreign policy resembles that of its ideological predecessor, Britain, in the nineteenth century.

For the above reasons, American military and foreign policy always operates at two levels:

1. At the public level we deny expediency, might, coercion, and forms of blackmail.
2. At the level of diplomacy, in order to achieve some degree of coordination and effectiveness with reluctant junior partners, we use precisely those methods we so anxiously repudiate.

The effect of conducting international relations at these two levels is that our foreign policy stances are full of ideological contradictions. With the highest moral principles we collaborate with dictators, fascists, communists, socialists and at times even with liberals and democrats. We support totalitarian regimes of every stripe, color, and persuasion while we attempt to find excuses based on moral terms for what are the logical bases of our leadership in the West. In the midst of this the American public, accustomed to a too rich moral cuisine, sometimes suffers political indigestion.

THE AMBIGUITIES OF WORLD POWER

Moral righteousness, while rarely controlling political and economic expediencies, has forced us to intervene in all areas of the world, where our dominance is threatened by "enemies" of all sorts, in order to preserve both our power and our virtue. No situation was too small to forestall American diplomatic interest or direct or indirect participation in it, and no distance was too great. President Dwight D. Eisenhower and Senator William Fulbright, among others, pointed out that not even America's great resources are sufficient to deal with all the challenges to its power, its righteousness, and its imagined dignity in all areas of the world.

Through all of recent history, however, there has been a consistency in American policy which cuts through moral and ideological issues. This consistency is based on continuous and direct opposition to communist penetration wherever it has occurred outside the Iron Curtain. This policy which was first articulated by Kennan* and carried out by Acheson and Dulles (as a consultant under Truman) and by Dulles under Eisenhower is the only fixed and constant policy the United States has had in the post-war years. To some extent, the policy arose in response to the tactics of Stalin and to the hard lines developed by Russian communists who at times carried out the Stalinist tradition in the post-Stalin era. By 1969 this same American policy of opposition to communist penetration operated primarily with respect to China.

Only the mutual possession of atomic and hydrogen bombs by the United States and Russia forced the United States to revise the policy of containment and forced Russia from time to time to adopt a less intransigent line. This mutual reassessment of policy shows that there has been at some level a recognition that brinksmanship involves such great risks that it would be in the interest of both countries to find some level of accommodation. Thus in the crises of Hungary and Cuba and the Israel-Arab war of 1967, one or both countries have backed down when it appeared that not doing so might widen the conflict. In the case of Vietnam, where Russia and the United States were indirectly opposed to each other, they maintained the fiction that they were not, so as to limit their differences in that area to that country. While it appears that both parties recognize the need for a new policy, their past habits and their past and present fears of granting too many concessions (as well as fears of being denounced

*Kennan originally stated this position for Europe and not as a global policy. Later, after the Chinese revolution, containment was applied as a world-wide policy.

as being betrayers of past ideological traditions) have prevented any resolution other than sporadic implementation of new policy gestures and *ad hoc* solutions to particular crises. Thus there are alterations of "hard" and "soft" lines toward each other, and a movement from crisis to crisis with no permanent solution either to the particular problems or to the one problem that troubles our time, the prevention of World War III.

In the meantime, the Soviet Union appears to be caught in a snare created by China under Mao's leadership: namely, that any time the Russians attempt to come to some kind of accommodation with the West they depart from the orthodoxy established by Lenin in the period immediately after the Russian Revolution. The Soviet Union is thus caught in a form of double-think diplomacy which, like the United States, forces them, while attempting to be accommodating also to be sufficiently aggressive, anti-Western and sabre-rattling in rhetoric and action to convince non-Russian communists that it is still orthodox in communism. Both the United States and the Soviet Union are caught in ideological and actual ambiguities which threaten their abilities to deal with each other and which reinforce their traditional, habitual, mutual hostility.

Maoist China's international position had the appearance of greater simplicity and clarity since it was an outsider to these forms of mutual accommodation. Within the framework of communist morality and rhetoric, the Chinese could blame Russian leadership for betraying the cause, and could rattle their sabres in a clear and simple form unencumbered by the apparent necessity for compromises. Whether China had the resources, the ability, the stability and, therefore, the desire to carry through with its threats is, if not unlikely, at least uncertain. Nevertheless, Chinese ideological pronouncements and combative spirit could evoke fears of world devastation, fears that have not declined with the continued development of their ability to manufacture and deliver hydrogen bombs. In the meantime, by the policy of encouraging "national liberation" movements such as that in Vietnam it could involve the United States and indirectly the Soviet Union in a bottomless mire of conflict, warfare, and expenditure of resources with almost no cost to itself except some limited amounts of material. Seen from the point of view of Chinese nationalism, the indigenous communist parties of Southeast Asia and the Maoists in the Western hemisphere are expendable in the same way communist parties were to the Soviet Union from the twenties to the fifties. In moral terms this is no doubt reprehensible.

However, it must not be forgotten that from a purely military point of view, the war in Vietnam initially represented for the United States an opportunity for invaluable training, operational exercises, and a chance to test military developments and material which heretofore had been untested, an opportunity whose full value we are sure the Pentagon appreciated even though it did not then speak about it. If, however, providing training had been a rationale for American intervention, it became inappropriate after the first few years of that war. By 1970 the American army was overtrained, perhaps for the wrong war. The irony here is that while the Chinese desired to embarrass the West with their policy of national liberation, they played directly into the hands of those groups in American society who are their most direct enemies, the warriors, militarists, and hawks. Because of these factors, the political and military policies of the Chinese were full of apparent contradictions and uncertainties which both the Russian and American governments found difficult to assess. The ambiguities which resulted from this situation could be more dangerous to world peace than outright and direct confrontation by opposing and violently hostile powers, for the United States and Russia can never be sure of the correctness of their policies until a mistake of such magnitude is made that they may lack the time to correct it. Never in the history of the world has it been more necessary for the underlying populations of the major countries of the world at large to justify to themselves their trust in the knowledge, wisdom, and sanity of their respective and collective leaders.

STRUGGLE FOR THE UNDERDEVELOPED WORLD

The centrality on a worldwide scale of the relationship between the United States and Russia, and the United States and China, has colored all other international relations, including those of the United Staes with the underdeveloped world. This is because each nation in the underdeveloped world represents not only a potential ally of the United States, but more important, a potential base for Russian or

Chinese influence. The role of the underdeveloped country as a potential ally, is especially crucial because frequently these governments have emerged from a revolutionary hostility to their former Western colonial masters and exploiters without, in spite of this resentment, developing internally stable societies that have a secure ideological and political base. Factionalism, brutal competition for dominance, internecine warfare, and the emergence of military totalitarianism are the chief characteristics of the governments of the underdeveloped world. To would-be leaders, political life in the underdeveloped nations appears to be full of ultimate opportunities. Thus the former colonial states are replete with adventurers, with prophets and saviors whose sense of salvation for themselves and their society has provided them with little awareness of the limits they confront as leaders within their society or as masters of their foreign policy. Tangible, immediate, and short-range adventuristic opportunities become guidelines for action and policy.

Due to their own weaknesses and the psychology of their own leadership, the former colonial states are virgin territory for any power that has an expansionist political ideology and that can offer economic or military aid. While these leaders are willing to make deals of all kinds, the lack of internal political and ideological stability means that no deal short of total domination by an outside power can be considered to be anything but temporary. The political instability and ambiguity allow the United States, Russia, Communist China, and in Latin America, Cuba, to confront each other in vaguely defined situations in almost all countries of the world. The vagueness of the definition of these situations adds to the potential for violence and civil war, as do the policies of the major powers, which intensify the already existing indigenous chaos.

Even where the underdeveloped country is not a new nation, as in Latin America, the historic pattern of ruthless and brutal exploitation by feudal and military upper classes over urban and rural proletariats has been so great as to make these lower classes virgin territory for any domestic or imported appeals that can express and channel their resentments. Thus in these nations Russian-, Chinese-, and Cuban-sponsored movements can find opportunities and followers who are willing to stir the brew. As a result the United States confronts Russia, China, and Cuba in these areas in much the same terms as in the former colonial nations.

Since the basic thrust of American foreign policy has been to prevent Russian, Chinese, or Cuban penetration of these states, the United States is driven to seek its indigenous allies wherever it can find them. Working in almost all parts of the world at all times, it frequently selects as allies the most reactionary, corrupt, feudal, and totalitarian elements within the countries which it regards as vital to its own interests. Out of an apparent sense of desperation, the United States at times seems to select as its allies what appears to us to be the most easily available candidates, neglecting such possibilities as might exist for developing regimes which could be democratic, relatively decent, somewhat clean or, at least, not too filthy.

Response to the needs of the moment appears to be a permanent policy. For the last twenty or twenty-five years the United States has had a long-term policy of short-term policies in all underdeveloped countries. The opportunities missed for pursuing more positive alternatives must be manifold. As a result, despite its ideology of moral superiority and its language of democracy, the United States is seen as the supporter of the oppressors and the most reactionary elements in local society. It appears that the only prerequisite to gaining U.S. support is a clear-cut expression of loyalty.

The logic of preventing Chinese or Russian domination of these societies is so persuasive and overwhelming that it overrules all past American policies. The traditional U.S. policy in Latin America was properly called imperialism, just as were the policies of England and France in Africa. In the earlier imperial epoch the military and political might of imperialistic nations was designed to provide support for domestic economic interests by protecting the sources of some raw materials and of some cheap labor, and to a minor extent, colonial markets. In economic terms, during the imperialistic period some relationship was maintained between the expenditures involved in maintaining military and political domination of the colonies and the expected economic benefits of imperialist activity. Imperialism was based upon an economic calculus. Both France's and England's willingness to free their former colonies were in part based on the excessive increase in the military costs of pacifying a population that had learned the value of political autonomy from the West. Even the granting of independence to former colonies was thus calculated in relation to the costs of maintaining control. Under the older system, the granting of independence was still part of an economic arithmetic.

THE PASSING OF ECONOMIC IMPERIALISM

Cold war politics in all of its ramifications has destroyed the primacy of economic imperialism as it existed in the nineteenth and early twentieth centuries. Since World War II, the stakes in international politics have become world domination and total control. When there is now the possibility of hydrogen bomb warfare, no costs are considered too high: the game of international politics can be played at an economic loss and still be regarded as successful. Modern imperialism is not geared to a simple economic calculus. Moreover, this new imperialism is a game which not only the capitalist powers can play: responding to the same situation and similar logic, both Russia and China have sacrificed their internal development for a chance to win some of the stakes in the world power conflict. Because Russia and China are at an earlier stage of accumulation, programs of foreign aid or political and military investments detract from their internal development at a time when the accumulation of capital and the satisfaction of a mass hunger for consumer goods are indispensable both to economic development and political stability. In fact, the United States is in a more favored position than the Soviet Union or Communist China because its military and economic expenditures in this race sustain certain sectors of the American economy, whereas similar expenditures on the part of Russia and China constitute a drain on their limited resources.

Russia is still in many ways an underdeveloped nation because its cold-war policies forced it to invest a major part of its capital resources in military production, and to export billions of rubles of unproductive capital in foreign military aid to allies who, like Egypt, did not know how to use it. In proportion to its domestic capital and consumption needs, Communist China's international capital commitments place it in even a worse position than Russia.

Both the Russians and the Chinese seem to have some sense of the limits of their capacity to invest their energies in international projects. The United States, especially under Lyndon B. Johnson and after Vietnam, only began to have a similar sense of limits. In this American extension of its international commitments, there are dangers for the United States economy. The primary danger is either inflation, which is the most visible result of large-scale increases in military expenditures or, more seriously, in the slightly longer run, the exhaustion and overexploitation of America's human and natural resources. In a sense, inflation is an indirect measure of the latter, which has never been directly measured by the economists.

It would appear, then, from the point of view of the United States, that this worldwide political struggle must be resolved lest the worldwide commitments of American resources result in the internal exhaustion of American vitality, just as the expansionist policies of ancient Rome caused the loss of Roman vitality. The weakness of American policy is its failure to understand the limits of its strength. Communist China, and apparently the Soviet Union, appear to be aware of this weakness. China's policy of creating or supporting local brush fires and insurrectionary movements even, when necessary, at the expense of indigenous Communist or subservient indigenous leaders may succeed in overcommitting the United States to vitality-exhausting policies at little or no expense to China itself. (The limits of this policy, however, are the inability of China to put out its own internal brush fires.) The direct encounter with China—vast, ambiguous, and expensive as it is—represents only a fraction of the total United States commitment.

The logic of America's present world position, then, has forced it to intervene in the internal affairs of all of the underdeveloped areas of the world. The negative policy of preventing communist expansion requires positive expenditures of people and resources to insure against it. As a result a whole host of institutions have been invented for the purpose of intervening in the political life of the underdeveloped world.

FORMS OF POLITICAL PENETRATION AND COORDINATION

The most obvious and direct form of political penetration and coordination is diplomatic representation: the requests, the demands, and the pressures applied through the normal channels of the State Department. However, State Department intervention is supplemented, directly and indirectly, by American aid, loans, military assistance, subsidies, food programs and many other forms of economic assistance policies. On their part, underdeveloped countries seek aid and assistance when in their attempts to hasten the pace of industrialization they find themselves without the financial resources necessary to sustain a viable economy. To support the projects they desire they are forced to come to the American government or to any of its numerous front organizations, including the various banks comprising the international banking system. Their requests for aid are usually considered and granted. This is true for two reasons:

1. Because of our central policy we are forced, whenever possible, to allow no government, no matter how bankrupt or corrupt, to fall into the hands of any anti-American opposition. Aid may be denied, delayed, or discussed indefinitely only in those instances where the recipient is unreliable or where there is a secondary backstage government capable of taking the place of the unsupported government.
2. The condition for receiving this aid is the acceptance of international political policies favorable to America's position in the cold war. India is a good example. In 1967 the Indian government, because of its need for aid, was forced to temper its resentments against the delay, indifference, inefficiency, and high-handedness of President Johnson and the State Department in providing aid.

Similarly, the United States canceled economic and military aid to Peru when the Peruvian government carried out what Washington regarded as excessive demands for retroactive compensation for oil royalties. The result was a breakdown in the Peruvian client relationship with the United States.

The idea that aid results in a form of simple domination over the aided nation is an oversimplification. These governments, even when favorable to the United States, are aware of the internal alternatives to their own regimes. When it is necessary to enhance their bargaining power, they can attempt to blackmail the United States by threatening to allow their regimes to fall. Since many of these governments are in fact precarious, the United States must frequently agree to relations that are not only short of domination but even frequently involve the acceptance of unfavorable compromises. The weakness of a dependent country may be the source of its greatest bargaining strength, but even with this kind of strength, the bargaining capacity of the dependent country is limited. Regional organizations such as the OAS, regional military pacts, the International Bank for Reconstruction and Development (the World Bank) the Import-Export Bank, and a whole host of world commodity agreement agencies serve as fronts by which American policy can be implemented with the collaboration of individual groups within the indigenous nations themselves. Usually the United States is only one of several participating partners in these organizations, but while it has only one vote, in almost all cases it has the markets or the money to implement or impede any policy agreed upon.

All of these forms of direct and indirect pressures on governments are not enough to guarantee their loyalty and stability. The instability of such governments is too well known to permit placing all one's eggs in so weak a basket. It is thus necessary to have secondary echelons of support and reserves in case the first line fails. These reserves are various.

American businesses often co-opt local leaders, suppliers, franchise importers, banks, and shipping and transportation elites. In being linked to American business these elite members act as points of penetration for United States policy, the more so as American international businesses must cooperate with the overall policies of their own government. Moreover, the local elites who cooperate with the United States are doubly paid off by the vast increase in opportunities for graft and theft of the other forms of American aid. It must be said, however, that American aid as such is not the source of this graft. It is rather that this *baksheesh* is the traditional form of paying the cost of administration in the feudal and preindustrial societies. As has been said of the Congolese politician, "He cannot be permanently bought, but only rented and then only for a day at a time." This sort of traditional power simply carries with it the privilege of being bought off. However, American aid increases the volume of graft without discount rates for quantity purchases. Since dealing with Americans sharply increases both profitability rates and commitments to the United States, large segments of the leaders of colonial societies must and do defer, at least minimally, to American expectations in the hope of continuing the flow of personal emoluments. These local elites would in other eras have been called quislings or rapscallions, living off their own populations. However, as they are themselves indigenous and frequently identified with the symbols of nationalism and independence, their role is less clearly visible to the rest of the domestic population.

But even the existence of co-opted local leaders is not enough to assure reliable governments. The CIA at a *sub rosa* level creates shadow governments which at times are prepared to replace existing governments if they are too unstable, incompetent, greedy, or undependable. Such subterranean institutions can always operate in the shadows and so can leave an appearance of ambiguity with respect to the purposes of their work. The myth, no doubt in part a fact, is that every Latin-American country has three governments—one on the way out, one in, and one in the wings. In truth there are usually two or three in the wings, leaving plenty of choice for all contingencies. As a result of these institutions there is even more societal instability than appears on the surface.

Lest one conclude that such diabolical designs operate with smoothness and dispatch, one must always remember the confusion and inefficiency of all large-scale operations. For example, the CIA may back a revolt while the State Department and local American businessmen support incumbents. At other times, just because of mistakes in timing, the rightist revolutionary group may tip its hand before the expected failure of the incumbent government. In such circumstances it can easily happen that two American-supported regimes may be fighting each other, and in doing so reflecting factional policy differences within the American group. Certainly, in all of these maneuvers a *sine qua non* for success is the secrecy of the CIA or the State Department. It is the secrecy itself which prevents more efficient coordination. The CIA, perhaps out of its emphasis on rigid efficiency, tends to tip its hand too soon. This frequently neutralizes the effects of its total operation by revealing the fact that an indigenous group is a puppet. When this happens, the interventionist policy boomerangs, and the indigenous population reacts more negatively than if no intervention had taken place. Blunders resulting from supersecret efficiency add to anti-American hostility. Moreover, such blunders provide grist for the propaganda mills of indigenous communist and other antigovernment factions which are also busily engaged in the same kind of maneuvers as the CIA, with respect to their sponsoring governments.

It is because of situations like these that the activities of the American philanthropic organizations are not only useful but extremely valuable. Simply because they are not directly and officially branches of the American government, they can co-opt local intellectual leaders, especially university officials and professors and aspirants to positions in organizations, schools, and institutes which the foundations themselves create. The purposes of foundation-created schools, projects, programs, and institutes are always the highest and, hence, morally blameless, so that in accepting foundation largesse people do not have to feel that they are explicitly tools of the American government or the foundation. The social and economic improvement of the underdeveloped country is thus linked to such *sub rosa* co-optation of university officials and professors. However, even more than is true of the United States, university youth and intellectuals have become aware of the processes of philanthropic co-optation. While they seem to be willing to accept the money, they define their existences as radicals by attempting in every way to disrupt the programs and agencies created not only by government, but also by private foundations.

The activities of such foundations and institutes appear to be nonpolitical with respect to the cold war. Their work and interest involve fertility control, population problems, health, agricultural productivity, urban planning, community development, education, agrarian reform, public housing, and so on. In connecting themselves to these activities, local professors and intellectual leaders inevitably are drawn into the orbit of the American sphere of local society. They begin to have Americans as friends, and their careers become attached to their American contacts. It is understandable that anyone whose economic and professional existence depends on such affiliations would find it disadvantageous to make an outright attack on the government and society that are the source of his well-being. Thus, whether intended or not, this philanthropic institutional cooptation silences potential opposition, especially in the intellectual strata, and may even create friends. Needless to say, those who are co-opted, particularly because they are the intelligentsia, are frequently aware of the fact and the consequences of their co-optation. In their awareness of their compromised position, they choose to be cynical and critical of American policy, government, and foundations, but because they are compromised they tend to confine the expression of this cynicism to private and intimate circles, hoping that someone else will play the public role of exposing and embarrassing the United States. If they themselves consider being anti-American, they do so with reference to the future—after the grant expires.

Even among those who are co-opted, there is a sympathy and sometimes secret collaboration with the left-wing opponents of American policy. Such scholars and intellectuals are frequently deeply anguished by their being ideological middlemen. Nevertheless, at any given moment, the policies of co-optation achieve the effect of neutralizing, sublimating, and silencing opposition. The exposure of such fronts, as in the case of Project Camelot, embarrasses both the project and its co-opted indigenous leaders. It results in anti-American propaganda, the collapse of the program, and the necessity to invent newer and more innocent-appearing programs.

Of course, the majority of American foundation executives and field workers are high-minded liberals, and are genuinely concerned with solving the problems of misery, poverty, ignorance, overpopulation, and disease wherever they exist. They welcome the opportunity to do meaningful work outside the framework of the crass materialism and tinniness of American commercial institutions. In this respect they are not unlike the missionaries who in earlier centuries, out of the highest purposes, paved the way for political and economic imperialism. In the same sense, the modern foundation missionaries produce consequences which are independent of their own intentions but which may not be far removed from the intentions of higher-level Machiavellians. The effects are the same as they were in the case of the missionaries, perhaps even more so, precisely because modern liberals are as high-minded as the missionaries, but are not people of God, and therefore do not have to act as if they were.

Yet, all of these modes of penetration, serious and expensive as they are, are minor in their effects on the total mass of the populace as compared with the propaganda value of American consumer goods and advertising. American products such as automobiles, refrigerators, Coke, transistors, television, plastics, toys, garments, and chrome automobile ornaments have an irresistible appeal. They symbolize a higher life devoid of misery, poverty, drabness, hopelessness—and what appears to the underdeveloped world as a secular version of heaven. The symbolic significance of American consumption models is so great that the gimcrackery of Western industrial countries almost exhausts the foreign reserves of many underdeveloped countries. In many ways, "Manhattan" is still being bought from the "Indians" in the four corners of the globe. Countries have been known to go bankrupt buying expensive gadgets, airplanes, and/or women. American consumption goods can have the same glamour, novelty, and excitement that toys have for children let loose in a department store. The United States as a consumption model seems to have captured the imagination of all countries and all their classes, so almost everyone seems to be willing to spend to the limit to acquire the plastic toy.

However, it is necessary to make a qualification here. Even though vast sums are spent on consumption, this does not account for all the capital drains that occur in underdeveloped countries. The other sources of loss of foreign exchange are the depositing of excess capital by the upper classes in foreign banks as a hedge against revolution, direct hoarding, and investing capital in land—which serves to increase the value of land beyond its productive value but produces no benefits other than a claim of social honor, since it evokes the image of a feudal, land-based, aristocratic past rather than the *nouveau riche* associations of commercial or industrial wealth.

While hedging themselves, the upper classes are likely to engage in higher forms of gimcrackery which consist of participation in the international jet-set society, where they spend capital on European and American imports, foreign residences, and on travel and play in Europe and America. The Latin-American contribution to international society constitutes another set of interconnections between the elites of the entire Western world. Combined with their European,

Middle Eastern, Southeast Asian, and African counterparts, the whole set comprises an international upper class which excludes only the Russians and the Chinese. But this exclusion probably holds only because China and the Soviet Union have not allowed members of their elites to participate in this worldwide system of social stratification.

Such members of the international social elite can be more than playboys. Because they represent or have connections with their respective domestic elites and institutional leaders, they can carry out formal and informal patterns of negotiations in unofficial capacities. Without publicity or official scrutiny or procedures, they can then set in motion forms of negotiation, coordination, and leadership between segments of the international institutional and diplomatic worlds. At times former leaders, for reasons of secrecy or fear of rebuff, may find it convenient to communicate through such jet-set high status socially connected individuals. In this respect it has not mattered if Averill Harriman has occupied an official position or not: He plays the same role on an informal as on a formal basis.

Such individuals at times occupy official positions primarily in the foreign services of their respective countries. Others operate as private individuals, but the patterns of their personal contacts and class contacts qualify them for their public roles.

Such an interinstitutional elite provides a necessary basis for achieving some forms of international coordination, can assist in the preparation of a revolution, a detente, an alliance, signing of a contract, arranging of an international political marriage, the division of spheres of influence and of international monetary cartel and patent agreements.

It is doubtful, however, that these types make international policy. Rather they implement and facilitate it. The UN and Washington, DC, provide focal meeting grounds for these widely dispersed groups, and the diplomatic corps of the entire world are absorbed into the culture of these centers.

At some level, everyone seems to understand that the United States is the dominant power of the world. The halo effect of this recognition is to produce some admiration for US technology and productivity. However, the very successes of the technology and the productivity are the bases, the operating instruments, on which resentment builds. The United States is resented because it has too much, gives too much, and yet cannot be wholly indulgent. The world's reaction is one of ambivalence, ambiguity, and resentment, perhaps because it is difficult to accept the full implications of American political, economic, and military dominance and intervention. It is thus natural that Americans and America should be hated in most areas in the world, but this is a point that most Americans, including our national leaders, are unwilling to accept. It is not enough that we influence or control policy. We must be respected and we must be loved. And we turn on those we manipulate when they do not love us for our manipulation. In this respect, the problems of American foreign policy are based only on the oversensitivity and righteousness of Americans. They are not "reality problems," unless we make them so by becoming vindictive or punitive to our allies and to the underdeveloped world.

15. *American society as a functioning system*

Ever since the beginnings of the Republic, American society has undergone a continuous revolution. The major generators of the latest revolution have been the development of large-scale bureaucratic industry and the counter-development of large-scale bureaucratic government. The growth of a vast federal budget has served to politicize all areas of American life, and since World War II has served to stabilize American economic prosperity. The bureaucratization of American society has resulted in the emergence of new classes which face new problems without secure traditions. A whole new set of philanthropic, welfare, and educational institutions have developed as a means of stabilizing and sustaining the society. Even with these new institutions, and because of them, whole new sets of problems have emerged for individuals, institutions, and classes.

The middle classes have been the major beneficiaries of the prosperity of the past twenty years. Not only have they been awarded an education and good jobs, but they have been given tax concessions and substantial aid in the form of commuter transportation subsidies and educational subsidies for their children. They have reacted to all these concessions in a variety of ways. One advanced segment of the middle class has emulated the "beautiful people" and repudiated its own traditional life styles. Another segment, many of whom are just moving into the middle class, are immigrants or children of immigrants who reject such radical life styles. They acquire the righteous and moral indignation traditional to the lower middle classes. But because the beautiful people, especially the youth, reject the old values and virtues for which the righteous have striven and sacrificed so much, they adopt a backlash psychology. It is especially pronounced because blacks of all classes are demanding the same kind of entry into American society which the new backlash classes have just achieved.

Labor has made its peace, though this peace has been bought at a relatively cheap social cost: promises of nominal wage increases if the unions will stop striking and asking for greater concessions than are politically feasible. The policy of recent administrations has been one of managed inflation for the purpose of rewarding both labor and management and avoiding unpredictable strikes and interference in the smooth operation of the society. Sometimes labor has seen itself as the victim of Keynesian economics, because the rewards it has received are relatively low. Sometimes it has threatened to withdraw its efforts, and at times it has had to strike, not against business, but (in the Kennedy and Johnson administrations) against government guidelines on permissible increases in its wages.

Businessmen have been satisfied by favorable tax policies, tax reductions, favorable interest rates and monetary policies, and, most of all, by huge federal expenditures for atomic science, electronic systems, missiles, and defense in general. One result of the volume of federal expenditures has been a revolution in government-business relations. Whereas in the 1930's government and big business saw each other as enemies and rivals, the effect of the constantly enlarging federal budgets, spent primarily for big business expansion and profits, has been to reduce, if not silence, big business opposition to government. This change has been so great that the Eastern fiscal and corporate giants work hand in hand with Democratic as well as Republican administrations in opposing the "political irrationality" of small businessmen who cling to Midwestern and nineteenth-century political mentalities. The Goldwater split within the Republican party was a split between those who would not and those who would cooperate in the consensus and pluralistic politics of the fifties and sixties.*

Until the seventies the universities enjoyed the abundance of national prosperity as distributed by federal budgets. As a result of dizzying amounts of aid to the universities, professors were provided with higher standards of living than they ever had achieved in the past, and younger professors now take this prosperity for granted. Their incomes rose while they were given reductions in work loads and increased opportunities to engage in practical or impractical research. As a result, university professors have become a pool of talent for the government, for business, and for the foundations. In their work for these agencies they help to create ideologies and to formulate technical government policies, and they are frequently instrumental in the manipulation of public opinion. Between the thirties and the sixties, intellectuals and college professors as a class have become coopted, deradicalized, and converted into technicians.

Until World War II, intellectuals were primarily an annoyance to the establishment. Since the rate of production of intellectuals had invariably exceeded the capacity of the economy to absorb them, before the war they were underrewarded, unappreciated, and regarded as superfluous. Responding to this condition, intellectuals attacked the society which rejected them. On the right and the left they were in the vanguard of revolutionary activities; deprived of material opportunities, they attacked the materialism of the business society. But after World War II, intellectuals were surprised to find themselves appreciated, employed, and rewarded, and they no longer found it easy to criticize a society that took such good care of them. Thus, in addition to becoming intellectual technicians, they became ideologists for a new society which they defended by attacking, among other things, other intellectuals who maintained their past ideologies.

The new radical youth and the younger professors, not having experienced the depression or any serious deprivation, attack the "system" for a number of reasons: some because the system is too materialistic,

* President Nixon has attempted to heal these divisions within the Republican party. He has leaned as much to the right as necessary to unify the party and, with respect to his "Southern strategy," to unify the nation. At the same time he has been unable to revoke the policy which the Republicans in the thirties called the fiscal madness of the Democratic party.

others, using the same rhetoric, because they lack the self-discipline to acquire the skills necessary to be coopted.

The earlier cooptation of the professors by foundations, the universities, and the government formed the basis of new institutions aimed at defining and influencing public opinion and social policy. The federal government initially realized the greatest gains from these new institutions. Only since American intervention in the war in Vietnam have some segments of the academic community shown a degree of independence. Apart from the youth, who have a vested interest in opposing the war, a part of the academic community has provided the most articulate critics of the Vietnam War policies. To a surprising degree they have helped to alter the climate of public opinion with regard to the war. In this respect the attempt to secure consensus has failed—and so has the attempt to secure a final victory in Vietnam.

Presidents Kennedy and Johnson raised the urban issue but failed in their attempts to solve the crisis of the cities and to win the new war on poverty. By recognizing the problem and then providing only token, fragilely built solutions, they created expectations and hopes which were not fulfilled. Both Presidents and their advisers were more anxious to placate the middle classes through tax relief and favorable spending policies than to solve the problems of the poor. President Nixon's contribution was to reflect and intensify the righteous indignation of the middle classes while cutting back funds available for solutions to the problems of poverty and the urban crisis. His advisers, like those of Kennedy and Johnson, have demonstrated considerable ingenuity in taming papier-mâché tigers, but in spite of these solutions, the real problems have intensified. Certainly the costs of the war in Vietnam contributed to these failures in each administration. But having roused hopes and expectations among the blacks, and having disappointed them, Kennedy and Johnson were rewarded with urban riots, violence, and burning and looting. These urban problems contributed to an alienation of the white middle and stable working classes, whom the Democratic administration attempted to placate by tax relief, a policy which failed in the long run. President Nixon promised law and order, tax relief, and an end to programs which coddled the poor. Of course he could not fulfill these promises, but in the meantime, he won the election.

In addition to these dramatic failures, the attempt by Kennedy and Johnson to create the machinery for the manufacture of consensus has not worked. The use of foundations and universities to define public issues has been relatively successful, but the new issues have most frequently been resolved by interest-group politics. President Johnson, by using budgetary devices, was able to purchase consensus on almost all issues except the war in Vietnam. That war virtually destroyed the consensus policy of both Kennedy and Johnson. The governmental and philanthropic machinery for implementing that policy still remains. The machinery is available to a Republican as well as a Democratic administration, if that administration can understand the political and social meaning of the federal budget. President Nixon has not yet been willing to commit himself. Pressures for minor budgetary savings have deprived him of much of the established opinion- and consensus-making machinery implicit in the federal budget. To save money and to lower taxes he alienated some groups who were otherwise cooptable. Most of these groups already belonged to the Democratic party. President Nixon has not used the universities, foundations, and government machinery available for consensus-making as did Presidents Kennedy and Johnson.

Those classes and groups which are not coopted by federal budget and monetary policies constitute a series of threats to the establishment. Until some means of coopting them is devised, they will always feel a sense of injustice about the inequitable distribution of economic opportunities and rewards of the society. Once the process by which classes are coopted becomes fully understood by all groups, each group facing the government becomes concerned not only with the amount of its *own* reward but also with the amount given to other groups who are being bought off. It is possible that an intellectual understanding of the system, in a sense, may defeat its operation as each class looks for a larger and larger slice of the pie. Opposition is possible even from those who are willing to be coopted, but who cannot be coopted because their demands rise faster than the prices offered.

Within every group there is the possibility that some of its members cannot be coopted even if they are economically rewarded. Groups and individuals may attack government policy on ideological, moral, ethical, or philosophical grounds as a form of protest which is seemingly independent of the process of cooptation. Thus an articulate but dedicated minority of the academic community began to protest against United States policy in Vietnam. Some youth who have not yet reached the age at which they are locked into the economic system still have some choice in defining their interests. They can, if they wish, object to and resist the consensus policy of the society because they are not yet aware of its direct material rewards which silence opposition. As youth acquires age and economic responsibilities, it becomes a more likely target for cooptation. Even considering these special situations, the possibilities of resistance exist only relative to the capacity of government to be able to afford dissent. In an affluent society it is literally possible for one hundred flowers (or weeds) to bloom because there will be almost no compelling reasons for a significant number of people to be attracted to any one cause. Opposition and dissent dissipates itself in the face of the comfort and satisfaction of those groups to whom its appeals are made. It is impossible to coopt some groups because their demands are for power, unearned prestige, and compliance with absolute ideals. These demands are made primarily by the affluent and by ideologues, both of whom are above monetary incentives. But their gripes and complaints are made at the personal level, or in areas that are not crucial, or in so many disorganized and fragmented ways that the protest does not affect the central structure of the society. These protests can, however, even if fragmented, threaten the sense of security of the leadership strata and of the middle and lower middle classes.

The Vietnam War, the activism of the students, and the urban riots have called into question, both politically and psychologically, the whole system of consensus instituted by Presidents Kennedy and Johnson. The sense of dissatisfaction among students and among groups not favored by consensus politics remains. Their levels of resistance have in fact been heightened because Nixon's victory was based partly on exploiting these dissatisfactions and because he is now obliged to resolve them. Academic intellectuals are as disenchanted with President Nixon as they were with Presidents Kennedy and Johnson when it became clear that neither had any intention of sharing power with them. All these intellectuals, however, expected greater rewards because they were either righteous or value neutral.

OTHER WEAKNESSES IN THE SYSTEM OF COOPTATION

Historically the Negro has been outside the policy of cooptation. He has been deprived of his elementary political rights in both South and North. In the South he has never (until recently) progressed beyond a slave psychology. In the North he has been politically ineffective because of poor voter registration, low political self-confidence, deficiencies in leadership, and social and political strife within the ghetto community.

Only with the civil rights revolt and the movements that have resulted from it have the blacks developed a political voice that can be heard in American society at large. This voice, in part, consists in the ability to produce riots, civil disorder, and other interferences with the routine operation of urban life. As Negroes became blacks and a substantial part of the urban electorate, they became conscious of their strength as an increasingly important factor in critical elections at local, state, and national levels. Because of this potential power, for the first time in American history the dominant white society has had to find ways to buy off the blacks. Hence the development of a politics of poverty.

The new federal and local poverty and community action programs have become vehicles by which middle-class black administrators, politicians, social workers, teachers, and community leaders are put on a government payroll. In addition to a salary, these community leaders and ideologues are also given an opportunity for constructive leadership which will, hopefully, absorb and deflect their political unrest. As coopted black leaders become concerned with the bureaucratic technicalities of such programs, they cease to be leaders of protest against white society: instead they develop their own vested interests in their well-paid positions. They do, however, use the rhetoric of protest as a put-on and a device to increase government and foundation budgets, and as a means of proving their leadership in the ghetto.

Poverty and education programs were originally designed to provide jobs in what turned out to be imaginary educational and training programs. These programs were, in fact, designed to sponge up the idle time and energy of the teeming masses, especially the youth, who then would not have time for civil disorder. Given this intention, much more money would have had to be spent to assure success. Bayard Rustin estimates the real cost (in 1966-value dollars) at more than $100 billion over twenty years.

The fact is that the poverty programs were not genuine and failed to provide opportunities which would have alleviated the fundamental economic disadvantages and impairments of the mass of blacks. They were recognized almost instantly as fraudulent, but of course the fraudulence did not prevent community leaders and ideologues from demanding and accepting token programs. The success of the programs really rested on the capacity of black leaders to be coopted. There was always the possibility that some black leaders and intellectuals would be uncooptable (some did accept jobs but used their new positions as platforms for escalating their demands). The other possibility was that if black leaders were coopted, new leaders would continuously emerge from below to remind the ghetto residents that the success of the poverty and education programs was measured primarily in jobs given to a previous layer of black leaders. A few who were not militants and therefore could have been coopted have refused to participate at all.

At another level, if the education and poverty programs do not produce genuine jobs, they may simply produce new and higher types of black failures. The participants in the program live in fear that budgets will be cut; they know that the programs train them only to ideologize, threaten, and collect a pay check. This produces a new type of colonial ghetto in which the leader is given a job to keep the masses pacified—but his ideology, pride, and interest force him to activate the masses. If they are successful, black community action and poverty programs would produce an indigenous caste system in which the black is isolated from the total society by means of education, social work, entertainment, and pseudo jobs. Black leadership already has a vested interest in the separateness, distinctiveness, and isolation of the races as a result of these programs.

A genuine economic and educational program for the poor would aim at destroying racial barriers to opportunities rather than emphasizing them, as has been the case up to now. Carrying out a nonracially oriented program would require programming in which jobs and economic opportunities would not be linked to race, so that the black could surrender his primarily racial identity and replace it with an economic identity. He would be entitled to concessions because he is poor rather than because he is black. He would then have a class identity corresponding with his continuously evolving interests as he moves upward economically and socially. Such programs have not yet been conceived because the politics of cooptation results in demands for rewards to blacks as blacks, rather than as separate individuals. Changes in these policies have been opposed both by the new black bourgeoisie and by black nationalist leaders who have sometimes gone to the extent of mobilizing their followers to demonstrate against urban poverty programs that are not based on community action.

In addition, of course, present programs are based on minimal expenditures to purchase a black leadership that already knows its own value. Since the beginning of poverty programs in the Kennedy administration, concessions to blacks have been microscopic in comparison with those granted to the farmer, the middle classes, the business classes, and defense industries. Thus for the blacks, the politics of consensus has meant the attempt to purchase their participation (perhaps passivity) at virtually no cost. To reward the black in proportion to his need or his numbers would mean deflecting resources from those who already receive a lion's share of the social rewards. It is specifically at this point that class and other vested interests re-emerge and oppose alternative distributions of the federal budget. It is precisely here that budgetary conservatism becomes fiscal racism.

Ironically, another major group that has gone unrewarded is the Southern redneck. As the enemy of the Southern black, he has been outside the mainstream of American society almost as much as his adversary. George Wallace has relied on traditional methods to mobilize this group, and President Nixon, at the national level, has attempted to block Wallace by coopting his program. Neither has so far been successful over the whole nation. The difficulties of rewarding the redneck are so great as to make it almost impossible. The Southern redneck demands no less than a restoration of a society which probably never existed and which is less and less possible even as a dream. Since the end of the Populist era, the redneck has been in psychological rebellion against the whole mainstream of Western society; insofar as he holds to his earlier values, it is impossible to fulfill his demands, there being no rational system of rewards which can gratify them. If the redneck is to be rewarded, it cannot come through the politics of consensus unless that consensus is between the rednecks and all other backlash groups. Such an alliance would indeed be a novelty in American history. In the meantime, the redneck remains the core audience at which backlash political movements are aimed. The extent to which such political movements can become national depends not only on the extent of the backlash sentiment but also on the ability of racist leaders to find political formulas that will reconcile redneck styles and politics with those of other similarly disaffected groups. So far, racist politicians have not succeeded in finding such formulas. If they do, the politics of race and resentment may totally defeat the politics of consensus.

The small businessman is, in much the same sense as the redneck, a victim of the direction of change in Western society. Large-scale business, with its rationality, technology, scientific knowhow, its capacity to assemble almost unlimited resources, and its ability to mine and to profit from the needs of a scientific-military society, has taken over most of the areas of opportunity formerly available to small business. In addition, the development of the mass market, mass distribution, and the franchise system have converted what were once local markets into a system of nationally organized local outlets. Thus small business sees itself continuously superseded by the giant corporation. The small businessman who was once a respected member of his community now finds employees of nationally organized industries occupying community positions that historically were occupied by him. As a consequence, the small businessman resents labor which, according to him, is too well paid for work not done and whose wage demands make it difficult for the businessman to make the level of profit he feels he should make. He sees himself in unfair competition with big business, which has the resources, markets, and technology that make small business more and more marginal. He sees the government, by its tax policies and by its expenditures, denying him his share and devaluating his work and usefulness to the community. He also sees the Negro profiting from his taxes through poverty and job programs which are "unnecessary, wasteful, and troublemaking." These programs drive his cost of wages up, thereby putting him in a wage-price squeeze. If his business is located in a ghetto, he sees himself as the primary target of race riots, looting, boycotts, and crime in the streets, and as a victim of subsidized competition from new but incompetent black businessmen. Because of these dissatisfactions and resentments, the small businessman represents a continuous source of resistance to the New Society and a potential supporter of backlash politics.

Although consumers are the largest group in our society, it is difficult to isolate their interests. In spite of efforts such as Ralph Nader's to serve the interests of consumers, they are not easily organized as a pressure group because most consumers, except for lower-class blacks, the ill, and the aged are also producers. In the total society, the producer's role tends to dominate the consumer's role, so that it has not been possible to organize consumers into a group sufficiently unified or powerful to be coopted.

The Keynesian solution rests on the willingness of substantial segments of the population to accept the basic premise of controlled government spending designed to stimulate consumption. This requires an element of economic and political rationality on the part of all groups who have an interest in maintaining the system. But the resentments of the redneck and the small businessman raise the possibility of a political irrationality in the form of a total attack on the system. First, as we have indicated, both groups are outside the main drift of American society, and second, the federal government up to now has not been able to find a means by which to reward either group sufficiently to pacify it. They are joined in their resentment by all those who experience anxieties caused by black rage and militancy. These include white policemen who are forced by their occupation to cope with race riots, looting, and the hostility, provocation, and resentment of blacks, and who must deal with these phenomena despite charges of police brutality, criticism by civil rights organizations, and review by their civilian political masters and the courts. The fact that behavior described as "police brutality" may be traditional police practice does not mitigate the resentment felt toward the police nor the desire of the police to escape from review, criticism, or limitations. White school teachers and trade union members resent, in the same sense, the increased competition from blacks and their demands for occupational entry into areas which whites have sought to monopolize by tenure rules, examinations, and seniority.

White immigrants and children of immigrants who have achieved, by virtue of twenty-five years of prosperity, a sense of their stake in American society (home, automobile, and television ownership, and college educations for their children) and a sense of being part of a new American establishment, have grown to resent the claims of the blacks to enter or share in that establishment. This is especially true when such groups live near or in the path of urban ghettos, where the growth of the ghetto is seen as a threat to their living space, their property values, their jobs, and to the new-found Americanism they now enjoy.

These groups, who make up a substantial part of the stable working classes and the lower middle classes, represent potential supporters for racists and backlash politics. Some of the working classes are torn between radical right-wing politics and conventional trade union support for New Deal liberalism.

The Goldwater and Wallace candidacies expressed these resentments in political terms. Both Senator Goldwater and Governor Wallace appealed to small business, Southern rednecks, and all those outside the framework of the present drift in national and economic affairs. They did this by attacking the Keynesian solution, the new black demands for economic and political equality, and the twentieth century in general. In 1964, Goldwaterism and the resentments it organized had no chance. One must bear in mind, however, that the Johnson administration in that campaign was at the high point of its success. Even today there is a chance that a major economic reverse, a crisis in international relations, an insult to American honor, continuous casualties in Vietnam, the eruption of other Vietnams, or repeated race riots can reinvoke the irrationality of those who are quiescent because their immediate economic interests have been satisfied.

President Nixon profited from some of these dissatisfactions and resentments, as did Governor Wallace, even though American prosperity during the election of 1968 was at an all-time high. But President Nixon does not have, as did President Johnson, a more conservative (but not racist) party to his right to absorb the dissatisfaction that would follow a failure on his part. As a result, the danger of an alliance of "little men," the so-called silent majority, will be greater in the future than in the past. An even more serious danger is the possibility of a more right-wing Republicanism gaining control of the Republican party. If either of these directions should be realized, the whole framework of American society could be radically changed, and political irrationality could be as destructive and as terrible in America as it has been in Europe.

THE AMERICAN ECONOMY AND THE UNDERDEVELOPED WORLD

Since World War II the United States has been "forced" to apply Keynesian concepts to international relations, even though it has not been fully conscious of their application in this area. For America a kind of practical Keynesian imperialism is at work.

The American economy escaped a depression through aid to its allies in the late thirties and early forties, and achieved economic prosperity as a result of war production during World War II. This same productivity built up during the war was applied after the war to foreign aid programs, first under the Marshall Plan and later to the underdeveloped world. Over the past twenty years these aid programs (industrial, commercial, and military), supported by federal expenditures, have provided additional markets for American productivity, and have helped to solve—temporarily—the "dilemma of capitalism." At the time of this writing, while aid programs have been and are being reduced, military and other programs, including the war in Vietnam, have helped to maintain the American economy at levels of almost full employment for skilled workers and technicians, and of very high profitability for those industries connected with war expenditures. Some cutbacks of military expenditures by the Nixon administration have already caused high levels of unemployment in war-industry towns.

This is not to say that the American economy can survive only through war, for war is actually a relatively inefficient solution to the dilemmas of capitalism: its consequences cannot be controlled. A war economy results in continuous inflationary pressures in some areas of the economy and serious dislocations in other areas. And it is almost impossible to control the expenditures for a war economy. The unpredictability of events and the need for psychological and military victories usually result in expenditures that transcend any rational economic or other type of planning. A war economy results in an overuse of both men and resources in ways which are likely to have no other consequences than to provide temporary employment during the course of the war.

We have already suggested two methods other than war which can use up or organize the same economic resources, and provide the same markets necessary for operating the economy effectively: (1) internal expenditures, and (2) aid programs to the underdeveloped world.

The issue of aid programs opens the whole question of the implications of the Keynesian revolution for the international economy. The dilemmas of capitalism, including its potential overproductivity and the difficulties of providing markets for it, are not problems at all for the underdeveloped nations. In contrast to the United States and other Western nations, the underdeveloped nations face fundamental problems of achieving enough income and productivity to maintain a standard of living capable of sustaining life. For the underdeveloped world, one of the major and unexpected results of the scientific revolution has been a significant reduction in death rates, especially infant mortality. But birth rates have remained at their usual levels, with the result that starvation and social dislocation have proved almost insurmountable problems for the governments of these countries.

Taking the world as a whole, there is probably more misery, more starvation, and lower standards of living in the twentieth century than in any other historical age. It is only in the light of this standard that the United States, with its high consumption, its high standard of living, and its senseless glut of productivity, becomes an embarrassment to itself and a source of envy, resentment, and admiration to all underdeveloped countries.

Exacerbating this attitude is the penetration of American industrial capital and American corporations into most countries of the world. American industrialists have, under pressure from the State Department, unwillingly declined invitations to set up factories in the Soviet Union, leaving this task to Italian capitalists. To the less-developed world, American penetration is viewed as a problem, for American productivity appears to have been gained at the expense of the underdeveloped world. While the underdeveloped world wants to share in the consumption standards and productivity of the United States, it feels that American imperialism denies it a just share. In addition, American foreign policy has defined itself as in conflict with Russian, Chinese, and Cuban communism, and is therefore labeled by the underdeveloped world as reactionary, exploitative, and feudalistic. To some extent the charge is true: the United States often supports the internal exploiters in underdeveloped countries and thus inherits, in addition to its own, the resentments directed at the internal exploiters.

This heritage of resentment is, in part, a product of the United States' position as the most highly developed industrial power in the world. It results also from the self-selected role of the United States as the principal opponent of communist penetration in the underdeveloped world.

In this position the United States might expect to be hated and resented by its clients, but Americans have shown no willingness to accept this enmity. With its ideology of being a leader of democratic ideals, America expects itself to be loved, admired, and followed simply because it has these ideals and virtues. When Americans learn to understand that they are not appreciated everywhere, they may be more realistic about the way in which they can deal with the underdeveloped world.

The other side of this coin is that the increasing poverty and misery of the underdeveloped world provide a bottomless reservoir of consumers necessary to sustain the increasing productivity of American industry—even if the underdeveloped countries do not have the means to pay for the needed goods.

The parallel between domestic and international Keynesianism is not wholly exact. First of all, it requires that the United States (and Europe and Russia) provide aid programs, resources, and capital export programs that are large enough to sustain American productivity even in the absence of wars. This would require expenditures of at least $25 billion annually for domestic and international aid programs to maintain the same level of prosperity afforded by the Vietnam War. If such a solution to the problem of aid and capital export could be found, then the United States could solve its own internal problems at the same time that it helps to reduce misery on a worldwide basis. *But* if this is to be politically effective, the pattern of aid must be different from that provided in the past, and it must be different from that provided by traditional foreign policy and aid programs.

Under Cold War political "imperialism," the price of economic support has been acceptance of American political leadership. If, however, we regard an aid program as necessary to the survival of the United States internally, then it would not be necessary to put political and economic stipulations on aid. By demanding political acquiescence as the price for aid, we increase the opposition to American policies and the resentment against us by those who receive the aid. American policies must appear to be genuinely altruistic in order to be genuinely selfish. This means that we must abandon attempts at political control through aid while we increase the amount of aid. Although this solution is totally out of temper with the American past, we would argue nevertheless that it is totally necessary as an economic solution to the fundamental problems of survival for the populations in both the developed and underdeveloped worlds. President Nixon appears to be a true American in that he shares the American sense of righteousness and agrees with President Johnson on the policy of using aid as a means of international control, despite speeches to the contrary. But Nixon appears unwilling to pay the economic, political, and military price of such programs. In the conflict between international control and traditional greed, the latter appears to have won.

Economically the Keynesian formula, if followed, seems capable of providing a solution both at home and abroad. But a precondition for such a solution is accepting the political rationality involved in Keynesian budgetary solutions to the dilemma of capitalism, and diminishing the resentments and irrationalities of those groups who have not profited from the Keynesian political economy.

FREEDOM AND BUREAUCRACY

Up to now, in this final chapter, we have been talking about problems and solutions which concern only the economic and political realities of American society. They do not touch the quality of American life, culture, and civilization. The problem of how America is to realize itself in terms of the higher values has been raised by, among others, Adlai Stevenson, John F. Kennedy, and John Kenneth Galbraith, all of whom have placed a higher priority on the issue of the quality of American life than on brute economic expansion. We would imagine that American culture is something other than that displayed in the styles of the beautiful people, the radical chic, and the multimedia, communitarian, and counter-cultures.

The solution of economic problems does not automatically resolve the issue of what America is to become as a civilization or as a "spiritual example." In fact, the very resolution of the economic problems *creates* new problems for the quality of American life.

The resolution of almost every world economic problem requires a greater harnessing of the world's populations and a tighter organization of individuals and groups. Bureaucracy is the major administrative vehicle of industrial society, in the United States as well as in the rest of the world. Thus the solution of almost every specific practical problem in the United States involves the extension of bureaucracy and a broader and deeper penetration of its effects in all areas of personal, social, and cultural experience. Bureaucracy deprives individuals of freedom and autonomy, not necessarily by coercion but rather by creating a favorable system of rewards for compliance with dehumanized, technical, and efficient patterns of performance. The development of the bureaucratic machine, nationally and internationally, results in a kind of bureaucratic ideology which would deprive all individuals of any independence from it. Bureaucrats develop a sense of their power and have a tendency to affirm their bureaucratic function by exercising this power against the individual and his unique, personal creativity. When the bureaucrat expresses himself through the exercise of the bureaucratic function, he opposes the personal inclinations of others to express themselves.

The key personal, social, and cultural problems that flow from the processes of bureaucratization are the following:

1. *The development of pleasant, comfortable, pre-manufactured patterns of conformity which destroy personal autonomy and individualism.* The individual loses the sense that his life has any meaning apart from these stylized forms, or the sense that he can take his own identity for granted in a way that allows him not to feel that all he thinks and does is external to a real self which he cannot express. In trying to achieve a real identity he seeks romantic escape into exotic

behavior and attitudes. Included in such escapes are freaking-out, self-delusion, self-destruction, and a senseless destruction of the "repressive" system without considering realizable alternatives.

2. *The bureaucratic overdevelopment of stylized patterns of opinion and tastes that deny not only the independence but also the capacity for independence to all individuals who are not members of the bureaucratic elites.* The elites have, as their job, the manufacturing of issues, opinions, thought patterns, and cultural tastes for the rest of society. It is in this function that coopted intellectuals are most dangerous. If this process becomes efficient enough, all independent thought, opinion, and taste is blotted out in a glut of canned, pre-manufactured thought forms. The problem is one of maintaining channels that will allow authentic expression in a world that is becoming increasingly bureaucratic in organization. In our contemporary society, pseudo-expressiveness that expresses nothing but self-preoccupation and self-withdrawal from all realities, including spiritual ones, becomes defined as expressiveness.

3. *The development in the most general sense of a quality or tone of life that reflects the tone and quality of the bureaucratic milieu and becomes a dominant public style.* Since all major and most minor institutions in the society have been infused with the spirit of bureaucracy, there is little to prevent the spirit of the bureaucrat from attaching to all life experiences. Should the spirit of bureaucracy be brought into the private sphere, the truly private will be driven still deeper into itself. In this event, society would no longer have the resources of creative individuals, resources which it needs for its own creative regeneration. Again, pseudo-individuality enables empty persons to defend themselves against the standardization of a bureaucratic culture.

4. *The development of means by which the bureaucratic and administrative elites can use their key positions in their own interests.* Excessive ambition and the quest for autonomy on the part of the bureaucrats can only be achieved at the price of the freedom of the rest of society. The Soviet Union, as portrayed by Solzhenitsyn, is the best example of this problem.

Potential solutions to these problems can only be sketched here. And as we are dealing with issues concerning the quality of American life, describing these solutions per se is of little avail. To the extent that there are any solutions, they must be lived and cannot be resolved by discussion.

The problem of conformity and one-dimensionality has more facets than has generally been imagined. As we have suggested, conformity is demanded by the objective, quasi-legal requirements of work in large-scale organizations, and by the opinion-forming and other mass media which provide pre-manufactured experiences and styles for individual consumption. Yet, in spite of this, the ambience of urban bureaucratic society offers opportunities for solutions to problems of identity and autonomy not found in simpler societies.

The freedom from work afforded by a short workday allows almost everyone except the overworked elites the leisure to develop personal styles, interests, and idiosyncrasies. Such leisure is not available in societies where the need for work and the length of the workday chain the individual to objective work that permits little individualization. But the simple availability of leisure is not enough. One must know what to do with his leisure once he has it. In this respect the mass media are neutral in that they can be ignored at will. One can insulate himself from the mass media simply by finding something better to do with his time.

Bureaucracy, in addition to being legalistic and precise in limiting the rights and duties of the official while on the job, implies that other forms of activity not covered by the rules are left to the discretion of the individual. The way in which the individual uses his private life before and after work is increasingly his own business, particularly in urban centers where one's work site and nonwork life are geographically separated. Frequently, however, the habits of blandness and compliance learned at work are carried over into the nonwork life. This happens not because the bureaucratic elites demand it but because the individual is unable to cope with the opportunities afforded him. If he wishes, in his nonwork life the individual can pursue his own interests, talents, and tastes without regard for the external constraints of bureaucracy. In the middle class, as we have noted, individual bureaucrats sometimes develop enough independence to become swingers, beats, hippies, beautiful people, and liberal and radical reformers. Unfortunately, these activities are often the expression of an attitude of negation and are therefore incapable of enriching life over any extended period of time.

The freedom available in bureaucratic mass society is only available to those who are capable of using it. The failure to use such freedom is less the failure of our economic institutions than it is the failure of the individual. In this respect, however, the failure of the individual is due partly to the failure of parents and educational institutions to take seriously these crises of identity and problems of conformity.

Because bureaucratic work appears incapable of channeling the creative energies released by favorable middle-class environments, forms of expression other than work must be found to absorb these emerging energies. This means that individuals must be taught or must somehow learn that self-expression and creativity can be realized in serious, nonvocational, but disciplined work. Parents and schools and colleges must in some way show the neophyte how to develop interests, skills, and tastes that are not necessarily vocationally connected. In the middle-class world, an education that prepares one only for work fails to prepare one for life, because the most serious aspects of life are no longer connected to work. If leisure and consumption are functions of life as well as economics, the truly significant aspects of life are neglected by occupational training. Our educational system has failed to demonstrate this to youth because it is primarily vocational in character. But it has also failed in a more serious sense by failing to set an example to youth of what it means to have a serious, disciplined, intrinsic interest in a subject. The new relevant education, consisting of rap sessions, T-groups, and communitarian freedom, accentuates the original problem because it accepts the fact that students will not and cannot make demands upon themselves.

While teachers and parents are ultimately responsible for this state of affairs, youth is also implicated. The failure of youth to realize the opportunities inherent in the imperfections of the bureaucratic world is to a large extent a failure of consciousness and of nerve. The failure of consciousness means simply that individuals fail to recognize the amount of freedom that is available if they would choose to use it. The failure of nerve is an unwillingness to test seriously the limits of their interests and talents by doing positive, creative work.

It appears that the specter of conformity, of restraints, of adult hypocrisy, and of the ratrace have so dominated youth that they have chosen to combat everything *en bloc* without fully realizing what it is they are fighting. In choosing to combat the "culture of conformity" and the "establishment" they have failed to see the lack of unity and solidarity of adult society and of the symbols they are fighting. They appear to be more interested in attacking that world than in extracting the degrees of freedom which it offers. By concentrating on rebellious attack or withdrawal, they demonstrate by their behavior that they reject the very freedom they claim their society denies them. Whether hippie, radical, or "existentially honest," their rebellion is less an affirmation of independent autonomous values and beliefs than an affirmation of quite the opposite. Their ideas are transfixed by the image of the ideas they oppose. As a result they achieve not the freedom they desire but only a symbolic affirmation of negation.

For the most part these youth, not yet committed to a job and still in possession of the freedom guaranteed by parental support, do not have to make the distinction between work and nonwork life. If they could escape from their symbolic rebellion and withdrawal, and could develop a sense of their own direction, it would release the energy necessary to create human or artistic cultures.

The failure of the youth to do more than rebel (or lament), and the failure of their elders to do much more than conform, are based on an initial misapprehension of the pressures to conform. Conformism results from a lack of confidence in the ability to pursue one's own inclinations. If individuals can learn to pursue their own personal demons without regard to assumed pressures for conformity, self-assurance and self-confidence are likely to result from the act itself. Doing what one wishes to do will in itself remove the sting of conformist pressures. The failure to exploit the tolerance in repressive tolerance is a major crime. The failure to inform youth of that tolerance is an even greater crime.

Exploitation of the opportunities in repressive tolerance is not necessarily a solution to political problems in American society. The inability of youth to find opportunities for disciplined self-development has been defined as a political problem. We believe that opportunities for cultural and self-realization are available for middle-class youth, but that those youth have frequently failed to exploit these opportunities. We also believe that opportunities for the expression of the political idealism of youth are available but have not been exploited in a sustained and disciplined way—as we shall make clear later.

When the conformist sees his values violated by others who do so with confidence and impunity, he becomes less confident in his conformist behavior. In a complex, pluralist society, the very act of living an autonomous life creates the conditions which validate that life for others. Such men as Eric Hoffer, Irving Howe, Philip Rahv, Stanley Edgar Hyman, Meyer Shapiro, Harold Rosenberg, Kenneth Burke, Lewis Mumford, Wallace Stevens, William Carlos Williams, William Faulkner, and Paul Goodman have demonstrated the possibilities inherent in nonconformist work despite the demands of a conformist world. If the individual has confidence in his own life styles and values, he need not feel oppressed by others who may disapprove.

This notion that pressures to conform are brought against one is as much a product of the individual's own willingness to accept such pressures as it is the existence of the pressure itself. Failure to realize this results in conformity as well as the unnecessary rebellion against it.

David Riesman suggests that it is possible to accept the responsibility for determining and shaping one's own life style. To do this, however, one must have confidence in one's own values, the self-discipline to acquire the skills and knowledge necessary to cultivate one's interests, and the nerve to try to be autonomous. A painter, novelist, poet, or artist of any sort who is productive acquires the skill, discipline, nerve, and industriousness necessary to the achievement of autonomy by the very act of his productivity. He discovers the possibility of autonomy by relentlessly doing his own work, the results of which, as they accumulate, provide him with a means for gaining confidence from the fact that he has already done something. Frequently such individuals have been forced to live off earnings from routine, uninteresting work while creating works for which there is no audience. They may find approval only after they become successful, though there is no guarantee that such approval will be forthcoming. The landscape is strewn with novel, but unsung, failures. But in achieving either success or failure, the price paid for autonomy is the disciplined attempt to achieve it. One need not be a genius. Anyone with talent or who is strongly interested in politics, art, music, literature, and so forth, need only pursue his interests. Disciplined pursuit of the interest results in the acquisition of sensitivity, knowledge, skill, and discrimination which validate the initial interest. The validation allows one to live and grow within the framework of his own values, tastes, and interests.

One cannot pursue this style without paying a price, which at times is high. It may involve isolation from one's immediate social environment, loss of friendship with the rest of the herd based on the common denominator of the herd's interests, or being regarded as odd, eccentric, irascible, and difficult to get along with. To live against such threats of disapproval requires nerve. In this sense, the failure of nerve is equivalent to the unwillingness to acquire the discipline, self-confidence, and interest to be free. We believe it is this failure, more than the constraints of the philistine, the community, or the commune, that is likely to produce conformity and the problems associated with it. Rebellion against the philistine or middle-class life style is a rebellion which lacks both the nerve and discipline to act upon the principles which evoke the rebellion. When one accepts the constraints of a radical cell or a new commune, he reasserts his conformity. Radical constraints usually demand self- and organized discipline. Communal restraints can be violated by splitting. The new radical politics have as their major virtue the inability to organize anything.

Regardless of the possibilities, it appears that the number of individuals who are capable of living affirmatively within the framework of autonomous values is small. One of the most difficult of human tasks seems to be to summon personal reserves of interest, self-discipline, and nerve that will allow one to be at least partially responsible for his own growth and autonomous development. The upper middle class, having been freed from economic necessity, seems to be particularly incapable of self-direction. Increasing numbers of middle-class youths have become aware of the demands for conformity placed upon them, and increasing numbers rebel but fail in their rebellion—often with frightening results.

Finding solutions to these problems depends upon the ability of the society to apply rationally resources and technology that are already available. But, in addition, self-discipline, self-control, and the development of personal and creative skills are means to self-realization and intelligent control of the social structure.

We have argued that segments of middle class youth, whose very affluence has allowed them to avoid the discipline necessary for mobility and caused them to escalate their demands upon the system, have developed an attitude of righteousness, mindlessness, and a quest for immediate and direct action. It is in this sense that radical, extremist youth is irrational. We have also indicated that past repressions and promises, followed by lack of fulfillment, have produced a black anger and rage that result in violence, riots, and uprisings that, no matter how understandable, produce no solutions to the problems that evoke the protests.

But neither of these problems of youths or blacks nor the failure to solve them, *in themselves* need threaten American society. Each solution to major social and economic problems is likely to result in an increasing cooptation of the protesting groups, so that in the long run the granting of rights and social concessions may modify undesirable conditions and social injustices.

The more serious problem is that the actions of radical youth and angry blacks may provoke the hostilities of lower-class, lower-middle-class, and middle-class whites, and create a backlash of irrationality which transcends its causes.

Until the mid-sixties the old redneck, racist, lower-class and lower-middle-class culture of resentment was on the decline. The new middle classes—smug, liberal, and striving for culture—were the bearers of an ideology of liberalism, reform, political honesty, and government intervention in the solution of all major social problems. The black revolution and the youth revolution have frightened the new lower middle class out of its apathy and its ethnic liberalism. The white working class and lower middle class increasingly see the blacks as threatening their property values, their jobs, their safety, their tenure, and the success they feel they have achieved by hard work. The youthful radical, the upper-middle-class radical, and, increasingly, the lower-middle-class radical, are threats to the very system that guaranteed their success. The new patriots want law and order, and if law and order means repression, an increasing number of middle- and working-class

Americans want it. Since the 1968 presidential election, almost every state and local election in the United States has seen the proponents of law and order victorious. The response of blacks and white radical youth to the threat or actuality of repression is to become more destructive, provocative, and violent, which in turn stimulates greater counter-violence and repression.

As the hostility between the radical and reactionary forces in American society continues to polarize, it becomes more and more difficult to gain political support for solutions to the *original* problems. The middle classes become less liberal. Budgetary racism becomes more pronounced. Taxpayers' rebellions become something to be reckoned with. Emotional, irrational, racial, and political antagonisms have become the central issues of the day, and manifest problems which might originally have been solved are now ignored. They cannot be ignored indefinitely, for failure to solve them only worsens the irrationalities that produced the problems in the first place.

If the only solution to our current problems is repression, then neither radical students nor blacks nor liberals can win. A bureaucratic mass society can be permissive or repressive; but if it becomes repressive, it can become totalitarian. The middle classes, along with the white working class and the upper classes, can be liberal, conservative, or totalitarian, depending on the state of their defensive anxieties. Under the impact of the black and youth revolutions, these classes are being driven to the right. Youth can be liberal or totalitarian; and radical youth, under the banner of freedom, are becoming totalitarian and are driving other groups to adopt some versions of totalitarian repressiveness. If this process should continue, then the reason involved in Keynesian political economy will give way to an economy supported by police and domestic military budgets. We believe America is well down the road toward this state of affairs.

STYLES FOR DISSENT

The other major problems of the quality of American life—that is, the destruction of an independent public opinion, the cancerous spread of a bureaucratic spirit, and the dominance of society by bureaucratic elites—can, for the purposes of discussing their solution, be treated as one problem. Its root cause is the use by centralized bureaucratic elites of the organizations which they control and the resources provided by giant budgets for their own interests. Through their control of the mass media they can provide pleasant entertainment and national morality dramas which can be passively and comfortably consumed without recourse to independent effort or thought.

Television has abundantly demonstrated its ability to take the sting out of poverty, black revolution, youth revolution, drugs, and educational problems simply by presenting them in situational comedies or in serious dramas. The media can emphasize or minimize social problems; under pressure from the Vice-President they can play up or play down crime, race riots, student rebellions, and the successes or failures of presidential administrations. Programs that respond seriously to such problems are believed so long as their message agrees with the interests or reinforces the prejudices of their audiences.

Opinion-making institutions can present and diffuse ideologies that justify the dominance of bureaucratic elites and can withhold information that conceals incompetence, malfeasance, and self-serving. By virtue of their favored positions, they attempt to immunize themselves from criticism while developing justifications that entitle them to the highest rewards our society can produce. In these respects, modern bureaucratic elites are no different from all elites of the past, for the self-rewarding and self-justifying aspects of elitehood are generic to its nature.

What is unique about the past thirty years is the ability of the elites not only to command the machines of information diffusion and information control, but also their ability to coopt the academic and intellectual strata into their public opinion and publicity organizations. Before World War II the intellectual and academic classes were isolated from the elite establishment because there were no means to reward them for conformity to elite demands. The prosperity of America has provided—via gigantic corporation budgets and government, foundation, and university grants and positions—the means to grant the material rewards which have converted many American intellectuals into active technicians and self-satisfied extollers and ideologists for America's major organizations and institutions. Academicians and intellectuals have found these new social rewards pleasant. When the funds are cut back and rewards are no longer forthcoming, many intellectuals begin to make mindless, senseless attacks upon the system which has heretofore kept them living in a style to which they have become only too accustomed. These intellectual critics are joined by youth who will later reach thirty, become professors, and accept the perquisites and emoluments of subsidized professorial life. They become highly principled in response to new-found idealism, empty leisure, and a quest for high-minded causes. The most gutless of professors and academic technicians have simply collapsed under the not-too-subtle threats and pressures of their students, and have proved their sympathies by leading the students—to promotion and tenure for themselves, and jail sentences and expulsion for the students.

The idea of a democracy demands that intellectually independent and capable individuals scrutinize the operations of society and speak out against the excesses of its "self-elected," "self-appointed," and co-opted leaders and representatives. More than ever before, the conditions of mass democracy demand that intellectuals play the role of tribune (but not of Caesar) of the people.

Traditional democratic theory has assumed that the various interest groups in society will check each other. In addition, the free press, independent of all external pressure, is supposed to reveal abuses and excesses of power. In reality, several factors limit these traditional solutions.

The legal, administrative, and economic complexity of the modern bureaucratic apparatus make it extremely difficult for anyone to scrutinize its informal operations. The social distance of the press (not to mention all other audiences) from the sources of decision make it difficult, though not impossible, for the press to overcome the problem of the management of news and opinion. The fear of retaliation by government agencies, when criticism of the press and television is made by such responsible figures as the Vice-President of the United States, can and must be a major concern not only to the news media but to all those who hope to retain some form of democracy in America. Gaining access to privileged information and to organizational secrets would require forms of counter-intelligence agencies that would be accountable to the public. The use of the ombudsman is a weak gesture in this direction.

A more difficult problem arises from the fact that the ethics of modern bureaucracy increasingly require that in situations of policy conflicts and other forms of organizational infighting, the responsible official solves his problem without recourse to the public and the press. The ethical imperative demands that differences be resolved *in camera*. By going to the press or to other outside pressure groups and audiences, the bureaucrat expands the scope of the battlefield and invites a counterattack that would expose his excesses and special privileges. Even Robert Kennedy and J. Edgar Hoover, who lost little love for each other, managed in 1967 to call a truce in their public argument over wiretapping. It seems clear that the various bureaucratic elites and the mass interest groups they represent are likely to try to prevent the public from gaining information that allows for independent, informed decisions.

Strong as these tendencies to secretiveness and allegiance may be, independent journalists, academicians, intellectuals, and congressmen have at times succeeded in serving as tribunes for the people. People like Ralph Nader, Jack Anderson and the late Drew Pearson, Harrison Salisbury, Martin Luther King, Jr., and Senators Estes Kefauver, Eugene McCarthy, and J. William Fulbright, and Congressman Wright Patman have at times dramatized issues and exposed abuses that would otherwise have been neglected.

Authors of books and editors of small magazines are in a unique position. Due to the relatively low cost of producing a book or small magazine as compared with producing a newspaper, mass magazine, or television program, it is still possible for writers to study and report independently on issues that are not, and frequently cannot be, treated by other media. The means for maintaining independent sources of information and points of view rests on the willingness of a relatively few intellectuals and writers to remain independent in spite of countless opportunities to surrender their autonomy in return for higher rewards in the mass media. More than at any time in the past, American society offers untold opportunities to sell out—ideologically as well as financially.

As methods for selling out to large-scale organizations become more refined and perfected, the sell-out as an act can become genteel, prestigious, respectable, and highly profitable. Yet it is some kind of tribute to the human spirit that the process of increasing the rewards for acquiescence and cooptability also generates a striving on the part of some for personal autonomy and independence which results in the continued expression of dissenting views. In spite of its lack of conventional rewards, our society depends on dissent. Whether such dissent will continue to reproduce itself is by no means certain or automatic. We can only hope that it will continue to exist, not because it can sometimes correct the abuses inherent in any elite-dominated society, but as a symbol that it can survive in spite of those abuses. No matter how fragile the thread of dissent appears to be, in spite of all those forces organized to achieve a comfortable acquiescence or a forced, gutless radicalism, the simple existence of genuine dissent is the last significant symbol of the free society.

For the politically sophisticated who are aware of the full potential of bureaucratic constraints, and of those who oppose them, there is an ethical imperative to expose, oppose, and define human limits to organized repressions. To expose fraud and to oppose excessive ambition from both left and right becomes a major form of political action.

But exposing the fraud, the self-seeking, and the incompetence of bureaucratic elites is not enough. At best it results in a correction of the random mistakes of bureaucrats. It cannot lead to changes in bureaucratic policy and structures. Yet radical structural changes do not offer a solution to the problems of American society either. A radical attack on bureaucracy is likely to result initially in vast bloodletting followed by the reinstitution of a bureaucratic terrorism more thorough and centralized than we can now imagine.

It is impossible for American society to return to a decentralized laissez-faire state, despite the wishes of young and old reactionaries. Government budgets will remain large, and bureaucracy will remain as the basic organizational feature of industrial society so long as industrial society is able to exist. The upper and middle classes will be composed of managerial, administrative, intellectual, technical, and professional personnel. Many members of these groups, because of their education and favored position, will have the problem of rising above the pedestrian and technical nature of their bureaucratic work. Cultural and political discontent is, and will continue to be, a chronic problem in all advanced industrial societies.

Political discontent can be resolved by providing substantive solutions—rather than vast structural changes—to the problems upon which the discontent becomes focused. John Dewey, in *The Quest for Certainty,* suggested that the history of the world was a quest for ultimate and final solutions. A structural change, perhaps produced by revolution, or by one big blow-up, has always appeared to promise a final solution to all the knotty and complex problems of society. But the very complexity of the issues in contemporary industrial society works against total solutions.

This means that youthful idealism must be channeled into action on the dozens of political issues to which a solution is possible. Concentrating on these issues means concentrating on the acquisition of specific interests and information. It means that youth (and, of course, adults) must acquire the skills for political action. These skills include bargaining, organizing, and demonstrating, to be sure, but also running mimeograph machines, knocking at doors, and being able to listen politely to those whom they regard as their inferiors. More than this, youth must learn that the political process is a continuous one in which there is no guarantee of victory. They will often lose battles, sometimes wars. At times they will find it necessary to make weak compromises that will tarnish the sincerity of their efforts. Moreover, they will discover, as all political activists in the past have discovered, that their political victories may result in more opportunities for profit and exploitation by the philistines they think they have defeated. They may have to face the even more disillusioning knowledge that victory by idealists may convert the idealists into self-serving, successful bureaucrats, hacks, or businessmen. Youth may recognize these metamorphoses when they see them in their friends, enemies, and parents. Fortunately or unfortunately, they may change their perspective only when it happens to themselves.

Having ideals and being willing to risk realizing them involves dangers. So far as we know, the only way to avoid these risks is through apathy, withdrawal from society, or the quest for violent self-destruction in the pursuit of total solutions.

If one must strike an optimistic note, it is this: modern bureaucracies fall short of being thorough in their repressiveness. They are too inefficient. Whether their efficiency is more dangerous than their mistakes is an open question. Modern extremist political movements are even less efficient. They are as likely to purge their friends as their enemies, and, in the long run, if they are successful, their only friend is the executioner.

V.

Postscript

16. American Society since the Golden Age of Capitalism

The period from the end of World War II to 1965 has been called the Golden Age of Western Capitalism. By Western capitalism we mean the capitalism of the United States, Western Europe and Japan. During that period, capitalism had reconstituted itself and solved the internal and external problems brought about by the great depression and by Fascism and Nazism.

Since 1965 these countries have experienced economic, political and social crises, including a crisis of legitimacy. These crises are characterized by unemployment, inflation, and the collapse of the international economic system. In part these crises were brought about by the failure of the international monetary system established after World War II and its inability to deal with such problems as inflation and the oil crisis. But in addition, the crisis has expressed itself in a failure to recapitalize American industry to sustain efficient industrial production and in new demands placed upon the economic system by previously unfavored groups. Previous successes in the Golden Age caused both rising expectations and a new democratic sense that all groups should experience a share in the prosperity of the Golden Age including the expectation of previously deprived groups that they make up for their past deprivation.

The failure to meet these expectations led, in the sixties and seventies, to a decline of civility, anomic riots and segmental political explosions. Modern western capitalism has thus become politically less stable, and subject to wide and often unpredictable sources of disturbance, violence, bombings and riots generated by often short-lived, relatively small political, ideological, religious, ethnic and nationalistic movements and fads.

This synoptic summary outlines many of the major political phenomenon of the late sixties and early seventies; but to understand these phenomena more fully one would first have to understand the Golden Age of the post-war period. Some of its characteristics we have outlined in this book.

The post-World War II expansion and prosperity was to a large extent underwritten by United States governmental deficit funding and monetary and taxation policies which subsidized not only the industrial expansion that guaranteed new markets but created and expanded new occupational classes. These new classes were in the service industries, especialy governmental, in education and in white collar managerial occupations. The expansion of these categories which were primarily absorbed as lower and middle level bureaucrats has led further to an expansion of leisure and culture and the industries designed to service them. The increase in white collar, service, managerial, administrative and professional occupations far exceeded the declines in employment in basic industries and agriculture and unemployment as a problem appeared to be solved.

This expansion, from the standpoint of western capitalism as a whole, was not only American, but involved the economic and political penetration of American institutions into all areas of the world, but especially among the Western European nations and other industrialized areas, excluding Russia and China. Similar processes of expansion occurred in all of these countries partly as the result of loan and aid programs. But such expansion appears to be part of a generalized process that seems to have occurred with some leads and lags at different levels in various areas of the entire world, excluding only China and Albania. It is difficult to determine whether American expansion was the cause of these worldwide trends, but one can say with some degree of certainty that where this expansion occurred its effects in any one country reinforced similar effects in other countries. Thus relatively continuous and stable expansion occurred at economic, political and cultural levels in the western capitalist world during the period from 1945–1965.

The overall expansion in the United States that was almost without interruption for 20 years led first to a sense of new opportunities for previously unfavored groups such as blacks, youth, working classes, and new immigrants, and in the cases of older working class groups, especially ethnic working classes and their children, the realization of new opportunities. For the older generation of industrial workers, the new opportunities were seen as a symbol of arrival and acceptance. In spite of the Great Depression, America had redeemed much of its promise by giving them steady work at relatively high wages, seniority in unionized plants and consumer's durables such as home ownership, automobiles, television, and home appliances. This has been called peoples' capitalism. For their children, those entering young adulthood in the 1960s, these new opportunities were increasingly taken for granted because they had been reared in an environment of prosperity. Thus for them the prosperity was seen as the basis for making further demands on the "system."

Of course, the rising expectations that were a result of the expansion and prosperity were not evenly spread across the national class structure or the society. Regional, national and international variations occurred. What can be said at most is that those groups who in their own life time experienced the sense of opportunity earliest in point of time, age, and generation stabilized their expectations earliest and tended to use that stabilized standard as a floor from which to make further demands. Thus the achievement of "success" tended to "pacify" the older working class who realized in their own lifetimes more material property than they had expected, and to dissatisfy both their children and other groups who either took that success for granted—and did not regard it as success—or entered the economic scene too late to participate in the affluence of the Golden Age.

A major aspect of the Golden Age at its economic and institutional level was that it was the product of both conscious and unstated agreements among the various *organized* political and economic segments of the society. Those agreements were that the respective parties to them would practice restraint on their demands on the system, would respect each others' "rights" and would not attack the system as a whole. It meant that organized labor would not make excessive wage demands upon industry, that industry would not make excessive price demands upon the public and that government through tax and monetary policy would provide a basic expansive economic framework and would referee the economic demands of all parties by jawboning, mediation, and defining and enforcing price and wage guidelines. In accepting this overall framework, the various parties to the agreements accepted the legitimacy of the new forms of Keynesian state capitalism.

Less organized groups in the society such as the middle classes, farmers, youth, and to a much less extent minority groups were "bought off" by favorable agricultural, educational and social welfare policies.

Yet by 1968, the system had begun to collapse and its collapse was made manifest by 1970, reaching extreme proportions in the economic decline of 1972–1973. By this time in the United States an annual inflation rate of 12 percent and an unemployment rate reaching its high point, which seemed to signal the collapse of the Keynesian system of state capitalism. Radical critics saw this as a new failure of capitalism, the long deferred crises or contradiction of capitalism or as a failure of the Keynesian solution to the contradiction of capitalism. Even those who had no ideological interest in seeing capitalism collapse, began to doubt whether the patchwork, Keynesian pragmatism constructed by Franklin Roosevelt and maintained and expanded by Truman, Eisenhower, Kennedy, and especially Johnson could continue to work.

Some academicians, segments of middle class youth, blacks and Spanish-speaking radical groups began even earlier in the sixties to reject a political-economic system which had been engineered partly for them without their consent by an establishment that appeared to control the system. At present it is even fashionable to predict the end of the system, capitalism and even western civilization. Prophets of despair who are not necessarily Marxists become the profiteers of doom, even if that doom is to arrive a hundred years or more in the future.

The question of whether the collapse of Keynesian state capitalism is permanent is perhaps the most profound question of our times. If it has collapsed, the consequences may be too far reaching and frightful to contemplate by all but committed romantic radicals, for the collapse would be more than a collapse of an economic and political arrangement, and could be, as viewed by some, the collapse of western civilization itself.

Whether in fact the system is collapsing or whether its recurring rises are merely re-adjustments of the western world system is the problem that now faces the United States only two centuries after the founding of the Republic and the publication of *The Wealth of Nations*.

We will first analyze in some detail more of the dynamics of the western system in order to trace out some additional causes of its apparent failure.

SOURCES OF STRAIN IN KEYNESIAN STATE CAPITALISM

The system of relatively full employment which was a consequence of Keynesian institutional arrangements caused, by its very nature, a gradual and continuous wage and price inflation. Relatively full employment has always resulted in pressures to raise wages, and high levels of consumption result in pressure on prices. Through the entire period of the fifties and sixties continuous rises in prices at about a 3 percent level were part of the consequence of the sustained prosperity, even when pressures for prices and wage increases were restrained by the implicit and explicit agreements upon which rests the political basis of the Keynesian political economy.

Increased levels of inflation were a product of the Vietnam war when military budgets of 25–35 billion were met by deficit spending rather than by new taxation, causing higher demand and prices than would otherwise have occurred. Moreover, the Vietnam war led large numbers of youth and ultimately the liberal middle classes to become disenchanted with or to reject the political framework which previously had supported them in their educational aspirations and lifestyles. At the same time, the continuing inflation caused substantial segments of the business community to question not only the Vietnam war but also the terms of the political and economic agreements they had made with organized labor and the administrators of wage-price guidelines. Throughout the sixties a substantial segment of the business community began to inquire into the level of unemployment that would be appropriate to control inflation and produce a disciplined labor force. The estimates ranged from 1½ percent early in the period to 3–4 percent by the mid-sixties.

When Richard Nixon became President the proposals to create a reserve pool of unemployment in order to lessen wage pressures and to diminish demand could be turned into policy directives. During President Nixon's first term the primary device used to control inflation and induce the necessary unemployment was monetary policy. Interest rates were raised with the hope that such increases in capital costs would limit expansion and thus halt inflation. Whether in fact these policies worked is difficult to estimate. Certainly unemployment increased, but the rate of inflation also increased. Moreover, it is not easy to ascertain whether the rate of inflation would have had an ever greater increase without such policies, but one can be sure that increased interest costs were inflationary with regard to short-term investment. Investors with short-term capital hoped that the increased capital costs would be absorbed by even greater rates of inflation. If the inflation rate was greater than the interest rate, inflation would then pay off the increased capital costs at a profit. Long-term investment at a 10 percent interest rate on money borrowed especially in plants which required long periods of time to construct (such as an atomic energy plant which might require 7–9 years to build) would make the costs prohibitive. Yet the effect of cutting expansion in these areas was not necessarily deflationary in the long run because high interest costs so incurred would discourage other production by making investment capital less available in areas where increased production would take off the market the expendable income that was in itself inflationary. The productivity that could result from lower interest rates would result in lower costs and would create the additional commodities that would absorb the excess expendable income and eliminate excess unmet demands as a source of inflationary pressure.

In the late sixties the expectation by businessmen of still higher interest rates resulted in a flow of capital into Western Europe and a decline in long-term capital investments in heavy industry in the

United States. Businessmen were followed in making foreign investments by institutional investors and money managers who saw opportunities for quick profits in European and Japanese money markets because of a continuing decline in the value of the dollar relative to other currencies. The already existing large stock of dollars in international markets which had accumulated throughout the period 1945–1965 were increased too by these new exports of business capital and resulted in a further decline of the value of the dollar. In addition hopes of even higher interest rates resulted in competitive investing in commercial paper with little or no productive result, and a rise in the cost of government borrowing especially for municipalities and state governments. By 1970, the outward flow of capital was so great that American exports were no longer competitive on the world's markets and the United States had accumulated embarrassingly large trade deficits which were the result in part of high levels of imports encouraged by domestic inflation. This forced a *de facto* devaluation of the American dollar which was the basis of the international monetary system. It further forced a formal devaluation by President Nixon in 1970 which tended to increase American domestic prices, encourage American exports and thus caused further inflation within the United States.

Both the inflation (whatever its causes) and President Nixon's electoral victory in 1972 ended the implicit political and economic agreements that constituted the basis of the Golden Age of American Capitalism. Prior to 1968, Democratic administrations and even the Eastern Republican establishment tended to restrain themselves with respect to increasing prices and taking a positive attitude towards labor. The small margin of the Republican victory in 1968 meant that an overall change in policy could not be conspicuously undertaken. In fact, President Nixon was careful to announce, "I am a Keynesian," at the same time that he began to subvert the agreements that were the basis of a Keynesian political economy. But while President Nixon maintained the rhetoric and the substance of Keynesian policy, he drastically changed the direction of that policy to favor certain segments of the business class, especially those on the outer rim. When businessmen recognized this shift in orientation and realized that the administration was favorable to their economic demands they felt free to increase prices without the restraints of wage-price guidelines. The Nixon administration subverted price and wage controls by eliminating limits on the price of raw materials, and on profits and dividends. This policy of leaky controls invited successive price increases, made mockery of the 5 percent statutory ceilings on wages and prices, and subjected only labor to its restraints. One can speculate that the wage-price control legislation was designed to fail. In part the approval for price increases was purchased by political contributions; in part businessmen may have understood that their past contributions assured a lack of interference with a policy of price inflation whether such policies were the result of explicit agreements or not.

From 1970 onwards, at increasing levels raids upon the consumer were organized first by smaller and later by big business. These raids were expressed in raising prices of milk, sugar, grains, meat, coffee, and soy beans. In part, some of these raids were the product of natural disasters in producing areas which, however, became a source of unusual profits for processors, distributors, and retailers. Others were the result of economic mismanagement as in the case of the sale of American grain to Russia and China—although some of the mismanagement must be seen as part of a public relations effort designed to further detente and to deflect attention away from Nixon's growing domestic problems.

The precipitating events of the depression of 1973–1974 were twofold: (1) the oil crisis and (2) the automobile price increases of 1973 and 1974. The oil crisis perhaps reflects the end product of a series of bungled attempts by American oil companies to avoid paying corporation taxes in the United States. To avoid domestic taxes the oil consortia arranged to have the oil producing countries change the label of what previously had been royalties into taxes: taxes to be paid to foreign governments could be subtracted from taxes to be paid to the government of the United States. In order to make this change, it was first necessary for the oil drilling companies to work out a uniform pricing and taxing scale among the oil producing countries. This meant that the previously disorganized and often hostile oil producing countries had to be organized, and it was undoubtedly the organizing genius of the American oil companies and the American State Department that made OPEC possible. This organizational achievement together with the withdrawal of the British Navy from the Persian Gulf and Indian Ocean made the Arabian Gulf states autonomous and permitted a unity among the Arab states which they had until then never been able to achieve. The first result of this unity was the expropriation of higher and higher percentages of the ownership of the oil drilling countries. The next were, after the Arab-Israel war of 1973, the oil embargo followed by a ten-fold increase in oil prices. The oil companies themselves compounded the problem by withholding delivery of in-shipment oil for American markets at the time of the crisis, creating further shortages that justified still larger price increases. Part of the strategy behind such withholding may have been the desire to raise the price of domestic oil and to de-regulate the natural gases. In these aspects then the action of the oil companies was another raid against the American consumer. The OPEC countries in following a policy of restriction of output, cartelization of production, and managed prices were pursuing a similar policy, though their methods resembled more the methods of the Standard Oil companies of the first decade of the 20th century. They had learned this lesson too from American monopoly capitalism.

From another point of view, the lesson of the oil crisis is that the Keynesian system is an international system which involves a policy of mutual self-restraint on the part of all of its participants, international as well as domestic. The OPEC countries as part of that international system, like the oil companies and an increasing part of American domestic and international corporations, rejected the restraint of a Keynesian system.

The immediate effect of the politics of oil was to fuel inflation not only in the direct costs of heating and transportation but in the total petrochemical industry that contributes to the cost of agricultural products, plastics and the industrial uses of energy.

The automobile companies exceeded the greed of the raw materials producers by raising prices 8 percent in 1973 and 11 percent in 1974. But unlike foods, the purchase of an automobile is postponable, and the immediate effect of increases in automobile prices of almost $2,000 per car was a drastic decline in automobile production and large-scale unemployment in the automobile and related industries.

This occurred at almost the same time that oil companies used the oil crisis as a screen for the consolidation and rationalization of the retail sales of gasoline. This entailed the elimination of independent gasoline retailers and single pump chain outlets in many rural parts of the country where these had existed since the twenties and thirties.

By 1973, unemployment had reached the level of 8.7 percent and inflation an annual level of 12 percent. In 1986 unemployment hovers around 7 percent and a non-inflationary equilibrium has been reached at much higher levels of prices, but not wages. This equilibrium, however, is threatened by large trade imbalances and the high carrying costs of the national debt.

SOCIAL AND POLITICAL ASPECTS OF ECONOMIC STRAINS

This historical overview of economic policy does not account for political changes which preceded and to a large extent helped to explain the economic changes. The reaction to the Vietnam war and the revolution of rising expectations among minority groups which in part was a product of court decisions, the civil rights legislation of the early sixties, and the war on poverty, caused a backlash in the election of 1968 which was expressed in more intensified form in the election of 1972.

It is difficult to determine whether President Nixon's response to students and urban riots in the 1968–1972 period was purely a calculated attempt to profit from the anxieties of the American middle class concerning the cultural and political revolution of the time or whether honest political righteousness was the dominant factor in the dirty tricks, Watergate crisis. Certainly a great many of President Nixon's house staff defended their crimes on the basis that only a Nixon victory in 1972 could save the United States from subversion or revolution. The two sets of motivations could have operated separately as apparently they did, and neither of these motives appeared to conflict with a determined policy of President Nixon to reward contributors or extort contributions in exchange for actual or implicit rights to raid both the treasury and the consumer.

But Watergate was more than either political righteousness or campaign politics, for it violated the very basis for legitimacy underpinning much of the American political system. The notion that government is responsible to its own laws has been a cardinal principle in American society no matter how often it has been dishonored in practice. It has been the basis for the cry "Turn the rascals out" from the time of the Florida land scandals to Teapot dome, and the defalcations of Sherman Adams and General Vaughan. But even given the negative reactions by large segments of the American middle and working classes to the youth and black rebellions of the late 1960s, the American public had a vast reluctance to turn the then most recent rascal out. Only the Saturday night massacre, the firing of Archibald Cox and the resignation of Elliot Richardson produced a constitutional crisis which, in turn, was intensified by the televising of the Ervin hearings and the publication of the tapes. Perhaps President Nixon's obscenity and the cold, calculating nature of his contempt for his subordinates, colleagues and the public was enough to produce the demand for impeachment and to force his resignation.

But the basic data about dirty tricks, the Watergate and Ellsberg break-ins, political favors for campaign contributions, as well as assaults on the press and political opposition were widely known, but not documented by public hearings, before the election of 1972. The Democratic congress, the general public and even Nixon supporters were not impelled toward taking action against the President until the continuously unfolding pattern of public exposure left these groups no other choice than to press for impeachment or forced resignation. Prior to the Saturday night massacre, the public was led by the belief that can be summarized as "Say it ain't so, Joe." No one wanted to believe that the President could be so despicable; or if he was, no one in office wanted to be the first to say so. In part, the refusal to accept the increasingly documented charges against President Nixon and his administration was based upon the acceptance by some groups of the argument that strong measures were necessary to repress the youth and black rebellions. Other groups were prone to accept the Nixon political strategy as part of the cost for favorable social and economic policies, and of possible international gains.

In short, Nixon in his economic and social policy was meeting the basic desires of a large part of the middle and upper clases, including their desire to curb some of the effects of the rise in expectations of youth and minority groups. But, in addition, President Nixon's policy of repression of youthful demonstrations against the Vietnam war, of the new moralities of rampant drugs, sexuality, dropping out and communalism, the rhetoric of black liberation, urban disorder and crime in the streets also were the source of anxieties for the lower middle and ethnic working classes as well as almost all classes in the rural fringes in the South and Southwest and in the small town heartland of mid-America.

Certainly, the anxieties of these groups could be catered to by cutbacks of poverty and welfare programs and of support to university education and the withdrawal of federal funds from cities with high densities of minority ethnic groups, especially in the industrial and Democratic northeast. Moreover, the expression of these anxieties and aggressiveness toward those groups who appeared to provoke the anxieties could be expressed in cuts in budgets of those programs that appeared to subsidize and support them. As a result, taxes could be cut and the incomes of favored groups maintained in a time of rising prices and budgetary squeezes by cutting expenditures on those who were regarded as socially, economically, or morally useless or dangerous. Thus the righteousness generated by hostility to the disturbers of the American dream as it was experienced by those who supported Nixon could be used in justifying economic policies which the embattled lower middle, middle and upper classes would support anyway. They could put all their rotten eggs in one basket.

The anxieties exposed by the black and youth rebellions permitted political attacks on the press, the liberal establishment, on congressional autonomy and on a federal bureaucracy which was largely a hold-over from the eight preceding years of Democratic administrations. President Nixon thus attempted to make these anxieties the basis of a total policy that would undermine all opposition to whatever policies he happened to support at the moment, but especially the opposition to the East Asian war that he had pledged to end.

The resignation of President Nixon solved for that moment the problems of political corruption and political legitimation. President Ford's emphasis on clean politics and on fair political tactics seemed initially to obscure all other issues including the issues of inflation, stagnation and the rising demands for political benefits by minority groups, blacks, environmentalists, and the exponents of the new cultural politics such as women, homosexuals, and lesbians.

President Ford may well have been an accidental president or, if one wishes to see it so, the political fall-out of Watergate. In terms of economic policy, he presented a substantially different approach from that of President Nixon. Nixon appeared primarily to be attempting to corrupt and deflect the Keynesian state system in order to reward political supporters of a new political establishment he was in the process of creating. President Ford, if one accepted both his political statements and his congressional record, appeared to be fundamentally opposed to the very idea of a Keynesian political economy. His rhetoric was that of deregulation and dismemberment of the bureaucratic governmental establishment, of support of the individualistic entrepreneur no matter how little the individual exists as an economic force and how greatly the corporation so exists, and of budget and tax cutting to provide discretionary income disposal for those groups thus freed from taxes and regulatory controls. To be sure his apparent natural inclinations were supported and encouraged by the apparently stronger rhetorical individualism of Ronald Reagan. Both appealed to those groups who felt they were overconstrained by the Keynesian political formula and both go back to a political rhetoric which was expressed in recent times only by Senator Goldwater in 1964 and by Alf Landon in 1936. Yet, it is not political tradition, by itself, that determines policy, for the inflation of the mid-sixties has to some extent affected everyone. The problem that then emerges ~~is~~: who is to bear the cost of inflation?

The major issue in American society since at least 1970 is to find some group other than one's own on which to displace these costs. Cuts in taxes, especially income and corporate taxes, place the increasing costs of inflation in the hands of others than those who have the greatest income. The addition of regressive taxes, especially social security taxes, increases the burden on those who have the least income. Cuts in welfare payments, of course, have hurt the "unworthy" poor and especially those unworthy poor who have made their poverty the basis for political demands. The termination of poverty programs has hurt the blacks and Spanish minorities who have dared to make their presence felt and who are "collectively" reputedly "responsible" for violence in the streets. At the same time increased budgets have been allocated to law enforcement agencies and institutions. Cuts in educational expenditures for students and research programs have disadvantaged working and middle class youth and their professors while research funds have been made increasingly available to applied sciences and to industry. To the extent that educational programs may be encouraged, they are designed to facilitate career education when unemployment makes careers more difficult to find.

Cut-backs in aid to the cities have the effect of penalizing all of the above groups, but especially the ethnic minorities who increasingly reside in the city. The suburbs and exurbs which are populated primarily by middle classes are largely exempt from such cuts. And these latter groups are likely to support such cuts justifying their support on the grounds of the law-abiding character and righteousness of the suburban and exurban way of life.

In the meantime, the cities have had to bear the burden of increased welfare payments caused by earlier migration from rural areas, and of maintaining the urban commercial and cultural facilities and services for commuters and tourists. They have had to absorb the rising wage costs of the urban civil service that partially maintains and supports the less favored groups mentioned above.

These cut-backs of urban services and urban welfare constitute a reversal of Keynesian fiscal policy of the Golden Age wherein the expansion of service industries and employment was one of the chief objectives of Keynesian economic policy. In addition the high interest rates designed to curb inflation have represented an increasing set of costs to municipal and state governments which, as a result, have been forced to further cut benefits to those groups that would otherwise have been supported by traditional Keynesianism.

American society in the Golden Age was a society based on continuous expansion, and part of that expansion was produced by deficit financing with the expectation that a continuously rising gross national product would cover the costs of borrowed capital. So long as gross national product rose, the method of financing would succeed. The recession of 1973–1974 made this policy unworkable and produced an urban crisis as municipal and state costs continued to rise because the earlier commitments were long-term ones and government income declined as a result of the downturn in gross national product. The cities, especially those in the Northeast, were forced to re-finance high interest rate debt at a time of declining tax bases and revenues. The decline in part has been generated by a long-term flight of middle classes to suburbs and a shift of industry to the suburbs which in part were financed or supported by federal highway and tax policy. As a result cities, up to now only in the Northeast, are increasingly forced to cut services and employment in major areas of municipal social programs and services at a time when mass employment in other segments of industry has not yet reabsorbed previous unemployment created in other sectors by industrial cutbacks in the period 1972–1974.

In part the decline of cities in the Northeast is caused by a flight of industry and jobs to the "sunbelt." The expansion in the latter area is partly the result of federal support of defense industries, and partly a result of the flight of industry to less unionized parts of the country and to places where lower levels of economic development have resulted in low taxes and the willingness of underdeveloped areas to assume part of the initial costs of such development.

SOCIETAL TRENDS IN AN ECONOMY OF SCARCITY

Whether these fiscal and moral crises are a permanent part of American life is yet to be assayed. Energy prices are not likely to return to pre-1973 prices, though their major inflationary effects have already been absorbed in present price structures. At the same time, the industrial world is still vulnerable to the same kinds of economic warfare and price uncertainty of that earlier period. The exploitation of new energy sources, whether oil fields in Alaska, the North Sea, Mexico, Korea, etc., do not as yet guarantee energy independence let alone lower prices since these areas are being explored and developed in the expectation that present or higher prices will prevail. The exploitation of American coal reserves has not proceeded at a rate sufficient to assure freedom from dependence on imported oil and atomic energy appears to be a victim of high interest rates and the lack of the ability of engineers to solve the major technical problems necessary for competitively efficient production, not to mention problems of safety and waste disposal. Solar energy so far appears to be a public relations solution to the energy problem.

The effect of the fiscal crisis of the cities has not yet been felt in its full intensity and in the extent of its full diffusion throughout the country.

The most resistant indicator of a return to previous economic levels has been unemployment levels which since late 1974 have remained at between 9½ and 8 percent and which have dropped only slowly and in small decrements over the past twelve years.

Other economic consequences of a declining rate of expansion are still to be felt. Throughout the fifties and sixties the educational establishment has been geared to producing an increasing proportion of the total population for college entrance and the achievement of baccalaureate and higher degrees. The assumption behind this expansion was that of a continuous expansion in the service segments of the society which was to be financed primarily by government. It was also supported by the expansion of the white collar and bureaucratic structure of industry. However, by the late sixties the number of white collar, bureaucratic, administrative, managerial and technical jobs appeared to have become stabilized. Even as this stabilization was occurring, the educational system and the expectations of youth were premised on the assumption that the same rate of expansion would continue. Since the early seventies educational institutions have been turning out degree holders for whom there are proportionately fewer and fewer jobs at the level for which the students are presumably prepared. The educational planners and youth have solved this problem by preparing students for taking jobs for which less and less preparation is necessary. Thus the college educated population increasingly takes jobs that previously did not require degrees, and degree holders work in marginal jobs, combinations of part-time jobs, arts and crafts, street vending jobs, are unemployed, or try to stay in college while waiting for jobs to become available.

The short-run effects of the new scarcity are curious and contradictory. The experience of scarcity is a new experience for most youth in the United States. The twenty-year revolution of rising expectations has been reversed by a decline in actual opportunity. In the short run youth has become desperate to get into the economic system before further declines in opportunity occur. This has tended to defuse the youth rebellion: an increasingly large percentage of youth attempt to become square and meet square occupational demands by minimal conformance. Because of these economic realities, youth increasingly express their dissatisfaction through forms of personal and cultural expression. While dress and tonsorial styles have become increasingly subdued in relation to the demands of the square market, the demands have been modified by employers because of their own habituation to the wearing of more extreme styles. Youth dissatisfaction thus takes the form of non-work related personal and cultural consumption. Hence, the smoking of pot becomes more and more acceptable though there appears to be a decline in hallucinogenic and hard drugs. These concessions and modifications have been a concession to the reality of the market place.

At another level non-conformance is expressed in new forms of sexual arrangements including open living together on the part of large numbers, grouping in urban and rural households, network systems of sexuality and commensalism, overt lesbian families and out of the closet homosexuality and same-sex marriages.

At the other extreme there are whole new systems of religious commitment and affiliation. These include attachment to new combinations of theology, mysticism, asceticism, communalism derived from Buddhism, Hinduism, primitive Christianity, early Judaism and Mohammadanism. In addition there has been a revival and expansion of earlier Anabaptist traditions as expressed in Jehovah's Witnesses, Seventh Day Adventists, Southern Baptists, and other Protestant traditions exemplified by such figures as Oral Roberts, Billy Graham, and the Reverend Moon. At a more secular level are the whole range of quasi-religions including Scientology, Transcendental meditation, co-counseling, psychological groupies, Erhard seminar training, and encounter grouping. At a still more secular level are Kung-fu, Karate and other forms of physical fitness perfectionisms.

All of these forms of religion are not to be taken as simple aberations and deviations. They represent at the most intimate and fundamental levels a rejection of rational industrial society, but this rejection does not constitute a direct political confrontation. They permit believers to live simultaneously within and outside the society by segmenting their public and private lives. They represent a more radical alternative to mass media consumption which attempts to accomplish the same purposes though managed from above and lived vicariously. At the personal and cultural levels these alternative life styles may well represent a radical rejection of the whole tradition of western society without particularly attacking its organizational or political structure. This change could well be a profound break with our past and appears to be independent of immediate fluctuations of the business cycle.

THE NEW DISENCHANTMENT

The prospects of long-term permanent unemployment of large segments of youth and blacks after a period of (a) rising expectations or (b) a desperate desire to "get back in" may have more disturbing implications. If it appears that it is impossible to get back in, then a sizeable segment of both black and new middle class populations may find it difficult to make ideological and cultural compromises with the system. A long-term prospect for American and Western society is that a permanently disaffected group may exist in the midst of an imperfectly stabilized neo-Keynesian society.

In urban areas this may mean a return to urban violence, greater growth of upper class ghettos to complement the existing lower class ghettos, and patterns of residential segregation and fortification which deny the existence of the city as an entity.

At the national and international scene, organized small scale adventurism appears to be a permanent way of life for some disaffected youth and some racial, minority and ethnic groups. The level of organization and size of such groups may be so low, however, that a solution to the damage these groups cause may not exist. Sporadic violence, bombings, assassinations and terrorism come to be accepted as part of the permanent cost of living in industrial society.

The problems in the underdeveloped world will undoubtedly be worse. There, problems of political instability will compete with problems of starvation, famine, genocide, and large-scale organized political extremism. The Western world could try to survive by making itself into a fortress hoping to isolate itself from the problems of the underdeveloped world, but not from its resources.

Whether the domestic and international problems of the United States and western society are solvable is an open question, but a precondition for an approach to their solution depends upon maintaining high levels of employment and productivity within a world of decreasing natural resources and increasing competition for them. It would appear that they might be solvable only if approached from a world-wide perspective, which seems even more dubious. But again, if they can be solved, they can only be solved when the underdeveloped world is given and is prepared to receive the benefits and the procedures of western technology and the constraints that accompany them. All but a few nations of the world are committed to industrialization and to the world credit system and cannot reverse their course. To be successful in this venture means the development of stable systems of production and distribution within an orderly and pacific political order, the development of narrow occupational, craft and administrative skills necessary to the industrial organization of society, the acquisition of motivational and consumption patterns that permit the accumulation of capital, the efficient utilization of capital provided by the capital-rich nations in the form of loans and aid, and the development of fiscal and monetary policies to protect themselves from domestic and foreign expropriation of their internal accumulation.

At present, the acquisition of these productive institutions and social characteristics has occurred in only a few of the developing nations. In part the image of western "consumerism," the attractiveness of industrial consumer goods ranging from trash and junk to consumer durables, is more visible than the production habits, motivation and discipline necessary to generate that consumerism. Western society achieved "consumerism" after decades and even centuries of primitive and secondary modes of capital accumulation. The new, developing, societies see the attractiveness of consumerism without being able to see the sacrifices that capitalism previously had imposed upon its own societies (though they have seen the sacrifices capitalism imposed upon colonial society). They would like to acquire the apparent fruits of industrialism without knowing how to generate the capital that produces those fruits.

The intense, immediate demand in the developing societies for industrially produced consumer goods, hampers the accumulation of capital. The desire to enjoy those goods, especially by the upper classes and political elites, *inhibits the development of a social character geared to* the acquisition of skills, and long-term planning which are the pre-conditions for industrialization. Only those underdeveloped countries that are rich in petroleum, fossil fuels and minerals for which there is a high international demand have the opportunity to acquire the capital and modern technology without the sacrifices associated with primitive capital accumulation. Only these countries can reach sophisticated levels of consumerism for significant numbers of their populations in relatively short periods of time.

Governments engaged in modernization thus are forced to use draconian measures to inhibit consumption among the masses, while they provide vast opportunities and little restraint to the entrepreneurial classes. But world-wide pressures for immediate personal gratification are so great that policies of repressive austerity are only partially successful even when politically possible.

The industrialized western nations face problems of maintaining systems of positive economic and political motivation. The achievement of affluence among its new middle classes has tended to erode the incentives for mobility, for discipline, for achievement, and for long-term personal planning. It has, in short, weakened if not made obsolete the Protestant Ethic. In the short run, the new scarcity has reinvoked the discipline for mobility among large parts of the middle classes but may embitter the new lower class ethnic aspirants who are denied opportunity after the desire to achieve economic and political mobility has been aroused in them. In the long run, the new scarcity may embitter substantial portions of the new middle classes and the rising ethnics who for different reasons may be frozen out of a productive role in the economy.

New forms of cleavage appear to be emerging in western society. On one side there is a dominant segment of population committed to the industrial structure of that society. This industrially committed segment is itself continuously sub-divided into small segments at various skill, occupational, industrial, managerial and income levels. The committed segment may range from semi-skilled workers to the managerial and financial upper classes. But this group is cut-off from a sub-proletariat which is denied economic opportunity as well as the chance to acquire the skills, motivation, and education to enter the industrially committed sectors of society.

This scarcity-induced exclusion from the fruits of consumer society cannot be anything other than a source for continuous protest, disruption and lawlessness for some groups. Such lawlessness exists more frequently and continuously at a personal level than at a political level; and such lawlessness serves to reinforce the boundaries between the committed and uncommitted segments of the society. Disease, poverty, alcoholism, vice, and a whole host of symptoms of despair and personal and social disorganization accompany lawlessness as the characteristics of scarcity induced and enforced exclusion.

A third major segment into which western society seems to subdivide itself is the "counter culture." Originating in the middle classes, segments of youth voluntarily segregate themselves from the committed world or drop out because the new scarcity may impose intellectual, academic, and personality demands upon them that are too severe for them to bear. At the same time because of the scarcity, "society" cannot or is unwilling to guarantee that the sacrifices necessary for commitment will be rewarded. In the sixties a ready-made cultural frame for dropping-out was constructed. Now the counter-culture includes ever expanding cults, "ideologies," organizational forms, experimentation for the achievement of personal salvation outside the system, and adventuristic political assaults on the system. The counter-culture is so varied, so unorganized and disorganized that it constitutes no major threat to the system, even though it appears to be a stable feature of western societies.

The only imaginable threat to the system posed by the disenfranchised subproletariat and the counter culture would be if its numbers were so large or its ethics were so pervasive that it destroyed the motivational schema that makes the committed industrial sector possible. The new scarcity seems to prevent such a possibility. Scarcity reinforces the motivation of the haves, as it strengthens the opposite motivation of the have-nots.

The "culture" of the counter-culture also permeates the life styles of those who are occupationally committed to the industrial establishment. Dress and tonsorial styles, sexual experimentation and new forms of sexuality, the use of marijuana (though not LSD), attraction to new forms of art, the multi-media, high and low porn and new forms of music have become chic and stylized among large segments of the "occupationally committed" at increasingly wider ranges of the occupational and age structures.

These "counter-cultural" elements become increasingly integrated into the "normal" culture, but a separation of cultural styles occurs at the level of work. Commitment to the industrial structure is increasingly confined to the place of work. It includes the acquisition, display and exercise of skill, craftsmanship and dedication to occupational task at hand. The private life with its acceptance of life style elements that previously might have been characterized as counter-cultural is rigidly separated from the work life of the individual.

Such a division of life into two spheres is facilitated by a greater permissiveness by employers of work-unrelated deviancy. Employers increasingly do not inquire into the non-work life of their employees.

At the same time, the attractiveness of the personal styles of the counter culture and the difficulty of maintaining a divided life continuously thrusts members of the industrially committed middle classes into the total world of the counter culture. The counter culture as a distinct, isolated segment of western society is thus fed by the young who are unable or unwilling to compete in the square world of commitment, and by those who have competed, often successfully, but who are unwilling or unable to maintain a divided life.

The separation of western society into three major distinct sectors appears to be a permanent feature of that society. The development of the counter-culture is one of the major products of the Golden Age of affluence. Affluence appears to have raised the level of idealism among scions of the middle classes to the point where a commitment to industrial society could not gratify that idealism. The new scarcity appears to have stabilized the counter culture and is likely to make it permanent. It does so because when scarcity produces increased competitiveness for education, jobs, and for self-discipline and personal achievement, the on-going counter culture provides new sets of culturally sanctioned alternatives for withdrawal from that society.

Scarcity also provides the basis for the increased segmentation and isolation of ethnic and racial groups and other sub-proletariats, but it does so in new ways. Because the new scarcity follows a period of rising expectations, heightened political aspirations and governmental sponsored mobility, the sense of failure and despair may be greater among these groups than would otherwise be expected.

American society has traditionally maintained a partially open society by providing at least the promise and often the actuality of opportunity. In part this was due to cheap land and natural resources much of which was made available from the public domain. In part the process of industrialization itself provided opportunities for the domestic lower classes and successive waves of European immigrants. In addition, substantial opportunities were provided by governmental fiscal and taxation policy. In the Golden Age extensive opportunity was provided by fiscal, budgetary, and tax policies. The new scarcity began in the recession of 1972, but was foreshadowed in 1968 by a switch in the beneficiaries of these federal budgetary policies. In 1986, the focus of federal policy appears to reserve the benefits of the economic system for those who have already arrived and to place the burden of the cost of inflation and unemployment on wage workers and those who have not arrived. This is a historic reversal of traditional federal policy, including not only that of President Johnson's 1965 policy to end poverty, but also a much older policy of the United States to provide opportunity to all but the slaves.

In the post-Golden Age this reversal serves to seal-off and make permanent the boundaries between the three major cultural and social segments of American and western societies. Downward mobility between the segments is always possible. Upward mobility within each segment is also possible, but upward mobility across the segments is increasingly denied and frustrated by current social policies.

If the traditional virtues of an open society are to be maintained a drastic reversal of social policy is necessary. But maintaining mobility and economic expansion will be increasingly difficult in a world where limitations of natural resources including energy and mineral and fossil fuels and even land are becoming increasingly apparent.

In the underdeveloped world all of the above problems occur at more extreme levels. Governmental policy may be less important as a barrier to opportunity than the almost insurmountable problems of developing societies to mobilize human energy, to achieve discipline, and to efficiently utilize capital.

Such barriers to development as noted may be less important to a few countries like Brazil, Iran and Saudi Arabia where the abundance of natural resources may provide the basis for the accumulation of capital without the rigors of primitive accumulation of capital, and with greater margins of safety for a more slowly developing industrially motivated labor force.

By and large, the underdeveloped world faces the prospect of a much smaller industrially committed labor force than in the west and a very much larger sub-proletariat. The uncommitted intelligentsia may be small in relation to the total population but relatively large in comparison to the committed industrial classes.

If civilization is defined as the possibility for increasingly larger segments of the population to achieve not only economic well-being but the prospect of realizing their potentials by the escape from misery, the prospects are indeed bleak.

In some societies the bleakness seems to be due to difficulties that are inherent in their history and situations. In other countries, like the United States, the difficulties are willed. The desire to achieve and maintain affluence at the expense of others becomes the basis for social policy, and produces an economically, culturally and socially closed world.

Bibliography

BOOKS

Baltzell, E. Digby. *Philadelphia Gentlemen: The Making of a National Upper Class*. New York: Free Press, 1958.

———. *The Protestant Establishment*. New York: Random House, 1964.

Banfield, Edward C. *Political Influence*. New York: Free Press, 1961.

Bensman, Joseph, and Arthur J. Vidich. *See* Vidich, Arthur J., and Joseph Bensman.

Berger, Bennett. *Working-Class Suburb: A Study of Auto Workers in Suburbia*. Berkeley: University of California Press, 1960.

Berle, Adolf A. *The 20th Century Capitalist Revolution*. New York: Harcourt, Brace & World, 1954.

———, and Gardiner C. Means. *The Modern Corporation and Private Property*. Chicago: Commerce Clearing House, 1932.

Boorstin, Daniel J. *The Genius of American Politics*. Chicago: University of Chicago Press, 1953.

Booth, Charles. *Charles Booth's London*. Edited by Albert Fried and Richard M. Elman. New York: Pantheon, 1968 (first published 1845).

Brady, Robert A. *Business as a System of Power*. New York: Columbia University Press, 1943.

Brown, Claude. *Manchild in the Promised Land*. New York: Macmillan, 1965.

Brown, Norman O. *Life Against Death*. New York: Random House, 1959.

Burnett, Hallie. *The Brain Pickers*. New York: Dell, 1958.

Burnham, James. *The Managerial Revolution*. New York: John Day, 1941.

Carr-Saunders, Alexander M., and P. A. Wilson. *The Professions.* Oxford: Clarendon Press, 1933.

Centers, Richard. *The Psychology of Social Classes.* Princeton: Princeton University Press, 1949.

Conant, James B. *The American High School Today.* New York: McGraw-Hill, 1959.

Conference on Economic Progress. *Poverty and Deprivation in the United States,* 1961 (The Keyserling Report).

Currie, Lauchlin B. *Accelerating Development: The Necessity and the Means.* New York: McGraw-Hill, 1966.

Dahl, Robert A. *Who Governs?: Democracy and Power in an American City.* New Haven: Yale University Press, 1961.

Dalton, Melville. *Men Who Manage: Fusions of Feeling and Theory in Administration.* New York: Wiley, 1959.

Davis, A., and Others. *Deep South: A Social Anthropological Study of Caste and Class.* Chicago: University of Chicago Press, 1965.

Drake, St. Clair, and Horace R. Cayton. *Black Metropolis.* New York: Harcourt, Brace & World, 1945.

Drucker, Peter F. *Concept of the Corporation.* Boston: Beacon Press, 1946.

———. *The New Society: The Anatomy of the Industrial Order.* New York: Harper & Row, 1950.

Erikson, Erik H. *Childhood and Society.* New York: W. W. Norton, 1950.

Flexner, James T. *Doctors on Horseback.* New York: Dover, 1968.

Frazier, E. Franklin. *Black Bourgeoisie.* New York: Free Press, 1957.

Freud, Sigmund. *The Future of an Illusion.* Translated by W. D. Robson-Scott. London: Hogarth Press and The Institute of Psychoanalysis, 1928.

Friedenberg, Edgar Z. *Coming of Age in America.* New York: Random House, 1963.

Galbraith, John Kenneth. *The Affluent Society.* Boston: Houghton Mifflin, 1958.

———. *The New Industrial State.* Boston: Houghton Mifflin, 1967.

Gans, Herbert J. *The Urban Villagers.* New York: Free Press, 1962.

Geertz, Clifford, ed. *Old Societies and New States.* New York: Free Press, 1963.

Gerth, Hans H., and C. Wright Mills. *Character and Social Structure.* New York: Harcourt, Brace & World, 1953.

Glaab, Charles N. *A History of Urban America.* New York: Macmillan, 1967.

Goffman, Erving. *Asylums: Essays on the Social Situation of Mental Patients and Other Inmates.* Garden City, N.Y.: Anchor Books, 1961.

———. *The Presentation of Self in Everyday Life.* Garden City, N.Y.: Doubleday, 1959.

Goodman, Paul. *Growing Up Absurd: Problems of Youth in the Organized System.* New York: Random House, 1960.

Halbwachs, Maurice. *Esquisse d'une Psychologie des Classes Sociales.* Paris, 1938.

Hamilton, Walton H. *The Politics of Industry: Five Lectures Delivered on the William W. Cook Foundation at the University of Michigan.* New York: Alfred A. Knopf, 1957.

Harrington, Michael. *The Other America.* New York: Macmillan, 1963.

Hawley, Cameron. *Executive Suite.* Boston: Houghton Mifflin, 1952.

Hollingshead, August B. *Elmtown's Youth.* New York: Wiley, 1949.

Hunter, Floyd. *Community Power Structure: A Study of Decision Makers.* Chapel Hill: University of North Carolina Press, 1953.

———. *Top Leadership, U.S.A.* Chapel Hill: University of North Carolina Press, 1959.

Kaufman, Harold. *Prestige Classes in a New York Rural Community.* Ithaca, N.Y.: Cornell University Agricultural Experimental Bulletin, March 1944.

Keats, John C. *The Crack in the Picture Window.* Boston: Houghton Mifflin, 1957.

Kelman, Steven. *Push Comes to Shove: The Escalation of Student Protest.* Boston: Houghton Mifflin, 1970.

Keniston, Kenneth. *The Uncommitted: Alienated Youth in American Society.* New York: Harcourt, Brace & World, 1965.

Keyserling, Leon H. *Progress or Poverty.* Washington Conference on Economic Progress, December 1964.

Kolko, Gabriel. *Wealth and Power in America.* New York: Frederick A. Praeger, 1962.

Laine, Mark. *The S Man.* Boston: Houghton Mifflin, 1961.

Lewis, Oscar. *Children of Sanchez: The Autobiography of a Mexican Family.* New York: Random House, 1961.

———. *La Vida.* New York: Random House, 1966.

Lipset, Seymour M., and Reinhard Bendix. *Social Mobility in Industrial Society.* Berkeley: University of California Press, 1959.

Lynd, Robert S., and Helen M. Lynd. *Middletown.* New York: Harcourt, Brace & World, 1929.

———. *Middletown in Transition.* New York: Harcourt, Brace & World, 1937.

MacIver, Robert. *Society.* New York: Holt, Rinehart & Winston, 1937.

Mannheim, Karl. *Essays on Sociology and Social Psychology.* Edited by Paul Kecskemeti. New York: Oxford University Press, 1953.

———. *Man and Society in an Age of Reconstruction.* London: Kegan Paul, Trench, Trubner, 1940.

Marcuse, Herbert. *Eros and Civilization.* Boston: Beacon Press, 1955.

———. *One-Dimensional Man.* Boston: Beacon Press, 1964.

Matlin, Norman. *The Educational Enclave: Coercive Bargaining in Colleges and Universities.* New York: Funk and Wagnalls, 1969.

Mead, George Herbert. *Mind, Self, and Society.* Chicago: University of Chicago Press, 1934.

Mead, Shepherd. *How To Succeed in Business Without Really Trying.* New York: Simon and Schuster, 1952.

Michels, Robert. *Political Parties.* Glencoe, Ill.: Free Press, 1958.

Mills, C. Wright. *The Power Elite.* New York: Oxford University Press, 1956.

———. *The Sociological Imagination.* New York: Oxford University Press, 1959.

———. *White Collar: The American Middle Classes.* New York: Oxford University Press, 1951.

Moore, Barrington. *Social Origins of Dictatorship and Democracy.* Boston: Beacon Press, 1966.

Moore, Robin. *Pitchman.* New York: Coward-McCann, 1956.

Moore, Wilbert. *Industrial Relations and the Social Order.* New York: Macmillan, 1951, rev. ed.

Neumann, Franz. *The Democratic and the Authoritarian State.* Edited and with a preface by Herbert Marcuse. New York: Free Press, 1957.

Nieburg, H. L. *In the Name of Science.* Chicago: Quadrangle, 1966.

Perlman, Selig. *A Theory of the Labor Movement.* New York: Macmillan, 1928.

Poggioli, Renato. *The Theory of the Avant-Garde.* Cambridge, Mass.: Harvard University Press, 1968.

Poll, Solomon. *The Hasidic Community of Williamsburg.* New York: Schocken Books, 1962.

Polsby, Nelson W. *Community Power and Political Theory.* New Haven: Yale University Press, 1963.

Presthus, Robert. *The Organizational Society: An Analysis and a Theory.* New York: Alfred A. Knopf, 1962.

Remarque, Erich Maria. *The Black Obelisk.* New York: Harcourt, Brace & World, 1957.

Riesman, David, in collaboration with Reuel Denney and Nathan Glazer. *The Lonely Crowd: A Study of the Changing American Character.* New Haven: Yale University Press, 1950.

Rossi, Peter, and Robert A. Dentler. *The Politics of Urban Renewal.* New York: Free Press, 1961.

Schumpeter, Joseph. *Capitalism, Socialism and Democracy.* New York: Harper & Row, 1950, 3rd ed.

Seeley, John R., Alexander Sim, and Elizabeth W. Loosely. *Crestwood Heights.* New York: Basic Books, 1956.

Simmons, J., and Barry Winograd. *It's Happening: A Portrait of the Youth Scene Today*. Santa Barbara, Calif.: Marc-Laird, 1966.

Spectorsky, A. C. *The Exurbanites*. Philadelphia: Lippincott, 1955.

Stein, Maurice. *The Eclipse of Community: An Interpretation of American Studies*. Princeton: Princeton University Press, 1960.

Tawney, R. H. *Equality*. London: Allen & Unwin, 1931.

Thomas, William I., and Florian Znaniecki. *The Polish Peasant in Europe and America*. Boston: Gorham Press, 1918–1920.

Thometz, Carol. *The Decision-Makers: The Power Structure of Dallas*. Dallas: Southern Methodist University Press, 1963.

Veblen, Thorstein. *Absentee Ownership and Business Enterprise in Recent Times*. New York: Augustus M. Kelley, 1964.

———. *Imperial Germany and the Industrial Revolution*. New York: Macmillan, 1915.

———. *The Theory of Business Enterprise*. New York: Scribner, 1904.

———. *The Theory of the Leisure Class: An Economic Study in the Evolution of Institutions*. New York: B. W. Huebsch, 1922.

Vidich, Arthur J., and Joseph Bensman. *Small Town in Mass Society*. Princeton: Princeton University Press, 1968, rev. ed.

Warner, W. Lloyd, and Paul S. Lunt. *The Social Life of a Modern Community*. New Haven: Yale University Press, 1941.

Weber, Max. *Essays in Sociology*. Translated, edited, and with an introduction by Hans H. Gerth and C. Wright Mills. New York: Oxford University Press, 1946.

———. *The Protestant Ethic and the Spirit of Capitalism*. New York: Scribner, 1930.

———. *The Theory of Social and Economic Organization*. Translated and edited by A. M. Henderson and Talcott Parsons. New York: Oxford University Press, 1947.

Weingarten, Samuel. *The Rationale for Corporation Giving: A Case Study of the General Electric Company*. Ann Arbor: University Microfilms, 1962.

Whyte, William H. *Is Anybody Listening?* New York: Simon and Schuster, 1950.

———. *The Organization Man*. New York: Simon and Schuster, 1956.

Wildavsky, Aaron. *Leadership in a Small Town*. Totowa, N.J.: Bedminster Press, 1964.

Yablonsky, Lewis. *The Violent Gang*. New York: Macmillan, 1962.

ARTICLES

Finestone, Harold. "Cats, Kicks and Color," *Social Problems*, V, No. 1 (1957), 3–13.

Fishman, Harry. "Historical Analysis of Economic and Political Relationships Between National Corporations, Banks and Community Organizations in Bridgeport." M.A. Thesis, New School for Social Research, New York, 1965.

Goffman, Erving. "Characteristics of Total Institutions," in Symposium on Preventive and Social Psychiatry (1957), pp. 43–84. Walter Reed Army Institute of Social Research.

Macdonald, Dwight. "Our Invisible Poor," *The New Yorker,* XXXVIII (January 19, 1963), 82–132.

Mills, C. Wright. "The Middle Classes in Middle-Sized Cities," *American Sociological Review,* XI, No. 5 (October 1946), 520–529.

Nieburg, H. L. "The Contract State: Government in the Economy," *Dissent* (September–October 1966), pp. 526–537.

Sapir, Edward. "Culture, Genuine and Spurious," *American Journal of Sociology,* XXIX (1924), 401–429. [Continued in Tumin, Melvin. *See* below.]

Tumin, Melvin. "Culture, Genuine and Spurious: A Re-evaluation," *American Sociological Review,* X, No. 2 (April 1945).

Wrong, Dennis. "The Case of the New York Review," *Commentary,* L, No. 5 (November 1970).

Index